What readers are saying about the Daughters of the Promise series

"In the fast paced world we live in, it is a blessing to be able to pick up the Daughters of the Promise series and be taken away mentally to a place where life is so much more. The love of family and friends, the bond that unites them all to one another and to God. Being able to focus on those precious moments in our lives that we typically let pass us by or take for granted. Beth Wiseman has such a gift in not only sharing this simpler way of life, but a way of truly putting us, the readers, there with them."

—Erin B.

"The story line and the people draw you into the story, it's written in such a way that you feel as though you are right there each and every day with them. The intrigue and the day-to-day living can be seen and felt with each and every word. It's a relief to let the worries of today dissolve as you are drawn back into a world of contentment and peace."

—Lori M.

"The Daughters of the Promise series is all about family, faith, friendship, and hard work. I love that the series gave you a look inside the Amish way of life, the closeness of community, simplicity, and how to live your best life outside what is happening in the world. Beth Wiseman brings each character to life in a way where you almost feel like you are there. Once you start this series, you look forward to the next one!"

—Cookie D.

"From the first sentence of the first Daughters of the Promise book, I was drawn into a lovely place where old friends and family reside. I feel happy there, I feel relaxed there, I am home there. Each book is like a welcome home hug. These books are so much more than books . . . they are blessings."

—Mandy B.

"I have and reread this series. The characters come alive in these books and you find yourself right there with them and rooting for them. Beth is a gifted writer, transporting you into the story. You won't be able to put these books down."

—Cheryl B.

Plain Peace

Also by Beth Wiseman

Plain Peace

BETH WISEMAN

THOMAS NELSON
Since 1798

NASHVILLE   DALLAS   MEXICO CITY   RIO DE JANEIRO

© 2013 by Elizabeth Wiseman Mackey

Published in Nashville, Tennessee, by Thomas Nelson. Thomas Nelson is a registered trademark of Thomas Nelson, Inc.

Thomas Nelson, Inc., titles may be purchased in bulk for educational, business, fund-raising, or sales promotional use. For information, please e-mail SpecialMarkets@ThomasNelson.com.

Publisher's Note: This novel is a work of fiction. Names, characters, places, and incidents are either products of the author's imagination or used fictitiously. All characters are fictional, and any similarity to people living or dead is purely coincidental.

Library of Congress Cataloging-in-Publication Data

Wiseman, Beth, 1962–
 Plain Peace / Beth Wiseman.
  pages cm. — (A Daughters of the Promise Novel)
 Summary: "Anna's grandfather seems determined to ruin her Rumspringa and any hopes she has of finding a husband. Anna Byler should be enjoying her Rumspringa as allowed by her faith. But because of the strict rules enforced by her grandfather, the available suitors in town are afraid to court her. Even Anna's grandmother is keeping a big secret from Anna's grandfather in an effort to keep the peace. Under her grandfather's oppressive watch, Anna begins to feel her faith slipping and wonders if God has forsaken her. Jacob Hostetler and his family have relocated to Lancaster County following a family tragedy in Ohio. As his family struggles to rebuild their lives, Jacob is forced to act as head of the household when his father is unable to cope with recent events. It's been a long time since Jacob has felt any joy. Until he meets Anna Byler. But will Anna's grandfather succeed at keeping them apart? And can Jacob put the past behind him and open his heart?"— Provided by publisher.
 ISBN 978-1-4016-8594-2 (Trade Paper)
 I. Amish—Fiction. 2. Lancaster County (Pa.)—Fiction. I. Title.
 PS3623.I83P565 2013
 813'.6—dc23   2013023671

Printed in the United States of America

13 14 15 16 17 18 RRD 6 5 4 3

To Richard Gabler

Daughters of the Promise
Community Tree

Bylers
Isaac ─┬─ Marianne

Elam (D) ─┬─ Suzy (D)   Jacob   Abe   Anna Mae   Margaret   Leah (D)

Anna

Hostetlers
John ─┬─ Cora

Huyards
Abraham (Abe) ─┬─ Mary Ellen (Stoltzfus)

Matthew   Luke   Linda (adopted)

Saunders
Kade ─┬─ Sadie

Tyler   Marie

Ebersols
Bishop's Grandchildren

Stephen   Hannah   Annie

Millers
Irma Rose (D) ─┬─ Jonas (D) — Lizzie

Sarah Jane

Lillian

Dronbergers
Josephine — Robert

Linda

Barbie Beiler
Bed & Breakfast

Fishers
Zeb ─┬─ Sarah (D)

Saul   Rubin   James   Hannah (D)

Stoltzfuses

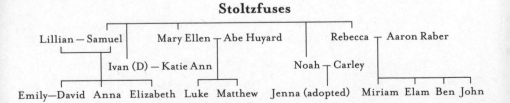

Lillian — Samuel   Mary Ellen ─┬─ Abe Huyard   Rebecca ─┬─ Aaron Raber

Ivan (D) — Katie Ann   Noah ─┬─ Carley

Emily — David   Anna   Elizabeth   Luke   Matthew   Jenna (adopted)   Miriam   Elam   Ben   John

Pennsylvania Dutch Glossary

Aamen—Amen
ach—oh
boppli—baby or babies
bruder/brieder—brother/brothers
daadi—grandfather
daed—dad
danki—thank you
dochder—daughter
Englisch—a non-Amish person (in Lancaster County)
fraa—wife
gut—good
haus—house
kaffi—coffee
kapp—prayer covering or cap
kinner—child, children or grandchildren
lieb—love
maedel—girl
mamm—mom
mammi—grandmother

mei—my

mudder—mother

Nee—no

onkel—uncle

Ordnung—the written and unwritten rules of the Amish; the
   understood behavior by which the Amish are expected to
   live, passed down from generation to generation. Most Amish
   know the rules by heart.

Pennsylvania Deitsch—the language most commonly used by the
   Amish. Although commonly known as Pennsylvania Dutch,
   the language is actually a form of German (*Deutsch*).

rumschpringe—running-around period when a teenager turns
   sixteen years old

schweschder/schweschdere—sister/sisters

sohn—son

Wie bischt?—How are you?

wunderbaar—wonderful

ya—yes

Yankee—a non-Amish person (in Middlefield, Ohio)

1

ANNA WATCHED OUT THE WINDOW AND WAITED UNTIL her grandfather's buggy rounded the corner before she pulled the bottle of pills from her apron pocket. She handed the prescription to her grandmother, resolved that she would never live the way her grandparents did—keeping secrets from each other. Even if her future husband did end up being the bishop like her grandfather.

"*Danki*, Anna." Marianne Byler popped two pills in her mouth and followed them down with a glass of water, then stashed the pills in her own apron pocket. Anna knew she wouldn't see the bottle again until it was empty and time for more, and she'd often wondered where her grandmother hid the bottle.

"The pharmacist said you've been out of refills for a few months, but Dr. Noah kept approving it. He won't fill it again, though, until you come for an office visit, and this isn't the full prescription." Anna began gathering up the dirty dinner dishes, glancing at her *mammi* a couple of times before adding, "So what will you do?" She piled the plates on the counter next to the sink and folded her arms across her chest.

Mammi dipped a dishrag into the soapy water and looked over her shoulder. "The Lord will provide."

"I sure hope so." *Mammi* never got worked up about anything, but sometimes Anna thought maybe she should.

It had been eight months since her grandfather had forbidden everyone in their district to visit Dr. Noah Stoltzfus's clinic. Anna wondered if *Daadi* would have made such a decision if he'd known that his own wife was so dependent on Dr. Noah, a secret *Mammi* had been keeping since way before the official ban. Anna glanced at the clock on the wall.

"Can I go now?" She tucked a strand of loose brown hair beneath her *kapp*, then smoothed the wrinkles from her black apron. "The volleyball game at the Lapps' *haus* started at one."

Mammi turned around, dried her hands on a kitchen towel, and leaned against the counter. "*Ya*, but be home in time to help with supper." She smiled, defining the lines around her tiny mouth and those feathering from the corners of her eyes. "And have fun."

Anna nodded, then hurried through the living room to the front door.

The Lapp farm was in walking distance. By the time she arrived, the court was filled with players.

"Come be on our side, Anna!" Emma Lapp waved, and once Anna was in place, she stared through the net at an unfamiliar face. She gawked long enough to almost get hit in the head with the ball but awkwardly bounced it away with her elbow instead. Luckily Emma got underneath it and made the point.

"That's Jacob Hostetler," Emma whispered in Anna's ear. "His family just moved here. They bought the old Zook place." Emma struggled to catch her breath as she brushed her palm against a sweaty forehead. "Hard to keep focused with him on the other side of the net, *ya?*" Emma grinned before she got back in place a few feet to Anna's right.

Anna tried to keep her eyes on the other team's server, but her gaze kept shifting back to Jacob Hostetler. Like most of the men this time of year, Jacob's face was bronzed by the summer sun, and his shoulders and arms looked like those of a man who'd been chopping wood since he was born—nineteen or twenty years ago, she guessed. If his tall and muscular physique wasn't enough to set any girl's heart to racing, he also had brown hair streaked with gold, his cropped bangs resting just above piercing blue eyes. When he looked at her, tiny dimples formed on either side of a flawless mouth.

She forced herself to look away from his perfectness and watched the volleyball coming in her direction. "Got it!" She wasn't as tall as most of the players on the team, so she had to jump really high to slam the ball over the net. And slam it she did—right into the side of Jacob's face.

"Are you okay?" She peered through the net. One side of Jacob's face was bright red. But he waved her off.

"*Ya, ya.* I'm fine."

The game went on for another forty-five minutes before Emma's *mamm* set refreshments on a nearby picnic table. Emma looped her arm through Anna's as they walked to the table, leaning over to whisper in her ear again. "Well, he's a looker, but have you ever seen a worse volleyball player in your life?"

Anna had been thinking the same thing. If Jacob did happen to make contact with the ball, it went flying wildly out of bounds every time. "Maybe they didn't play volleyball where he comes from." She paused. "Where does he come from? Do you know?"

"Somewhere in Ohio. Middlefield, I think."

Emma was tall with auburn hair, bright green eyes, and a figure with exactly the right amount of curves. She could have her pick of any guy in Paradise, Pennsylvania. Anna wondered if Jacob would add himself to Emma's list of suitors. Would he be the one Emma finally latched onto? Both Emma and Anna would be nineteen in February, so they were looking for that special someone.

Although Anna didn't have a single prospect on the horizon.

Once everyone was gathered around the table, they all bowed their heads for a silent prayer, then dug into the chips, dips, cookies, and punch. Anna was thankful for the shade of the tree above them and the gentle breeze. It was fiercely hot for June.

"*Danki* for inviting me today." Jacob reached for a chip as he glanced around at the seven other people snacking. His voice was deep even though he spoke softly, the hint of a blush in his cheeks.

Anna knew that pride was a sin, that looks were not supposed to be important, but this fellow had been abundantly blessed just the same. Apparently Anna herself had not. Otherwise, surely at least one member of their district would have wanted to date her.

Ben Raber introduced everyone and spoke up on behalf of the group. "*Gut* to have you." He paused as he reached for a cookie. "So tell us about you. About your family."

Anna held her breath as she waited for Jacob to answer, assuming he probably had a perfect family with wonderful parents and a herd of brothers and sisters. Doubtful that both his parents had been killed in a buggy accident when he was three and that he'd been raised by his grandparents, as she had.

"It's *mei mamm* and *daed*, and I have two *schweschdere* and two *brieder.*"

Of course you do. Anna took a large bite out of a chocolate chip cookie.

"And one of *mei schweschdere* is named Anna," Jacob added, winking at her. "But we call her Anna Mae."

Anna felt sure the earth was shifting beneath her feet, but with her cheeks packed with cookie, all she could do was attempt to smile and nod. She didn't recall ever feeling so weak in the knees.

A short while later Anna helped Emma and her mother clean up while the older males—those in their *rumschpringe*—went to the barn and the two younger children went home.

"I think the new fellow took a liking to Anna." Emma smiled as she handed her mother an empty bowl.

"I'm not surprised." Sarah Lapp put the bowl in the sink as she turned to Anna. "You're a beautiful young woman."

Compared to your dochder? Are you kidding me? Anna forced a smile, knowing both Emma and her mother were mistaken, but proud of the fact that she could honestly say she'd never been jealous of Emma. Her best friend was as beautiful on the inside as she was on the outside, and she'd never been anything but wonderful to Anna. "But you're wrong," she said to Emma after her mother had excused herself.

"Hmm. We'll see." Emma giggled.

Jacob listened to Ben Raber and Rubin Fisher talking about what a hard winter they'd had last year, and he nodded when the conversation seemed to call for it, but all he could think about was what might be waiting for him at home. Playing volleyball had been a great distraction—even though he was lousy at it. Spending a few hours with people his age who didn't know about his past almost made him feel like a normal person again, and it was nice to have a Saturday off from work. But reality loomed about six miles down the road, and he didn't think that moving would fix anything. They were a messed-up family, and geography wasn't going to change that.

Despite his worries, Jacob's ears perked up when he heard Ben mention Anna Byler. Watching her through the volleyball net had been the highlight of the day. Several ringlets of light brown hair had fallen from beneath her *kapp* during the games, enough to make him wonder if she had long wavy curls that cascaded to her waist when it wasn't wound in a bun beneath her prayer covering. He'd tried to hold her gaze for more than a few seconds, but she'd kept pulling her deep brown eyes away from his. She was by far the prettiest girl there.

"What?" Jacob interrupted Ben, who by now had turned the conversation to fishing. "What did you say before about Anna Byler?"

Ben grinned. "I said I think Anna gets prettier every time I see her." He paused and scratched his chin. "But I also said it's too bad she's undateable."

Jacob leaned back against the wall of the barn and looped his thumbs beneath his suspenders. "What do you mean, undateable?" *If anyone's not fit to date, it's me.*

Rubin chuckled as he sat down on a square bale of hay. "I thought I saw you giving Anna the eye." He shook his head. "Don't even waste your time. I don't think that girl has been on one date." He looked at Ben. "Do you think anyone has ever even taken her home from a singing?"

Ben shook his head from where he was standing a few feet away. "*Nee.*"

Jacob frowned, wondering what could be so wrong with her.

"It's her grandfather." Ben pulled a cigar from his pocket and ran it beneath his nose, breathing in the aroma. "She lives with her grandparents, and no one will go near her because of him." He lit the cigar, took a few puffs, then passed it to Rubin. "Anna's *daadi* had been a minister for years, and he was a scary man in that role. Last October he became bishop, and it's gotten worse. He's changing everything around here, and not for the *gut*."

Jacob shook his head when Rubin passed the cigar to him. People in his district didn't smoke. "Is this allowed?" He nodded toward Rubin as Rubin took another puff.

"*Ach*, it used to be." Rubin gave the cigar back to Ben. "The men have always gathered in the barn, especially after a meal, to share stories and smoke cigars. But Bishop Byler put an end to all smoking. And cell phones. And a whole bunch of other stuff."

Jacob automatically reached for the cell phone in his pocket, glad that it hadn't rung since yesterday. He held it up. "Guess I better get rid of this." That would give him a good excuse to distance himself a little more from his past. Without the cell phone, no one could find him.

"We had a strict bishop in Ohio too." Jacob paused, reaching for the cigar, then coughed after he took a puff. "How bad can he be?"

Ben raised his eyebrows and laughed. "*Ach*, you'll see. He's as mean a man as I've ever known, and I bet he keeps Anna locked in her room half the time."

Jacob scowled. "What? I doubt that. And how'd he get to be bishop if he's so mean?"

"You know how it works—all done by the lot," Rubin said.

"And I'm guessing back when he was first nominated to be a deacon or minister, he must have had everyone tricked into believing he was a *gut* guy."

Jacob knew exactly how it worked. A man must receive three nominations to be considered for a role as deacon or minister, then all candidates would walk into a room with hymnals laid out before them. One of the books contained a piece of paper with a scripture reading on it. Whoever picked that particular book was God's chosen one to minister. The same process was used to pick a bishop. These were sacred callings.

"What about the deacons and ministers? Do they agree with him? In Ohio, some things were put to a vote before anything could be changed in the *Ordnung.*" Jacob took another drag from the cigar and coughed again, thinking he wouldn't miss this particular ban.

"But that's the problem," Ben said. "Our *Ordnung* has never been changed, upgraded, or whatever you call it. Bishop Byler and the ministers and deacons are just enforcing what's already in the *Ordnung.* Our parents say things have just been kind of overlooked for years, but now Bishop Byler is taking everything back to the old ways."

"Do your parents agree with him?"

"Not really. But no one wants to stand up to him and face being shunned—or even if not shunned, shamed." Rubin stubbed out the cigar and put it back in his pocket.

Jacob pushed back the rim of his straw hat. "That doesn't sound *mean*, just strict."

Ben chuckled. "*Ach*, well . . . then you go right on over there and ask Anna Byler on a date or to a Sunday singing."

"I never said I wanted to ask her out." Jacob thought she was beautiful, and she seemed to have a playful spirit, something he found attractive in a woman. But he wasn't planning on dating anyone, despite his mother's encouragement to do so. "I doubt a man of God like the bishop would lock his granddaughter in her room or willingly be mean to anyone. He probably just doesn't want his district changing with the times. Lots of bishops are that way."

Rubin took off his hat and ran his forearm across his forehead. "Well, I'd sure ask her out if it weren't for her grandfather. The bishop we used to have was strict, but nothing like this. Bishop Ebersol was a wise old man. He knew when it was okay to bend the rules. Bishop Byler doesn't bend on anything, but we're stuck with him until he dies."

Anna kept one hand tightly over her mouth as tears streamed down her cheeks. She'd come to tell the men that Emma's mother had dessert and coffee set out for them in the kitchen, but she'd stopped outside the barn door when she heard her name. *Is this really what they think of* Daadi?

She knew her grandfather was strict. Too strict. Her grandmother was proof of that, hiding prescriptions from her own husband because he preferred her treatment to come from the homeopathic doctor in town. And those herbal remedies had worked . . . at first. But when the symptoms grew worse, he had refused to back down, so *Mammi* had gone to Dr. Noah behind his back. Anna suspected she hid more than just medications. Maybe all married couples lived like that—keeping things from one another just to keep the peace. Anna would never want to do that.

But she also knew that her grandfather loved her and her grandmother and all the people in his district. *Stuck with him until he dies? These jerks don't know him as a person, don't know what his motivations are.* The only one who seemed to get it—maybe—was the new guy, Jacob. Trembling, she kept her hand over her mouth and listened.

"The biggest thing folks are upset about is not being able to go to Dr. Noah's clinic."

Anna leaned an ear closer and recognized Rubin as the one speaking.

"Noah Stoltzfus was shunned by the community a really long time ago. He wrote a book or something." Rubin paused. "Anyway, he came back and wanted to make up for the way he'd acted by opening a clinic. He'd gotten him a doctoring degree, and he opened a clinic within buggy distance for most of the Amish folks here. It was his way of giving back to the community, he used to say. And his wife, Carley, used to work at the front desk. *Gut* people and related to some of the families here in our district. At first our old bishop—Bishop Ebersol—wouldn't let anyone go to Dr. Noah's clinic, but eventually he gave in because he knew it was the best thing for the community. The hospital is too far to reach by buggy. Most of us could get to Dr. Noah's clinic by buggy, and lots of times he drove to our *haus* if it was an emergency."

"Not anymore." Anna heard Ben jump in. "Almost all of Dr. Noah's patients were Amish. I heard he might even close down his clinic now. A real shame." He paused, and Anna could hear rustling, as if someone had stood up or moved around. "And I know it's Bishop Byler's fault that Lizzie Miller died a couple of months ago. Sarah Jane begged Bishop Byler to let Dr. Noah treat her stepmother, saying the distance to Lancaster was too far for the old woman, even by car. I was young when Lizzie's husband died, but Jonas was somewhat of a legend around here, and I doubt he'd be too happy that Bishop Byler practically killed his wife."

Anna gasped before she rushed into the barn, not even attempting to hide the tears rolling down her cheeks. "Liar! You're a liar, Ben!" Anna turned and pointed a finger at Rubin. "And I wouldn't go out with you, Rubin Fisher, if you were the last man on the planet!"

Ben moved toward her, but Anna backed up and held a palm out in front of her. "You're so wrong about him, about *Daadi*! About everything!" Anna knew for sure that her grandfather had nothing to do with Lizzie Miller's death. He'd gone to their house several times and offered to have a driver take Lizzie to the hospital. Anna and her grandparents had always included Lizzie in their prayers. This was a nasty rumor—one of many, Anna was sure.

"We're sorry, Anna." Rubin was walking closer to her too. "We didn't know you were out there listening." He raised one eyebrow. "Eavesdropping?"

"Shut up, Rubin! Just shut up!"

Then before she said things that went against her upbringing, she ran out the door, across the yard, and toward the road. Once she got to Black Horse Road, she crossed the street and ran as fast as she could through the field toward home. She hadn't gotten very far when she heard footsteps rustling in the high weeds behind her. She looked back to see Jacob Hostetler.

She turned around, tried to catch her breath, then yelled, "Don't follow me, Jacob. I want to be left alone."

When he kept on running toward her, Anna spun back around and ran faster until she couldn't hear Jacob behind her anymore.

Still in the field, she fell to her hands and knees and sobbed. She loved her *daadi*. She loved both her grandparents. They were the only parents she'd ever known. They'd been strict, no doubt, but she'd never felt unloved and had certainly never been locked in her room. *Jerks.*

She cried harder as anger at the men pressed down on her.

But even worse was having to admit to herself that some of what Ben and Rubin said was the truth.

2

JACOB COULD HAVE RUN FASTER AND CAUGHT UP WITH Anna, but he'd respected her wishes and turned around. During his walk home, he wondered if what Ben and Rubin said was true—and if it was . . . poor Anna. Thinking about her provided a temporary distraction from his own problems, but as his family's farm came into view, the heaviness settled around his heart. Mealtime was always the worst.

Jacob spotted Eli and Abraham outside as he neared the house—an enormous farmhouse that had been restored before Jacob's family had made the move from Ohio. The Amish family who owned the farm had chosen to downsize because the father had taken ill. With a fresh coat of white paint on the outside, a new tin roof, and a white picket fence, it should have been the most inviting house on the road. But as Jacob drew nearer, he could see that his mother and sisters still hadn't done anything with the flowerbeds that ran the length of the porch. They remained as barren as all their hearts.

"Need some help?" Jacob walked to where his brothers were brushing down Bolt, a retired racehorse they had bought when they arrived in Paradise.

"*Nee*, we got it." Eli ran the brush the length of the animal, who bobbed his head in pleasure over the rubdown. The little spot of white between the horse's ears seemed to twinkle against his glossy black hide.

Jacob nodded to his twelve-year-old brother, then eased around to where Abe was standing. The seven-year-old reached as high as he could, smoothing the animal's sweaty flanks.

"Bolt looks worn out." Jacob scratched the horse on the snout.

"Mary Jane and Anna Mae went visiting." Eli stowed the brush in the bucket, then grabbed the reins, clicking his tongue for Bolt to follow him to the barn.

"That's *gut*." Jacob tagged along behind his brothers, raising his hand to his forehead to block the setting sun. "Where'd they go?"

Eli shrugged as he led the horse into the stall. "I don't know. *Mamm* just told them they needed to go make friends with the neighboring families. They didn't want to, though."

Jacob sighed, sad to hear that Mary Jane and Anna Mae hadn't made the choice to venture out on their own. "You all need to make some new friends."

"What for?" Eli shrugged.

"I played volleyball today, and I met some fine folks." But Jacob had gone only to set an example for his siblings, and now he almost felt guilty for enjoying it.

Eli closed the latch on the stall, then whirled around. "I had plenty of friends back home, and I don't know why we moved to this stupid place." Eli rushed off, and even though Jacob called after him, the boy kept going.

Jacob leaned down in front of Abe, playfully tipping the boy's straw hat until it covered his eyes. "You want to make some new friends, don't you, little man?"

Abe pushed his hat back, and Jacob could see that Mary Jane had cut their youngest sibling's blond bangs much too short again. "I guess so."

Jacob straightened. "Let's go wash for supper. Just keep praying, Abe. Everything is going to be okay." He put his hand on his brother's back, and they walked toward the house, stopping at the water pump outside before they climbed the porch steps.

As they walked into the living room, Jacob breathed in the aroma of freshly baked bread, and for a few seconds there was a sense of normality. In the kitchen, Anna Mae and Mary Jane were setting out jams, jellies, and bread while their mother stirred something on the stovetop.

"How was the volleyball game?" *Mamm* kept stirring but turned around and smiled. Cora Hostetler did her best to put on a happy face each day for her family, but the dark circles under her eyes told another tale. Jacob still had lots of sleepless nights as well.

"*Gut.* Nice folks." He took his seat at the large oak table in the middle of the spacious kitchen, as did Abe and Eli. "Although I'm still no *gut* at volleyball." He chuckled, hoping to get a glimpse of joy . . . out of anyone.

"You don't realize your own strength." Mary Jane set a bowl of mashed potatoes in the middle of the table, the hint of a smile on her face. "That's why you always knock it out of bounds."

"Maybe." Jacob leaned back in his chair as his sisters set the table. It was hard to believe that the twins had started their *rumschpringe*, although you'd never have known it. They weren't taking advantage of the freedoms that went along with the running-around period. "Where's *Daed*?"

"He is . . . resting." *Mamm* avoided everyone's eyes as she ladled gravy into a small bowl. "I'll take him a plate later."

Jacob scooted his chair closer to the table and didn't say anything. This was how it was most nights—their father either resting or not feeling well. John Hostetler rarely ate breakfast with the family either. He left before anyone got up, farmed all day, and went to his room. Jacob hadn't even seen him in two days. *Daed* didn't want help out in the fields, so Jacob had gotten himself a job in town at the lumberyard. Eli was working too, tending to a widow's farm animals. Both Jacob and Eli were glad not to be in the fields, but Jacob missed the way things used to be.

The girls did most of the farm chores—milked the cows, gathered eggs, and mowed the yard—as well as helping *Mamm* with the sewing, cooking, and cleaning. Young Abe fed the pigs, goats, and horses, and Jacob was sure the girls pawned off some of their easier chores on him. He hoped someone would feel motivated to plant the flowerbeds soon.

Once everyone was seated, the family bowed their heads in silent prayer before beginning to fill their plates. Jacob glanced at his father's empty chair at the end of the table, then envisioned the spot where Leah used to sit.

Why can't God put the pieces of our lives back together again?

Anna pushed peas around on her plate as Ben's and Rubin's words echoed in her ears. Without lifting her head, she raised her eyes to her grandfather and watched him taking a bite of butter bread. He was the only father she'd ever known, even though she'd always called him *daadi* instead of *daed*, the same way she called her grandmother *mammi* and not *mamm*. *Mammi* had explained that it was out of respect for Anna's parents. "They will always be your parents," she'd said from the time Anna was young, although Anna had no memories of them.

She forced a bite of peas into her mouth, chewing slowly, her mind whirling with conflicting thoughts. She loved her grandfather and couldn't stand the way some people perceived him, yet part of her understood the criticism. *Does everyone think he is a bad bishop?*

Glancing around the kitchen, she realized it was perfectly displayed the way her grandfather wanted everyone in their district to live. All of their windows in the entire house were covered with green shades, something that used to be uniform within the district. Many had veered from that, but Anna knew her grandfather was making house calls to correct that.

Her eyes drifted to the countertop, bare except for the canisters that held baking ingredients. No trinkets or decorative tins. No vases. Nothing out of place. The white clapboard walls were bare too, without even a calendar or clock. Three years ago they'd finally gotten a gas oven—after a spark from the wood-burning stove started a fire in the kitchen. There were no propane lights, just lanterns, and the modest home was furnished only by simple pieces her grandfather had built. Some of the pieces were fifty years old, like the oak coffee table in the living room. The sturdy table would probably last forever.

"How was the volleyball game?" Her grandfather didn't look up as he scooped another forkful of pot roast.

"*Gut.*" She paused, still watching him. She'd always known that he was strict and was aware that he'd grown even sterner as a bishop. But until today she hadn't realized how much some people disliked him. "There's a new family in town, living in the old Zook place."

Daadi nodded, finally looking up at her. "*Ya, ya.* I hope they will be at worship tomorrow."

Anna thought about Jacob and wondered if it was just a matter of time before he disliked her grandfather too. Probably.

She studied her grandmother's plate, noticing that she didn't have any bread or buttered noodles on it. As usual, she had her bottle of cinnamon pills from the homeopathic doctor on the table. Her grandmother would take two when she was done eating, and they'd help curb the glucose spike that usually happened a couple of hours after a meal. Then she'd most likely go upstairs and take the pills from Dr. Noah, the ones *Daadi* didn't know about, a form of insulin. Anna had asked her grandmother repeatedly why she didn't just tell him that she needed the prescription pills. *Mammi* just shook her head and said it was better this way. It wasn't exactly lying, but it wasn't being honest either.

"I paid a visit to Sadie and Kade Saunders this afternoon since they'll be hosting worship service tomorrow." Her grandfather reached for another piece of butter bread. "It pleases me that their family follows the *Ordnung* in almost everything they do." *Daadi* paused to scoop mashed potatoes onto his slice of bread, something he'd done for as long as Anna could remember. "And they are raising fine *kinner*, an even harder job than most since young Tyler is special." He took a bite of the potato bread, as he often called it. "And if an *Englisch* man like Kade can convert to our ways, adhere to the *Ordnung*, and follow the rules set forth by the Lord, then the rest of the district should be able to follow his fine example." *Daadi* gave a taut nod, almost dipping his gray beard into his plate.

Anna remembered years ago when Kade came into their lives with his young autistic son, Tyler. He'd married Sadie, who was a widow, and they'd gone on to have a daughter, Marie. Anna could also recall how unhappy her grandfather had been about the arrangement in the beginning. He'd been sure that Kade would never be able to make the switch from wealthy *Englisch* man to a baptized member of their community.

But *Daadi* had come around. He wasn't as rigid as some believed. Anna thought again about Rubin's and Ben's cutting remarks. It shook her to think they blamed her grandfather for Lizzie Miller's death. *Ridiculous*. She was lost in her thoughts when someone knocked at the door.

Daadi groaned. "Who would be calling at the supper hour?" He shook his head, and Anna's grandmother got up quickly from the table and headed toward the living room.

Marianne glared at Hector and spoke in a whisper. "What are you doing here?" She took the small box from his hands, shaking her head. "This is *not* our agreed upon time." She paused, blowing out a breath of frustration. "And what are you doing here on a Saturday anyway?"

"I couldn't help it, Mrs. Byler. I had tons of deliveries today, and I'm running behind schedule." Hector shrugged, his dark hair wet with sweat, his brown eyes begging for forgiveness. "And this package was marked for Saturday delivery." He gave a quick wave before running down the porch steps and back to his UPS truck.

She closed the door, hurried to her room, and stashed the box under the bed for now. *What was Hector thinking?* That young man knew to only come between noon and three on weekdays, when Isaac was working in the fields and Anna was out delivering bread, jams, and noodles to the bakeries or running other errands.

As Marianne crossed through the living room toward the kitchen, she took a deep breath, then swallowed hard when she saw her husband standing at the window with the shade pulled out slightly, peering outside.

"What is UPS doing here?" Isaac glanced at Marianne before he looked back out the window. Marianne didn't want to lie, but she certainly couldn't tell her husband the truth. He turned to face her, his eyebrows drawn. "Did we get a gift?"

Not exactly. "I . . . uh . . . ordered something." Marianne raised her chin and clasped her hands in front of her.

Isaac walked closer. "What?"

Marianne swallowed hard again. "It's . . . it's a surprise." She squared her shoulders and tried to stand taller. Her husband's shoulders had slumped over the years, but he still towered over her, and his hazel eyes were searching hers. She made herself meet his gaze.

"Maybe your birthday present, *Daadi*," Anna said from the doorway into the kitchen.

Marianne didn't breathe for a few seconds, knowing she'd lie if she had to. She didn't feel good about that, but if Isaac knew the truth . . .

"My birthday isn't until October." Isaac frowned before crossing over to his rocking chair. Marianne's pulse slowly returned to normal as she made her way back to the kitchen to help Anna clean up.

"So, what's in the box?" Anna whispered as she filled the sink with warm water. "It *is* a bit early for a birthday present for *Daadi*."

Marianne planned to have another chat with Hector the next time she saw him. This incident was putting her in a terrible situation. "A surprise." She took a deep breath, hoping for a smooth transition to a new subject. "How is Emma's *mudder*? I heard Sarah had been down with a cold."

"She seemed okay." Anna handed Marianne a stack of dirty dishes, and thankfully the conversation didn't return to the UPS delivery.

When they were done in the kitchen, they joined Isaac for devotions, then Anna excused herself.

"*Mei maedel* seemed quiet." Isaac closed the Bible, eased off his reading glasses, and rubbed his eyes for a few seconds. "Did she say anything to you about a problem?"

Marianne had noticed this too, but she'd been so preoccupied with Hector's mistake that she hadn't questioned the girl. "She didn't say that anything was wrong." She stood up and waited for Isaac. He put his glasses on the coffee table, and they both made their way to their downstairs bedroom. She waited until he was in the bathtub before she retrieved the package from underneath the bed.

She peeked out of the bedroom door and looked right and left. Once she was sure Anna was still upstairs, she carried the package and a lantern to the basement door beneath the stairs and tiptoed down the narrow steps. As much as she wanted to open the package now, it was too risky. She scurried to the closet in the corner, eased the door open, and placed the box on one of the shelves.

The spacious closet had once served as a storage area for brooms, cleaning supplies, and the like, but they had added on to the house, and now there was sufficient room on the first floor for stowing those things. Rarely did anyone but Marianne go into the basement these days. Isaac's knees prevented him from going down the steep steps, and Anna had no need to be down there since they'd added a large pantry off the kitchen for storing canned goods.

Marianne breathed a sigh of relief when she crawled into bed. Isaac was still in the bathroom, and she hadn't been caught.

Jacob set the lantern on the nightstand by the bed, then tucked Abe in after they said their prayers. His youngest brother had been sleeping in one of the twin beds in Jacob's room since they'd moved in a couple of weeks ago.

Back home, Abe had shared a room with Eli. But Abe had frequent nightmares, and tending to him had left Eli exhausted all the time. Jacob had offered to let Abe sleep in his room for a while so that Eli could get a restful night's sleep. Jacob wasn't sleeping well anyway, and as the oldest, he felt like he should take care of Abe. He was trying to set a good example for his siblings, so they could try to get back to some form of normal. His father had just checked out of life, and Jacob knew why, even though he didn't agree with his father's way of handling things. Unfortunately, that left Jacob in charge, trying to make sense out of everything.

"Do you like it here?" Abe said as Jacob climbed in bed. The boy spoke in a whisper, almost as if he was afraid to ask the question.

Jacob fluffed his pillow and crossed his ankles beneath the light blanket, thankful for the breeze blowing in through the open window. "*Ya,* I do. It's a *gut* move for us, Abe." He snubbed out the lantern but stayed sitting up, locking his hands behind his head. "You'll think so too, once you make some new friends."

As the wind stirred the tree branches outside the window, shadows from the leaves danced across the ceiling, and Jacob leaned his head back and focused on the rhythmic movement while remembering their life back in Ohio. He could feel Abe's pain, but he worked hard these days to hide his emotions in front of his family.

"Do you think Leah can see us?" Abe was still whispering.

"I don't know. Maybe." Jacob rubbed his eyes, hoping that sleep would come. "But I'm sure she's having fun in heaven." He paused as he eased himself down and pulled the sheet to his chest. "And I know she'd want you to make lots of friends and not to worry about her."

He closed his eyes and pictured Leah's face—her soft blue eyes, her dainty features, and the way tendrils of hair, pale as a field of grain, often escaped her *kapp.* Leah had lit up any room she was in, and everyone had loved her.

Jacob fought the tears building in his eyes. Each night when darkness fell across the room, it encircled his heart as well, the thoughts and memories overwhelming him. It was during these times that he allowed himself to feel the pain.

Cora crawled into bed beside her husband and wondered if he'd ever touch her again. John's head was buried in a book, his way of avoiding her and conversation. As she rubbed lotion on her hands and arms, she worried how long her husband was going to punish himself for Leah's death. It had been over a year now, and none of them had really recovered. In fact, the first-year anniversary in May had seemed to make things worse, especially for John.

But life had to go on. Even Jacob was making strides by attending the volleyball game today, and her oldest son constantly encouraged the other *kinner* to make new friends. But Cora knew that Jacob was hurting as much as all of them.

She took a deep breath, dreading another confrontation with her husband, yet so tired from trying to be both parents. "Eli seems very bitter about the move," she said as she placed the lotion on her nightstand.

John didn't look up from his book. "He will adjust."

Cora bit her lip. If she pushed, this conversation could become a full-blown argument. But God didn't seem to be hearing her prayers these days, so she at least needed her husband to show some understanding. "You have to talk to him, John. Jacob does his best with both the younger boys, but they need their father. You can't keep . . ." She trailed off when John snapped the book closed, then quickly snubbed out the lantern.

"Another long day. I'm going to sleep." He lay back down and turned on his side, his back to her.

As she sat in the darkness, a part of her wanted to reach over and shove him, smack him on the back . . . something . . . to snap him out of this depression he was in. Instead, she eased into the covers, snuggled up against him, and draped one arm across his waist. When he tensed up, she moved over and put some distance between them. Hurt and anger wrapped around her so tightly she almost couldn't breathe. Didn't her husband understand that Leah's passing was hard on all of them? How could he just detach himself from life like this? He wouldn't have allowed another member of the family to behave like this if the circumstances of the accident were different.

Cora had told him repeatedly that he was not responsible for their daughter's death. "This was God's will," she'd told him many times. "As awful as it is, we must go on."

But John couldn't seem to get past it. She'd hoped he would be better, a bit back to his old self, once they'd distanced themselves from Middlefield. Leaving family and friends behind had been difficult, but staying had been impossible. The memory of Leah dying in front of all of them on their own farm was too much to bear, especially as spring neared and the prospect of plowing loomed.

The Zooks had agreed to plow and plant before leaving this farm—a true blessing. None of them, John especially, wanted to go anywhere near a plow this year.

Cora pulled her knees to her chest beneath the sheet, tucked her head, and cried the way she did most nights, her body trembling, her heart broken. *Please roll over and hold me, John. Comfort me.*

It took all of her daytime strength to be strong for her grieving children, but shouldn't she be able to rely on her husband for comfort? He was the man of the household, but sometimes she could barely stand to be in the same bed with him. And that was confusing.

In her mind she knew her husband wasn't responsible for Leah's death. It was God's will to take their eldest daughter home at the tender age of twenty. But when the lights were out, when John was cold and distant, and when her own grief overwhelmed her . . . it *was* John she blamed.

3

SUNDAY MORNING ANNA DIDN'T THINK WORSHIP would end soon enough. She stared straight ahead throughout the service without hearing much of what her grandfather or the other ministers had to say. Instead, she spent her time wondering how many people in the barn disliked her grandfather as much as Rubin and Ben did.

Without moving her head, she glanced to her left toward Sarah Jane Miller. Did Sarah Jane really believe that *Daadi* was responsible for her stepmother's death? Lizzie was sick for a long time, and Anna didn't think that anything her grandfather had done would have made a difference one way or another. But apparently others didn't feel the same way. Anna's heart hurt to think members of their district thought so unkindly of her grandfather. He was too strict. That was true. But he was also a loving man trying to do what he believed was right in God's eyes.

Twice during the service she caught the new fellow, Jacob Hostetler, staring at her. She knew it was because of her display the day before after the volleyball game. Jacob probably thought she was childish, running off and crying like that. But Ben and Rubin had said cruel things, things Anna had a hard time shaking.

She allowed herself a quick glance at Jacob. Their eyes met, and she thought she saw the hint of a smile. *Why?* Someone who looked like Jacob could have anyone he wanted in their district. Someone beautiful like Emma.

Anna pulled her eyes away, but when she looked back at Jacob a few moments later, his gaze was still fixed on her, and this time he did smile. Her heart raced as she quickly looked away, not wanting to get her hopes up that someone like Jacob might be interested in her. Maybe he felt sorry for her, after hearing all the things that Ben and Rubin had said, then seeing her run off crying. That was it. Pity.

She lifted her chin, pressed her lips together, and tried not to look his way. But as her grandfather concluded the service, her eyes drifted in Jacob's direction. Sure enough, he smiled again. Anna felt her cheeks warming, and while she couldn't help but question his intentions, she found herself conjuring up a plan.

She waited until after the noon meal and cleanup before she approached Jacob. He was standing among a group of fellows, including Rubin and Ben. She avoided everyone's eyes but Jacob's. "Can I talk to you for a minute, please?" Anna swallowed hard as she wondered what they all must be thinking.

Jacob grinned as he tipped back the rim of his hat. "*Ya.* Sure."

Anna turned, and without looking back, she walked around the corner of the barn. The Saunders had a small home, but they had an enormous barn where they could hold worship service. She could hear footsteps behind her but waited until she was clear of the crowd to turn around. Taking a deep breath, she knew this would be the boldest thing she'd ever done.

"Hello," she said softly, attempting a smile.

"*Wie bischt?*"

Anna swallowed hard as her heart thumped in her chest, but
Jacob strode up to her with the confidence of a hundred men, his
perfect lips curled up into a grin and his eyes twinkling. How
could anyone look this good? And why in the world would he even
consider accepting her proposal?

"Would you like to take me to the singing tonight?" Anna
blurted it out, then held her breath as she watched him rub his
chin, frowning. Ach, nee . . . *he's going to turn me down.* "I'm sorry.
Never mind." She shook her head, backed up, then turned around.
She'd only taken a few steps when Jacob called her name. Biting
her lip, she slowly turned.

"*Ya,* I'd like to take you to the singing." Jacob frowned again,
and for someone who *said* one thing, he sure looked like he felt differently. "There's just one problem."

Anna shook her head again, feeling ridiculous. "*Nee, nee.* It's okay."

Jacob eased a step closer to her, and it took her a few moments
to realize she was holding her breath. "The problem is that I don't
have my own buggy." His face reddened as he looked at the ground,
then back up at her. "We only brought one buggy from Middlefield.
I'm hoping to have *mei* own soon, but right now, I have to check with
my folks."

Anna let out the breath she was holding, unsure what to say.
Maybe that's just an excuse. She looked down, kicked at the grass with
one foot, and shook her head. "It's really okay, and—"

"Wait. I'll be right back." He held up a finger. "Don't go away."

Anna waited as he disappeared around the corner. She knew it
was only a matter of time before Jacob became interested in Emma
or one of the other girls in their district. But in the meantime,
maybe they could help each other.

She thought again about what Ben and Rubin had told Jacob—
that she was undateable. She leaned against the barn, bent her knee,
and propped one foot against the siding, knowing Jacob would
come back and say he wasn't able to use his parents' buggy.

Jacob spotted his father standing under an old oak tree on the
north side of the Saunders' house. He sighed. He'd rather seek
permission from his mother, but she was nowhere in sight, and
if he didn't hurry, Anna might leave or change her mind. Jacob
approached his father slowly. He'd been surprised that his father
joined them for church service at the Saunders'. But he was glad
too, though *Daed* hadn't had much to say. He had missed his father.
But here *Daed* was right now, and for the first time in over a year,
Jacob was feeling almost cheerful.

"*Daed* . . ." He stopped a few feet away.

"*Ya?*" His father squinted in the midday sun, his eyes as dark as
the circles beneath them, and Jacob nearly changed his mind about
asking him anything. But the thought of spending time with Anna
prodded him forward.

"I . . . I was wondering if I could use the buggy tonight." Jacob
scratched his nose and avoided his father's eyes.

"*Ya*, I don't see why not."

Jacob stared at his father. *Don't you even want to know what for?* He
knew his mother would be excited that he was doing something
social again. His father, however, didn't care what he did. What
any of them did. "*Danki.*"

He rushed back to where he'd left Anna standing on the other
side of the barn, trying to leave his sadness behind. He relaxed

when he saw that she'd waited for him. "It's no problem. What time should I pick you up?"

She stood taller and raised both eyebrows. "Uh . . . I guess four o'clock?"

Jacob felt a strange feeling in the pit of his stomach. He'd gone out with a few girls back home, but none as beautiful as Anna. He was looking forward to getting to know her better, and he hadn't looked forward to anything in a long time. "*Gut, gut.* Just tell me where to pick you up, and I'll be there." He thought about her grandfather and what Rubin and Ben had said, and for just an instant he wondered if he should have declined her invitation. But then she smiled, and Jacob realized he was more than willing to face her scary grandfather if it meant spending time with her.

"You know . . ." She stepped closer to him. "My grandfather isn't an evil man like Ben and Rubin made him out to be." She paused and took a deep breath, then grinned. "And he surely doesn't lock me in my room."

Jacob had suspected Rubin and Ben were exaggerating about the bishop, but he still felt relief flood over him. "I didn't believe what they were saying, and I'm sorry they upset you so much. Lots of bishops are strict, but they just want what's best for the district."

"*Ya!*" She bounced up on her toes, and a beautiful smile filled her face. "Exactly. I'm so glad you understand that. I wish everyone around here did." Frowning, she shook her head and went on. "Anyway, I appreciate you agreeing to take me to the singing. It . . . it isn't like a *date* or anything. I just thought if some of the other guys here saw me going out with you, then they'd know I'm allowed, that my grandfather isn't such a scary man." She blushed as she glanced down at the ground. "Although . . ." She shrugged. "Maybe there's another reason no one has asked me out."

Jacob opened his mouth to tell her that her grandfather was definitely the problem, that otherwise she would have been asked out dozens of times. But he said nothing, feeling like he'd been kicked in the gut. He'd thought maybe Anna was interested in him. It had never occurred to him that she might be using the new guy to let those in the district know she was allowed to date.

"Four o'clock sounds great," he finally said. He forced himself to smile, knowing this could be a mistake. Did she see through him? Could she tell that he felt on the verge of tears half the time? Or did she just not find him the least bit attractive? Either way, he knew he wasn't a good catch. Grief sucked the life out of him sometimes. But the deed was done, and at least it might set a good example for his brothers and sisters, show that he was getting on with his life.

For a short while today he'd felt like it might be true. But Anna had straightened him out about her intentions, and now he just felt sad. And a bit bitter.

Anna waited until they were almost home before she mentioned the singing to her grandparents. She leaned forward into the front seat of the buggy and clenched the leather backrest in front of her. *"Daadi?"*

Her grandfather gave a brief glance in her direction as he flicked the reins for the horse to pick up the pace. *"Ya?"*

"A—a . . ." She'd always hoped this day would arrive, and she'd always thought her grandfather would allow her to be picked up for a singing, but now that the moment was upon her, she wasn't sure.

"Spit it out, child." *Daadi* glanced at her again. "What is it?"

"A—a . . . um . . . boy would like to take me to the singing tonight. Is it all right?" She squeezed her eyes closed for a few moments until she felt the buggy slowing down. She opened her eyes to see her grandfather pulling back on the reins.

"What's this?" He narrowed his eyebrows into a frown and peered over at Anna's grandmother. "Did you know about this?"

Mammi shook her head. *"Nee,* but I think it is *gut.* She has been of age, Isaac, for a while."

Anna tightened her grip on the seat and waited.

"Who is this boy?" *Daadi* was still frowning and keeping the horse at a slow trot.

"Jacob Hostetler, the new boy from Ohio." Anna bit her bottom lip, glancing at her grandmother, but *Mammi* just stared straight ahead.

"We know nothing about his family." *Daadi* continued to scowl, but Anna felt hopeful that he hadn't outright denied her request. She waited for her grandmother to back her up again, but Anna supposed *Mammi's* earlier comment was all the help she was going to get.

"He seems nice, *Daadi,* and this would be a way for me to get to know more about his family." Anna knew her grandfather liked to be well-informed about members in their district, especially the new families.

She waited, the *clip-clop* of hooves growing louder against the silence. After another minute or so, her grandfather spoke up.

"He will come and talk with me first. You will not just jump in his buggy and leave. I didn't have an opportunity to properly meet him today." *Daadi* gave a taut nod of his head, and Anna wondered if she'd even get to the singing once her grandfather got done with Jacob. But this was probably the best she could hope for, and she'd take it.

"*Ya*. I will have him come in and talk to you and *Mammi* when he gets here." Anna released her grip on the seat and leaned back. She felt lucky to have nabbed this opportunity before Jacob chose someone else in the community. She knew someone like him would never really be interested in her, but going with him tonight would at least show boys like Ben and Rubin that she was allowed to date. Not that she'd ever go out with either one of them, but they were bigmouths and would spread the word. Maybe someone else would show an interest.

Jacob changed his shirt before he went downstairs. His excitement about Anna asking him to the singing had provided a welcome distraction from his troubles. But knowing that she was using him put a damper on the plan. Had everyone really been so fearful of her grandfather that they hadn't asked her out? Jacob would have gladly faced off with her grandfather for a chance to go out with her. But he sure wished the circumstances this afternoon were different.

His mother and the twins were in the living room knitting when he walked in, and he figured his brothers were outside.

"Where's *Daed*?" Jacob poked his head into the kitchen before his mother answered but saw no sign of his father.

"He's resting right now." *Mamm* didn't look up.

"He's *always* resting." Jacob shook his head as he pulled his hat from the rack.

She looked up but ignored his comment. "I think it's wonderful that you've found someone to take to the singing already." *Mamm* glanced at Anna Mae and Mary Jane. "Maybe your *schweschdere* would like to go?"

"This is a date, *Mamm*." Jacob put one hand on his hip and shifted his weight. "But you know I'll take the twins if they want to go." He glanced at his sisters, wishing they would go—and wishing they wouldn't go. They both shook their heads, leaving him relieved and sad.

By the time he arrived at Anna's house, his stomach was churning. He hoped Anna would wait for him outside, but after everything he'd heard about her grandfather, he was sure it wouldn't be that easy. Once Bolt was tethered, he walked across the yard and up the porch steps. Anna's house was big like his own and appeared freshly painted. The porch decking was light gray, and two white rocking chairs sat on either side of a plain white table. Not surprisingly, there were no wind chimes or other decorations on the porch, but it was nice to see the colorful assortment of blooms in the flowerbeds.

He knocked on the door, stood taller, and took a deep breath. Anna answered right away. She wore a burgundy-colored dress beneath a black apron, and she was smiling. Jacob couldn't get over how pretty she was. She could have anyone that she wanted, someone far better looking and more suitable than him. But this was God's plan, he supposed, so Jacob would do his part—letting the district know that her grandfather would let her date.

His stomach lurched as Anna stepped aside so he could come in.

"*Mammi* and *Daadi* would like to meet you before we go." She was still smiling, and Jacob wished they were going out under different circumstances. A *real* date.

"*Ya.* Sure." Jacob crossed the threshold, and he recognized the aroma of freshly baked bread mixed with something else he couldn't quite identify. Their living room was the plainest he'd ever seen, and his own family was going to be in trouble if this was how Bishop Byler expected everyone's home to be. There was a small, tan couch, two wooden rocking chairs, a simple coffee table, two lanterns on the mantel, and . . . He glanced around. That was it. No propane lighting, no wall decorations whatsoever. Not even a clock. He quickly looked to his right when heavy footsteps grew louder.

Bishop Byler hadn't looked all that scary at worship service earlier. But now that the man was in his own home, scowling, Jacob could see what all the fuss was about. The bishop was a tall man with slumped broad shoulders, and as he looped his thumbs beneath his suspenders and frowned, Jacob wondered what he was in for.

"*Mei maedel* does not kiss on dates, and she must be home by seven o'clock." Bishop Byler raised his chin, stroked his gray beard, and peered at Jacob. "Understood?"

Jacob felt his face reddening. A quick glance at Anna found hers to be a bright crimson as well.

"*Ya.* Yes, sir." Jacob pushed back the rim of his hat and nodded, hoping this portion of the date would go quickly. "I will have her home by seven."

Bishop Byler folded his arms across his chest. "And what else?"

Jacob glanced again at Anna, who was now hanging her head. "I—I . . . uh . . . no kissing."

"*Ach*, good grief, Isaac. Leave the boy alone."

Jacob had met Marianne Byler earlier in the day, and he was glad to see her entering the room now. "Nice to see you again,

Jacob." She gave his hand a squeeze and smiled at Anna. "You *kin-ner* go on now, and have a *gut* time."

Jacob waited for a cue from Anna, and when she waved for him to follow, he did so quickly.

Marianne closed the door behind Anna and her date, then whipped around to face her husband. "Why did you embarrass them both like that?"

Isaac raised his chin, frowning. "Why did you speak to me in such a way in my own home, in front of the *kinner*?"

"I'm sorry, Isaac." Marianne softened her voice to appease him. "But don't you ever wonder why no young lads have come calling for Anna? They're scared of you. And now, finally, a new boy in town comes a-courtin', and you're gonna scare him off."

Her husband walked to the couch and sat down. He picked up his Bible and his reading glasses, slipping the spectacles on his face. "He needs to be scared. Not just any young man deserves to be with our Anna. This Jacob must prove himself worthy first."

Marianne sat down beside him and touched him gently on the leg. "My dear, Anna must make her own choice for a husband, but if you scare away all her options, she'll have to settle for whoever is brave enough to face you. Do you want that?"

He turned the page in the Bible and pushed his glasses up on his nose before turning to face her. "I was a young man once. I know how they are."

Marianne grinned. "*Ya*, I know. I remember how *you* were too." She tapped a finger to her chin. "And if I recall, *mei daed* was just as worried about me as you are about Anna. But you must trust her to make *gut* decisions." She leaned over and kissed him on the cheek. "Why don't you take a nap, and I'll cook us some supper."

"A nap does sound *gut*." Isaac pulled his glasses off and put them on the coffee table. "See you in a bit." He kissed her before heading to their bedroom, and Marianne hurried to the kitchen. She pulled out a tub of leftover stew and quickly set it on the stove, turning the knob to low.

Once she could hear Isaac snoring, she tiptoed to the basement entrance, eased the door open, and hurried down the stairs.

4

ANNA WISHED SHE'D NEVER ASKED JACOB TO THE SING-
ing. He was sure to tell people what her grandfather had said. And
even if her friends saw her on a date, they'd eventually learn the
truth—how Anna had asked Jacob out. *Why didn't I think of that?* But
the silence in the buggy was too awkward not to say something
and try to make the best of it.

"*Danki* for taking me to the singing. And I'm sorry about *mei
daadi.*" She turned to face him, wishing this was a real date—one
he'd asked her on because he was interested in getting to know her
better.

"*Ach,* it's okay. He's just looking out for his little girl." Jacob
flashed his perfect smile, and she again wondered why he even
agreed to this. He could easily have gotten out of it by just saying
he didn't have his own buggy.

She pulled her eyes from his. "It was just so embarrassing."
She let out a heavy sigh, but Jacob chuckled. She lifted her head.
"What's so funny?"

"I was just thinking how goofy I must have looked. I could feel
my face turning red, and I wasn't sure what to say." He clicked his
tongue until his horse picked up the pace.

Anna twisted slightly in the seat to face him. "Under the

circumstances, I think you did just fine." She paused, twirling the string from her *kapp* around her finger. "Are you going to tell everyone what my grandfather said?"

His smile faded. "*Nee*, Anna. I won't tell anyone. I don't want to blow your chances of someone asking you out." He paused, still not smiling. "I'll tell everyone—Rubin and Ben included—that it was very easy, taking you out and facing your grandfather."

The edge in his voice was confusing, but Anna cringed just the same. "Ew. I don't want to go out with Rubin or Ben, so I really don't care what you tell them."

"So do you have someone else in mind?"

Anna kept her eyes on him, even though his gaze was straight ahead. He wasn't even pretending this was a real date. Part of her had hoped he would, even if just for the afternoon. No one in her district was as handsome as he was, plus he'd raced after her when she was upset and been brave enough to face her grandfather. She sighed. It would still be nice getting to know him, even though she knew he'd end up with someone who was a better match. Like Emma.

"There's no one in particular I'm interested in," she finally said. *Except maybe you.* At one time she'd had a crush on Jesse Dienner. He'd married a girl named Shelby, someone new to their district, so that had ended that. But maybe if Jacob stayed true to his word and didn't mention her grandfather's grilling, someone unexpected would ask her out.

They were quiet for a while as the buggy rolled down the gravel road. The Huyards were hosting the singing, and they lived about six miles outside of Paradise. Whoever held worship service usually hosted the singing in the evenings, but Sadie and Kade didn't have children old enough to participate, so the Huyards had offered to have the gathering at their house.

With two miles to go, the tension was thick, so Anna spoke up again. "Emma said she thought you moved from Middlefield, Ohio." She paused. "I guess that would explain this black buggy, as opposed to the gray ones we all have." She'd also noticed the slight differences in his clothing, and she was glad her grandfather hadn't mentioned anything about that. Usually a new family was given time to adhere to the rules of a new district.

"*Ya*. We moved here a couple of weeks ago."

"What made you move to Lancaster County?"

He shifted his weight in the seat, his eyes forward, and just shrugged. "Needed a change."

Anna pursed her lips together, knowing she could be a nosy Nellie sometimes. But curiosity won out. "Did you leave family behind?"

"*Ya.*"

Hmm . . . "I bet that was hard."

"*Ya.*"

Anna released the string of her prayer covering and dropped her hands to her lap. "I've never been outside of Pennsylvania."

"You're kidding? Not even on a vacation?" Jacob turned to face her, frowning.

"We don't go on vacations." She twisted in her seat. "Have you traveled a lot? Have you been on an airplane? What about Florida? Lots of folks around here vacation in Florida."

"I've traveled a little, and yes, I've been on an airplane."

She gasped slightly. "Really? Where did you go?"

Jacob pulled back on the reins and the buggy slowed. He

reached in his pants pocket, apologizing as he put a cell phone
to his ear. Anna had never had a mobile phone, and while they'd
been widely accepted by Bishop Ebersol, eight months ago her
grandfather had forbidden them completely. She knew that many
members of the community still used them for business but kept
them hidden.

Anna watched as Jacob's eyes widened. He pulled back on the
reins until the horse was completely stopped. "I'm on my way."
He glanced at Anna. "I have someone with me." He paused, nod-
ding. "Okay."

"Is everything all right?" she asked as he set the phone on the
seat in between them.

"*Nee.* I have to go home. Right now. It's *mei bruder. Mamm* said
something is wrong with him, but she was crying and I couldn't
understand her." He slapped the horse with the reins and yelled
for him to take off. "I'm closer to my *haus* than yours. Do you
mind coming with me? I'm sorry about this." His mouth was tight,
his jaw clenched.

"Of course not. Do you need to call an ambulance? Or I know
some drivers for hire."

"I don't think so." He shook his head. "I mean . . . I don't know.
I don't know what's wrong."

He yelled again, picked up the pace even more, and Anna held
on for dear life as the buggy hit a rut in the road. She bounced in
her seat, but Jacob didn't seem to notice, his eyes focused on the
road in front of them. As the horse's speed increased, so did the
flurry of dust beneath its hooves, and after a taste of it, Anna kept
her mouth clamped shut. She wasn't sure she'd ridden this fast in
a buggy before.

A few minutes later Jacob slowed the buggy in front of his house. It didn't look much different from when the Zooks lived there, except that Lena and her daughters had always kept the flowerbeds plush with greenery and flowers. Jacob's mother and sisters must not have had time to tend to them yet.

"What's wrong?" Jacob jumped out of the buggy as soon as it was stopped and ran toward the little boy who stood in front. "Abe, what is it? What's wrong with Eli?"

The boy glanced at Anna, his face wet with tears, then back at Jacob. "Who's that?"

"That's Anna. Now what's wrong with Eli?" Jacob grabbed the boy by his shoulders. "Where is he?"

They waited, but Abe just shrugged.

"Never mind." Jacob let go of the boy and glanced at Anna. "I'll be back." Then he bolted toward the house and took the porch steps two at a time. Anna stepped out of the buggy and walked around to where Abe was standing.

"Anything I can do to help?" She extended her hand to him. "I'm Anna."

He hesitated, then latched on. "I'm Abe." He let go quickly, then rubbed his nose. "I don't think there's nothin' you can do." He dashed around her, up the porch steps, and into the house. He couldn't have been more than six or seven.

Feeling awkward, she sat back down on the passenger seat in the buggy and chewed on one of her fingernails. She jumped when she heard Jacob's cell phone ringing next to her on the seat. Glancing down, she saw the name *Carolyn*.

Eli sat crouched in the corner of the living room, covering his face with his hands. Shards of glass and pieces of a broken lantern surrounded him, and his left hand was covered in blood. Their mother was crouched near her son, but she wasn't touching him.

"I can't find your father," *Mamm* whispered, shaking her head. "And he screams when I get too close to him."

Jacob turned toward the door as his youngest brother burst in. "Abe, go upstairs." Jacob waved a hand toward the stairs. "Go on, now. Do as I say."

Abe hesitated, then darted up the stairs. Jacob edged a little closer to Eli. "Where are Anna Mae and Mary Jane?" he asked his mother.

"They left awhile ago to pick berries." *Mamm* shrugged, swiping at her eyes. "They should have been back by now." She took a couple of steps toward Eli. "Eli, let me just clean this glass up, and I'll make you—"

"Get away from me!" Eli didn't look up as he yelled. Their mother stepped back and looked at Jacob. "What should we do?" she mouthed.

Jacob stood taller and spoke firmly. "Eli, you've cut your hand, and *Mamm* needs to tend to it. I'll clean up this glass."

"Go away, Jacob!" Eli brought his knees to his chest and buried his head, his bloodstained hands wrapped around himself. "It should have been me! I should have been the one who died, not Leah." Eli's shoulders shook as he sobbed, and he looked much younger than his twelve years.

Jacob eased toward Eli and squatted in front of him. He spoke softly. "*Nee*, Eli. That's not true." He touched his brother lightly on the arm. "It was God's will what happened to Leah." Jacob cringed, knowing how many times he had questioned the Lord's will over the past year. He knew it was even harder for Eli to understand the reasoning behind their sister's death. "*Mamm* needs to tend to your hand."

Eli lifted his head, his bottom lip trembling, his nose and cheeks bright red. "I was always the one on that side of the plow. Leah only took over because I was tired."

Jacob swallowed back a lump in his throat as he stared into his brother's eyes. "*Nee*, Eli. Things happen according to God's plan, not ours. God numbers our days. It was Leah's time." Even as he spoke the words, he had trouble believing them. "Now, you let *Mamm* tend to your hand." He reached for Eli's hand, and after a quick inspection, he could tell it wouldn't need stitches.

"*Daed* hates me. That's why he's never around." A tear rolled down Eli's cheek as Jacob accepted a wet rag from his mother and began dabbing the cut. For the first time, he had an urge to punch his father.

"That's not true." *Mamm* stepped closer, but Eli kept his eyes on Jacob's, waiting for a response.

"*Mamm's* right. That's not true. *Daed* feels responsible for Leah's death, like you do." Jacob paused, wondering if in some way each one of them felt responsible. Jacob knew he did. When she slipped, he'd been the one closest to her. Why hadn't he moved quicker and latched onto her arm? "And both of you are wrong. You can't carry that false burden, Eli. It isn't right."

"Then why is *Daed* doing it?" Eli cringed as Jacob finished wiping blood from his hand. Jacob didn't have an answer for his brother.

"Come on. Get up so we can clean this glass up." He glanced around the area. "What happened, anyway?"

Eli hung his head and spoke in a whisper. "I got mad and threw it down."

Jacob let out a heavy sigh. "Well, at least it wasn't lit." He stood up, offered Eli a hand, and pulled him to his feet. "Go on upstairs. I'll clean this up."

"Where's your friend? Is she still waiting outside?" *Mamm* had left and returned with a broom and dustpan. She started sweeping the glass into a pile, still sniffling. Jacob couldn't remember seeing his mother cry before Leah's death. Now it seemed that everything caused her to weep. Knowing he should be sensitive to that, he still spoke harshly to her.

"*Ya, Mamm.* She's outside. Would you have wanted me to bring her in to see this?" Jacob put his hands on his hips. "And where is *Daed*, anyway? Guess he isn't *resting*. Where is he?"

Mamm squatted and scooped the broken glass into the dustpan, shaking her head. "I don't know."

Jacob was quiet for a few moments as he watched a tear roll down his mother's cheek. "Do you want me to stay? Are you gonna be all right?"

"*Nee, nee.*" She stood up. "I'll be fine. You go be with your friend. I shouldn't have called, but . . ." She pulled a tissue from her apron pocket and dabbed at her eyes. "But Eli was yelling, and I was worried he'd hurt himself even more."

Jacob nodded. At twelve, Eli was as big as their mother—hard for her to control when he was so upset.

"I think I should take Anna home and then come back here." He sighed. Anna's plan had already robbed the outing of any potential joy. With this added to the mix, he was ready to just be alone.

"*Nee.*" *Mamm* actually stomped one foot. "You go, Jacob. You go and don't think about any of this. I shouldn't have called you. This is your father's job to—" She stopped, pressed her lips together, then locked eyes with Jacob. "Go. And have a *gut* time."

Jacob wasn't sure that was possible, but he knew he'd left Anna outside for too long already. "I'll think about it."

Mamm kissed him on the cheek before he walked back outside. Anna was sitting in the passenger seat, probably wondering why he was so rude to leave her outside. He wasn't sure how to explain things to her in a way that wouldn't make his family sound as broken as they were.

He untied Bolt and climbed into the seat beside her. "Anna, I'm so sorry to leave you outside like that. There was a problem with *mei bruder.*"

She started shaking her head right away. "Don't apologize. Really. Family must come first." She turned in her seat to face him. "Is everything okay?"

Jacob eased the buggy backward and got it turned around. "*Ya.* Sure." He wondered how convincing he was, since all he really wanted to do was cry—and a nineteen-year-old man just didn't do that. He got Bolt into a steady trot down the driveway, then onto the gravel road. The last thing he felt like doing was being around a crowd of people.

"*Nee.* I don't think everything is okay. And, Jacob, if you'd like to just take me home and be with your family, please know that's all right."

Her voice was soft and compassionate, her eyes sincere. He thought for a few moments before he answered her.

"How would you feel if we just get some coffee somewhere instead of going to the singing?" Then he remembered her plan to show him off to everyone, to let them know she was available for dating. *"Ach,* never mind. I know you wanted to go to—"

"I'd love to." She sat taller, batting her beautiful eyes at him.

"Really?" He swallowed hard, wondering how much to tell her over coffee. If she knew what a wreck his family was, she'd probably steer clear of him from now on. But his need to talk to someone his own age was outweighing concerns over what she might think of him. He'd tried to talk to Carolyn before he left, but she always seemed impatient for him to get over Leah, get past it, accept the accident as God's will and move on. He'd tried to do that, but talking about it would have helped. He'd only gone out with Carolyn a couple of times, but they'd grown up together. Jacob had expected her to be more understanding.

"If you turn left when you get to Lincoln Highway, there's a diner. It's pretty new. I haven't been there, but I heard it's good." Anna's smile seemed genuine, and Jacob nodded. Even if she didn't want to be more than friends, he could use a friend right now. Maybe he'd just tell her everything.

Or maybe not.

Marianne felt a thrill as she tiptoed down the basement stairs, along with a tiny tingle of guilt. She knew she shouldn't be keeping secrets from her husband, but all those years of living with her husband's authoritative ways had driven her to it. At least that's what she kept telling herself.

Stretching high on her toes, she reached atop the door frame and felt around for her key. Once it was in the lock, she turned the knob and walked into the closet, which was more like a small room. She flipped the switch on the battery-operated light she had hung on the wall inside the door, then she pulled her small box from the shelf and eased into her padded armchair in the corner of the small space. As she struggled to open the box, her heart raced. Even though Hector's timing had been terrible, she'd been waiting for this package to arrive. She pulled the cell phone from its container, excited to have Internet to order things with the credit card she'd gotten recently. Isaac would come unhinged if he knew she had a credit card, but having to send money orders for all her purchases had become a hindrance. And she was careful to pay the bill in full each month.

After she read the instructions, she realized she would have to find a place to charge the phone before she could use it. She glanced around at everything she'd collected over the years. It was nothing short of a miracle that Anna hadn't been more suspicious and found all of her goodies, but she suspected her granddaughter would keep her secret. It was all harmless enough.

She put the phone in her lap and reached for her aromatherapy lotion from Bath & Body Works and lathered the silky fragrance on her dry hands. She'd been ordering soaps, lotions, shampoo, and even laundry detergent through the mail for some time now—all items she used to make from scratch. Isaac never took notice of such things, and if Anna knew—which she likely did—she never said anything. Making them had become a struggle when Marianne's arthritis acted up, and she didn't want to ask Anna to take on anything else. Her granddaughter had plenty to do already.

Marianne did her shopping when no one was home. She had a pile of catalogs and *Englisch* magazines stacked on one of the shelves, and over the years she had begun to order other items. She reached

for the Sears catalog. Next on her list was a bright pink sweater
with pearl buttons. She'd never owned anything like it, though
she'd loved the color since she was a young girl. Even though she
would never be able to wear the sweater anywhere but this room, it
would give her comfort to wrap up in its softness, enjoy her hand
lotion, and read one of the many books she'd bought.

The little tingle of guilt returned, but she knew it would go
away. She'd married Isaac before she had an opportunity to have
much of a *rumschpringe*. Maybe she wouldn't have felt the need for
such luxuries if she had taken advantage of her running-around
period. But honestly, where was the harm?

She glanced around at the items she'd collected over the years,
thinking the Lord would understand.

Even if her husband wouldn't.

5

ANNA'S HEART WAS HEAVY AS SHE LISTENED TO JACOB explain about his oldest sister's death. The more he talked, the more she could feel his pain—and how much his family meant to him. Guilt flooded over her about the way she'd guessed his family to be perfect.

"I don't remember my parents' dying, and I just can't imagine what that must have been like for all of you."

Jacob took a sip of coffee, set it down, and shook his head. "I've burdened you with my problems since we got here. Tell me about your life, your grandparents."

Anna shrugged. "Well, let's see. I believe you already know that *mei daadi* is very strict." She paused as she circled the rim of her cup with her finger. "And *mei mammi* is one of the kindest people there is, even though . . ." Pausing, she met his eyes. "Don't get me wrong—I know that the man is the head of the household. But *Mammi* keeps a lot of secrets from *Daadi* because she feels he's too strict about some things."

"Do you? Think he's too strict?" Jacob was so easy on the eyes that Anna was finding it hard to keep her thoughts straight.

"Uh, *ya*. I do. But he means well, and he truly loves everyone in our district." She pinched off a piece of pretzel and dipped it in cheese sauce. "I could live on pretzels, I think."

He smiled. "For me, it's whoopee pies. Leah used to make the best ones."

Anna pinched another piece but then just sat there, staring at Jacob. He wasn't just great looking. He was also devoted to his family and sought peace in his heart. But his spirit was broken, and she wondered about his faith. Anna often felt like she was on a battlefield when it came to her faith—God on one side, her grandfather on the other—both shooting directives at her that often clashed. Sometimes what she felt in her heart, what she believed God wanted, was not the same as what her grandfather wanted. But she had to live with her *daadi*, so she tried to balance what she believed was the right way to live.

"It sounds like you and Leah were very close." Anna finally dipped the pretzel and took another bite.

"*Ya.* I'll be twenty in March. Leah would have been twenty-one in April." He took a sip of coffee, a faraway look in his eyes. "She was promised to a *gut* fellow back in Middlefield. He took her death as hard as the rest of us."

"We don't have to talk about this anymore if you don't want to." Anna took a deep breath and bit her lip. "I mean, I'm enjoying getting to know you, but I don't want you to feel—"

"*Nee.* It's *gut* to talk about Leah." He smiled. "I want to always remember how great she was." He tipped his head to one side. "You have the same light that Leah had."

Anna blushed. "Really?"

"*Ya.* You're easy to be around like she was."

She hung on the compliment for a few moments, then changed the subject to work, and she learned that Jacob worked at the lumberyard. She told him that she delivered *Mammi's* baked goods to local bakeries and detailed a bit about her days, the chores she took care of.

Their time together was casual, comfortable, and the most fun she'd had in a long while.

"It's nearing seven o'clock. I guess we need to go." Jacob glanced around the diner. "I don't see our waitress."

Anna didn't either, but she recognized the woman walking toward them. Lucy Turner. Lucy's hair was shorter and a different color now, but this was definitely the *Englisch* woman who'd wrecked Katie Ann and Ivan Stoltzfus's marriage. Anna never quite knew what to say to her.

"Here's your check." Lucy smiled as she put the bill on the table. "Cindy's shift ended—Oh hi, Anna."

"Hello, Lucy . . . Um, how's Benjamin doing?"

Anna and Lucy stumbled through an awkward conversation while Jacob went to pay the check. Lucy hurried off to check on other customers just as Jacob returned. "You know the waitress?" he asked.

"Not well. I babysat for her once." No point in spreading gossip. Jacob was bound to hear about Lucy Turner soon enough. Anna stood and smoothed the wrinkles from her dress. "*Danki* for the coffee . . . and the company."

Jacob nodded, and they headed for the exit. Fifteen minutes later they were pulling into Anna's driveway.

"Ten minutes to spare," Jacob said as he eyed the clock on his cell phone. Grinning, he added, "Guess this will have to go."

"*Daadi* is pretty strict about the use of cell phones." Anna shook her head as she stepped out of the buggy. Jacob quickly walked around to where she was standing.

"Do you, uh, want to do this again? Maybe go to the pizza place for supper sometime?" Jacob pushed back the tip of his straw hat and kept his eyes on hers.

Anna couldn't believe it. A real date—one she hadn't initiated. "Sure."

Jacob smiled. "What about Saturday?"

"Okay." Anna suddenly felt tongue-tied and couldn't even look at him.

"Great. See you then. Four o'clock?"

Anna nodded. "I better go in."

Jacob just stood there, kicking at the ground for a few moments. They'd talked about so much, it seemed like a hug was in order, but she wasn't sure what to do. She took a few steps backward, keeping her eyes on him, then gave a quick wave before she turned and ran up the porch steps. She was anxious to tell her grandparents about Jacob and his family.

And she was particularly anxious about Saturday night.

When she walked in, both of her grandparents were standing side by side in the living room, both frowning.

"Isaac, you remember what I told you," *Mammi* whispered as Anna closed the door behind her.

Her grandfather moved quickly toward her and grabbed her arm. Hard. He'd never done such a thing. "Where have you been?" he asked, his eyebrows drawn in.

"I . . . I was at the coffee shop, and—" She blinked a few times, hoping she wouldn't cry, but his forceful hold told her she was in big trouble.

"Emma came by looking for you. She said you never made it to the singing, and she was worried about you." *Daadi* finally let go of her arm, but he threw his next words at her like stones. "You will not see that boy again."

She put a hand to her heart and blinked back tears. "What? You haven't let me explain. There was—"

"Go now! Upstairs to your room." Her grandfather pointed toward the stairs.

Anna looked at her grandmother, but *Mammi's* hands hung at her sides, and she was staring at the floor.

"There was a reason we didn't go to the singing, and if you'd just let me—"

Daadi took a step toward her. He had never hit her except to spank her as a child, but the way his fists were clenched at his sides was enough to send her running to the stairs.

She slammed her bedroom door behind her, and with the mindset of someone half her age, she said aloud, "Oh, I will see him again. And you can't stop me."

Marianne glared at her husband before she stomped to their bedroom. Isaac was quickly on her heels.

"Why such a look? Do you want our girl off running wild, going with boys to places we have not approved of? She didn't go to the singing like she said."

Marianne sat down on the bed, slipped off her black leather shoes, and slid her socked feet into a pair of slippers. Sighing, she looked up at her husband. "You will push her away from us, Isaac. You didn't even give the child a chance to explain."

Isaac pulled his hat off and tossed it onto the bed, then stroked his beard as he sat down beside her. "We don't know that boy. He should have taken her where he said he was taking her, and that's all. There is no excuse. And I saw how worried you were when Emma came calling and said she wasn't at the singing."

Marianne scratched her forehead, feeling a headache coming on. She'd only had a tiny piece of shoofly pie, but her sugar was surely spiking. She felt a bit dizzy and not in the mood for a confrontation with her husband. Over the years she'd learned to just let things go. But when it came to Anna, she felt inclined to stick up for her granddaughter.

"*Ya*, I was worried, but not terribly alarmed. And Anna came home on time, apparently with an explanation." She turned to Isaac and frowned. "But you wouldn't let her speak."

"Young people Anna's age need discipline. You know that."

"Now, Isaac . . . if you'll recall, we were married by the time we were Anna's age. She's eighteen years old, and she's not even participated in much of a *rumschpringe*, so you need to give the girl some freedoms." *Or she'll end up like me—hiding things in the basement.*

Isaac ran his hand the length of his beard again, then stood and walked to the window. He raised the green shade and peered outside. "So much danger out there."

"But we must trust the Lord to keep Anna safe. That's all we can do." Marianne walked to the window and wrapped her arms around Isaac's waist. She knew what he was thinking. *The way He kept Elam and Suzy safe.*

It had taken Marianne years to get past the deaths of their beloved son and daughter-in-law. She wasn't sure that you ever really recover from something like that. But she'd made her peace with it. And with God. Marianne wasn't sure that Isaac had ever done that. Not really. He ruled with an iron fist, an enforcer of the rules, but with a heart so fragile that if anyone could see inside of him, they'd know the fear that drove him. That was why he reacted so harshly today. He was afraid something would happen to Anna. But their granddaughter wasn't baptized yet, and Marianne didn't want Isaac pushing her to a life in the outside world.

Isaac turned to face her. "I still do not want her seeing that boy. He looks like a fancy fellow anyway. He is not right for her."

Marianne chuckled. Briefly. "*Ach*, Isaac, the boy is very handsome. I can see why Anna wants to get to know him."

"*Nee*. She will not see him."

Isaac walked to the bathroom and closed the door behind him. Marianne just shook her head.

It was ten o'clock Sunday evening when Cora's husband strolled into the bedroom like he hadn't a care in the world, and it didn't take her long to recognize the smell of alcohol on his breath. Jake Troyer made the wine in his basement even though the bishop had forbidden it. And it hadn't taken John long to learn about it once they moved here.

Cora's chest tightened as she recalled the events of the day. There was the situation with Eli. Plus she'd forgotten about bread in the oven and burned two loaves, then later had to run interference between Mary Jane and Anna Mae when they got into a silly squabble over who would clean the bathtubs. She was exhausted, and the last thing she wanted to deal with was a drunken husband who had disappeared not long after they returned from church.

"Where have you been?" She eased her hands onto her hips and spoke through clenched teeth.

John scratched his nose, then belched as he glared at her. He might as well have slapped her across the face. "Ran some errands."

"This late? And on a Sunday?" Cora's heart was pounding in her chest as the possibilities ran through her mind. At Jake's house? Another woman's? Drinking out somewhere in public?

"Ya." He shuffled to the bathroom and slammed the door behind him.

Cora sat down on the bed, her lip trembling. She was so tired of crying. And so tired of living like this. She knew that *Yankees* sometimes went to a counselor for depression. No. Not *Yankees*. *Englisch*—that's what everyone here called the non-Amish. Her friend Barbara, who was *Englisch*, had gone to such a person after her two miscarriages. Maybe John needed someone to talk to. Maybe they all did.

When John came out of the bathroom in his pajama bottoms and white T-shirt, he walked around to his side of the bed and got underneath the covers. Cora hadn't moved from her spot on the bed. Within a minute, her husband was snoring.

Anna couldn't believe her grandfather hadn't given her a chance to explain. Did he trust her so little that he thought she'd be off doing something she shouldn't? She pulled her brush from the drawer of her nightstand and ran it through her hair, thinking about Jacob. No way was she going to miss going out with him Saturday, even if she had to sneak out of the house to do so. Finally, someone seemed to have an interest in her, someone incredibly handsome and nice. She'd adhered to all of her grandfather's rules over the years—most of them, at least—and she'd never given her grandparents any real trouble. It wasn't right for him to treat her this way.

She snuggled beneath the sheet, wondering how she would manage to get away for her date. She'd barely gotten settled in and was enjoying a nice breeze blowing through the opened window when she heard a rustling outside.

Raccoons. She'd been battling with them in her garden for over a month. The sneaky little fellows seemed to have a special fondness for strawberries. Sighing, she slowly sat up, though there wasn't much she could do right now. Tomorrow she'd have to put more mothballs around the fence edges. The mothballs seemed to deter them. For the most part.

She yawned as she got out of bed and walked to the window. She peered across the yard toward her lush garden filled with strawberries, tomatoes, hull peas, celery, peppers, and various other vegetables. Her grandfather had installed a solar light—the only kind he would allow—out by the garden to dissuade the critters from going over the fence. It was bright enough for her to see movement, but she couldn't tell if it was the raccoons or maybe a deer trying to poke his nose between the wire mesh. Their home was far from the main road, and although her grandfather only grew hay on a few acres, their five-hundred-acre spread was home to lots of wildlife. Anna loved watching the deer dart across the open field, especially when they had little ones in tow, but she wasn't fond of them eating her vegetables.

She blinked a few times and tried to get her eyes to adjust to the hazy movement beneath the solar light, which was only at its brightest after several days of full sun. The skies had clouded up the last few afternoons, so the light was dim, and she couldn't tell what critter was stealing from her. She walked back to her night-stand, bumping her leg on the corner of the bed, then felt around in the drawer until she found a pair of binoculars she kept for this very purpose. She had to know what she was battling and if she needed to secure her garden even more.

Careful of the bedpost, she felt her way back to the window and raised the binoculars to her eyes. She moved them around until she was centered on the garden, then she turned the dials until the area came into focus.

She gasped when the intruder came into view.

6

NOAH STOLTZFUS, MD.

Noah picked up the nameplate on his desk and stared at it. He'd worked hard to become a doctor—at great personal cost. And over the past few years, he had almost felt like he'd redeemed himself for leaving his people. Apparently the new bishop didn't agree.

He set the nameplate back on his desk and leaned back in his tan leather chair, wondering if today would be as quiet as yesterday . . . and the day before that . . . and the past few months before that.

"Dr. Stoltzfus?"

Noah raised an eyebrow and sat taller when he heard Francine's voice. "Yes?"

"There's someone here to see you. Alice Turner."

Noah remembered the woman. That wasn't hard since they'd only had six patients last week, but Alice stood out for other reasons. She'd come in without an appointment and refused to see the doctor, just kept asking Francine what she could take for an earache. Eventually Noah had emerged from his office and convinced the woman, who was obviously in a lot of pain, to let him look at her ear. Even then she'd protested, insisting she couldn't pay for his services. In the end, Noah had given her some antibiotics and eardrops that he had on hand in the office and hadn't charged her anything.

"Should I bring her back?" Francine was asking.

"Sure. That's fine." He didn't have anything else to do at the moment. He eased his chair back and stood when he heard footsteps coming down the hallway. Francine ushered the woman into Noah's office, then left.

Alice looked exactly like she had last week. She even wore the same clothes—a faded green dress that hung to her knees and worn white tennis shoes. Her tousled gray hair was loosely pulled into a bun, and the lines of time covered her face. She was a tiny little thing, and Noah didn't think she weighed more than eighty pounds. He wondered what her story was. He'd have bet money that she had an interesting one.

"Hello, Mrs. Turner," he said when she edged closer. "How's your ear?"

The woman squinted like maybe she didn't hear him, but then she held out a paper bag. "I brought you some strawberries. You said you like them."

Noah took the bag and peeked inside to find at least two dozen plump berries. "These look great, but you didn't need to do that."

"You like them, right? You'll eat them?" She crinkled her nose, sniffled, then squinted again.

Noah smiled. "Yes, I will. Thank you very much for bringing these to me."

"What other fruit do you like?" The older woman scratched the side of her face, and Noah noticed the action left a smudge of black on her cheek. He glanced at her hands, hoping she wouldn't ask him to eat one of the strawberries before he had a chance to wash them.

"I like all kinds of fruits. And vegetables." He put the bag on his desk and sat back down. "But, Mrs. Turner, I was happy to help you with your earache. You don't owe me anything."

She scratched her cheek again, and Noah noticed the dirt thick beneath her nails. He'd suspected she might be homeless when she was here before, but this visit almost assured it. And there was a distinct odor in the room. He wanted to do something for her, but he didn't want to insult her either. There was no telling when she'd last had a good meal. And where did she get the strawberries?

"Do you have a large garden?" Noah leaned back in his chair, recalling years past when he'd had a room full of patients waiting and no time for this sort of chitchat. "Or do you just grow strawberries?"

Mrs. Turner took a step forward so that now she was right on the other side of Noah's desk. She pressed her thin lips together and let out a breath of air through her nose, then said, "You saved my life."

Noah shook his head. "No, no. You just had an earache, and I gave you some medication that evidently helped."

She wagged her small head back and forth so hard that more strands of gray hair came loose from her bun. "No. I was hurtin' real bad. Thought I might die or go plumb insane from the ringing I heard. I was about to jump out in front of a car and end it all." She flattened her palms on the edge of his desk and leaned forward. "You saved me from doing that. I wouldn't have met the Lord if I'd have done that."

"Well, I was happy to help." Noah smiled. His practice was shot, but at least he'd been able to help this lost soul.

She pointed a finger at him and squeezed her lips together again. "I'll see you soon. I always pay my debts!"

She spun around and left his office. Noah sighed. *I'm sure I'll be available.*

He picked up his cell phone to call Carley. Jenna had been sick the past few days with a nasty cold, and he wanted to check on both his wife and daughter. But before he made the call, his thoughts shifted back to Bishop Byler.

The man had only been upholding a rule that had long been in place. Noah had been shunned for leaving the community following baptism and also for writing a book about his Amish upbringing—a subject matter that hadn't sat well with members of the community, especially his family. According to the *Ordnung*, no one in the community should have had anything to do with him. But his family had forgiven him anyway, and old Bishop Ebersol had made allowances so that community members could visit Noah's clinic.

Isaac Byler was a tough old coot, though, and he was determined that no Amish member of his district would come near the clinic for any reason. Noah had tried to talk to him several times, but the bishop wouldn't give him the time of day. That had been eight months ago. He wondered if it would be worth it to try again. Maybe he'd been pressured enough by the community to consider lifting the ban.

If the bishop didn't bend, Noah would have to consider relocating his practice. In the heart of Amish country—and way off the beaten path—his clinic wasn't frequented by many *Englisch*, as the Amish called them.

He let out a heavy sigh and called Carley. Maybe he'd just take off early and spend time with his two favorite girls.

Anna hadn't said anything to her grandparents about the woman she saw in the garden late last night. In truth, she hadn't said much of anything to her grandparents at all. She was angry with *Daadi* for not listening, upset with *Mammi* for not standing up for her, and feeling a little guilty for thinking about sneaking out on Saturday—though she'd do it if she had to.

An early morning inspection showed that the old woman had robbed her of almost all of the ripe strawberries she would have picked today. Critters she could tend with, but she wasn't sure what to do about an old woman picking in her garden well after dark. If she was so desperate to do such a thing, surely she was hungry.

Anna dressed for bed Monday night wishing she could talk to Emma about Jacob. But *Mammi* had kept her busy longer than usual delivering bread, jams, jellies, and homemade noodles. Her grandmother had also asked her to buy a few things from the grocery store—without mentioning it to her grandfather, of course.

When Anna returned home shortly before the supper hour, *Daadi* was out in the barn and *Mammi* was in the basement. Anna wasn't sure what her grandmother kept down there, but she knew the little room stayed locked, and *Mammi* spent a lot of time in it. Once when Anna asked her about it, her grandmother said it was her prayer closet. Anna suspected more was going on down there than meditation or prayer.

It was barely after dark when she settled into bed, but four o'clock came early each morning. And she'd nearly drifted off to sleep when she heard the familiar rustling sound in her garden. She grabbed her binoculars and found her way to the window, shocked to see the old woman in her garden again. *What is she going to steal this time?*

Anna felt around her bedroom until she found her robe hanging on the peg, then slid into her slippers. She didn't want to alarm the intruder by lighting a lantern. She tiptoed down the stairs, noting her grandparents' door was shut. Holding her breath, she turned the knob on the back door, thinking she would sneak out, then make her way along the side of the house to get a closer look at the woman.

She took slow, careful steps up against the side of the house, hoping her own rustling didn't send the woman running. As she grew nearer, she saw that the woman was facing away from her, with one arm raised high above her head. Anna boldly walked across the yard toward the garden.

"Hey!" Her heart raced as the tiny figure spun around. It took her a few seconds to make out the details of the woman's face. "*Mammi*, what in the world are you doing out here?"

Her grandmother quickly stuffed her hands in her apron pockets, and Anna wondered if she'd gone mad.

"It's late. What are you doing wandering around out here?" Anna asked again.

Mammi lifted her eyebrows and puckered her lips. She reminded Anna of a small child who'd just gotten caught with her hand in the cookie jar.

"It's a full moon." *Mammi* pointed toward the stars. "I was making a wish."

Anna planted her hands on her hips. "*Ya*, I'm sure that's it. And was it a full moon last night too?"

Her grandmother lifted her chin. "What are you talking about?"

Anna shook her head. "Come on. It's late. Let's go in."

Is that what it had come to? Now her grandmother was lying to her.

As *Mammi* got in step behind her, Anna slowed her pace and turned around to face her grandmother. "What did you do with all the strawberries?"

"What strawberries?"

Anna grinned at *Mammi's* wide-eyed innocence, then at a bulge in her apron pocket. "What's in your pocket?"

"My hands." Her grandmother scooted around her and hurried to the house.

Like dealing with a child. Anna shook her head and followed her inside, hoping she wouldn't venture out again.

And still wondering what had happened to all the strawberries.

Marianne slipped quietly back into her bedroom and stashed her nonworking cell phone between the mattresses. *Dumb phone.*

She'd gone to Barbie Beiler's house earlier in the day to charge her new phone. Barbie owned Beiler's Bed and Breakfast, and the *Englisch* woman had always been a good friend to the Amish folks. Some of her husband's kin were Amish. Barbie had helped her set up the phone, but now that she was on her own, Marianne couldn't remember how to work it. She couldn't seem to get on the Internet or even tell if she had a signal. Barbie had called the device a smartphone. Marianne didn't think it was very smart at all—and it was making her feel dumber by the moment.

At this point she'd pushed so many different buttons on the screen that she was lost. Barbie was leaving for her annual trip to Florida tomorrow morning, so Marianne was wondering who else she could get to help her.

Isaac would flip his lid if he knew she'd purchased the portable phone—even more so if he knew how much she'd spent on it. But she'd been saving her money from bakery sales for a long time. Her shopping had been limited because she didn't have Internet access, but then she'd learned that the newer phones could connect you right to the Internet. She didn't really understand how that all worked, but she knew it would be faster and easier than catalog orders. So she'd heard. If the phone would work.

Thankfully, Isaac was still snoring as she crawled underneath the sheet. She appreciated not having to make up something to tell him. When she couldn't drift off to sleep, she thought back to when she started collecting her little luxury items. Anna had still been quite young. And to tell the truth, she wasn't sure she could have survived living with Isaac for all these years without her little hobby. But at the end of the day, like now, the deceit still bothered her.

It occurred to her that maybe that was why sleep never came easy.

By Thursday morning, Jacob was getting more and more excited about his date with Anna. He'd already cleared using the buggy with his mother. It would take awhile for him to save enough money from his work at the lumberyard to buy his own buggy. In the past, he would have asked his father to help him, but he didn't ask *Daed* much of anything these days. And he'd noticed that his father had stayed out late the other night. He hated the way his mother often looked like she'd been crying, with dark circles underneath her eyes. He was resenting his father more and more.

But today he was trying to focus on something happier—on Anna. She'd let him talk about Leah and listened with compassion instead of trying to pretend nothing had happened the way

Carolyn had. Jacob needed someone to talk to, a friend. And it didn't hurt that Anna was the prettiest girl he'd ever met. He was looking forward to getting to know her better.

Mary Jane slowed the buggy in front of Lindemann's Lumberyard.

"I'll see you at three." Jacob stepped out of the buggy. "Sorry you keep having to bring me and pick me up, but otherwise you all would be stuck without a buggy all day."

"It's okay. I know you're trying to save money for your own buggy. And you can't really walk to your job the way Eli can."

Jacob waved as he crossed in front of the buggy. He wished Mary Jane and Anna Mae would get jobs, even if just part-time, so they'd be around people and hopefully make some friends. Back in Middlefield they'd been very social, but they didn't seem to have an interest in much of anything these days. What was it going to take for them all to move on?

He pulled the door open and glanced at the clock on the wall. Five minutes early.

"Good morning, Jacob." Glenda Myers was the *Yankee*—no, *Englisch*—girl who ran the cash register in the front of the store. She was about his age, and she made him uncomfortable. Her blouses were always low cut, her jeans a size too small, and there was something seductive about her eyes, maybe the way she wore her makeup. She'd asked him to lunch twice, and both times he'd come up with an excuse not to go. *Mamm* always sent him to work with a lunch anyway.

He gave a quick wave in her direction, forcing a smile, then headed to aisle four to take up where he'd left off the day before—unpacking and stocking a shipment of nails. It was easy work and kept his mind occupied.

Anna was in the kitchen pulling two loaves of bread from the oven when her grandmother entered the room.

"I've got three batches of snickerdoodles and three pans of peanut blossoms cooling on the rack, and everything else is already packed to take to the market and the bakeries." Anna took off her oven mitts, placed them on the counter, and turned to face her grandmother. "*Mammi*, I need you to convince *Daadi* to let me go out with Jacob on Saturday. He's the first person brave enough to face *Daadi*, and I really like him."

Her grandmother poured herself a cup of coffee and sat down in a kitchen chair. "I tried, *mei maedel*. But Jacob didn't take you where he said he would, and that didn't sit well with your grandfather."

Anna pulled out the chair across from *Mammi* and sat down. "But there was a *gut* reason. Jacob's *bruder* cut himself on a piece of glass. His *mamm* was desperate for some help, and their *daed* wasn't anywhere around." Anna shook her head as she recalled the details Jacob had shared with her. "Their *schweschder* was killed, *Mammi*. She fell off the plow, hit her head on the corner of it, and died in front of all of them. The whole family is grieving, needless to say. That's why they left Middlefield to start over. But Jacob said his father blames himself and that he stays upstairs or is gone when he's not in the fields or the barn."

Mammi kept her head down as she spoke. "*Ach*, that's terrible. I feel for all of them." She looked up, her eyes soft. "I understand their pain. I really do."

"I know you do. And I know *Daadi* does too. Please talk to him,

Mammi. Tell him what happened, and convince him to let me go on Saturday. Jacob did the responsible thing. He's a *gut* person." She paused, biting her bottom lip. "Please, *Mammi.*"

"I will try, dear." *Mammi* let out a heavy sigh. "But your grand-father won't like to hear that the boy has a cell phone. And that his *mudder* does too."

"Maybe just don't mention that part." Anna realized that she was getting more and more like her grandmother by hiding things from *Daadi.* It wasn't right, and she knew it. God had chosen her grandfather for this role. But that left her questioning His will. Why would the Lord put someone in charge of their district who refused to consider the members' feelings, who just did whatever he wanted, no matter how unreasonable? And her grandfather would hold the position until he died. Anna loved *Daadi,* and she hoped he would be with them for a long time, but what would it take to get him to ease up?

She knew he kept a list of violations. She'd seen it the other day on the kitchen table. The Huyards were using a gas lawn mower instead of the accepted push mower. Rumor had it that the Rabers had a deep freeze in their mudroom and were running a long extension cord from the *Englisch* neighbors' house instead of storing their meat in rented lockers like others in their district. Leroy Glick had been seen using a skid loader to scoop manure, something that used to be common until her grandfather became bishop. And Mary King was letting her daughters wear light-colored dresses, pink and other pastels. Anna knew they'd all be getting a visit.

Marianne's heart hurt for Cora Hostetler. She'd met the woman briefly at worship service but had no idea they'd lost a child.

"I think I'll pay Cora a visit. I'll take her some snickerdoodles too." Marianne stood up from the kitchen chair, slowly straightening her stiff back. "And I'll try to talk to your *daadi* tonight, Anna, but no guarantees."

"Danki." Anna threw her arms around Marianne's neck. Marianne had never seen the girl so interested in a boy before. Maybe no one had been worth fighting for until now.

"Like I said, no guarantees." She smiled. "Do you want the topless buggy or the other one?"

"It's hot and sunny. If you want me to take the open buggy, that's fine with me. I know your face burns easily." Anna walked to the counter and packed some of the cookies into a Tupperware container. "Here. These are for the Hostetlers." She set the sealed container on the table, then loaded up the rest of the cookies and six loaves of bread. "I'm going."

Marianne kept her seat for a while, drumming her fingers as she thought about her visit to see Cora. Then she went to her bedroom, reached between the mattresses, and found her new cell phone. Anna had said that Cora had a phone. Depending on how the visit went, maybe Cora would show Marianne what she was doing wrong. As she slipped into her black leather shoes, she wondered if Cora could be trusted. Would she tell someone that the bishop's own wife was in violation of his rules?

She looked down at the device and thought about how much simpler life would be if she was able to buy her favorite hand cream online using her phone. And what about the pink sweater she'd been eyeing? She stuffed the phone in her apron pocket, picked up the snickerdoodles, and walked outside. Anna had already gotten her horse and buggy ready, so she was quickly on her way.

She both anticipated and dreaded the visit. As much as she sympathized with Cora, their chat was bound to open up old wounds. There was nothing she could say to Cora that would ease her pain. But she was going to try, just the same.

And if she could get her cell phone working, that would be a bonus.

Cora was enjoying some quiet time—a rarity in her busy household. Anna Mae and Mary Jane had taken Abe with them to town. Eli was working at Widow Kauffman's farm. John was in the fields, and Jacob was at work.

She eased her feet up on the coffee table and picked up a gardening magazine she'd gotten in town, hoping it would inspire her to get to work on her flowerbeds. She'd only flipped through a few pages when she heard a buggy coming up the driveway. She should have known the quiet time wouldn't last, but who could be visiting? She hadn't really reached out to anyone in the community. Peering out the window in the living room, she saw a tiny gray-haired woman easing herself out of the buggy. Cora walked to the door and waited on the other side of the screen as the woman tethered the horse, then walked up the porch steps.

"*Wie bischt?* I'm Marianne Byler. I wanted to come welcome you to Paradise."

Cora had seen the woman at worship service. Marianne had a warm, kind smile. But she was the bishop's wife. And Cora had heard about Bishop Byler's strict ways just through casual conversations following worship service. He wasn't very well liked, and Cora instantly wondered if Marianne was here to spy on her. Cora wished they had taken the time to research the bishop here before they'd moved. The last thing they needed was trouble of any kind. But she pushed the door open and stepped aside so Marianne could enter.

"I'm Cora Hostetler. *Danki* for coming." She motioned Marianne into the living room and watched as Marianne's eyes scanned the room. Cora was sure it was much too fancy for her—or her husband's—taste. Cora had two landscape pictures on the wall along with a decorative calendar. The mantel held several ballerina figurines, gifts from a *Yankee* friend who knew Cora had read a book about the dancers as a child and been fascinated by them. And if Marianne wanted a tour of the rest of the house, Cora was in trouble. With three children in their *rumschpringe*, there was no telling what they all had in their rooms. She'd spotted earplugs and all kinds of electrical devices while cleaning.

"These are for you, dear." Marianne handed her a container. "Snickerdoodles. We're famous for them around here. We sell them to all the bakeries." She grinned. "Secret family recipe."

"*Danki*. Please sit down. Can I get you some *kaffi* or tea?" Cora sat down on the couch after Marianne chose one of their blue recliners.

"*Nee*." Marianne waved a hand in the air. "I'm fine." She took a long look around the living room. "You have a lovely home."

Cora smiled tentatively as she waited for Marianne to tell her that it was too decorative, but instead Marianne started to tell her about the local Sisters' Day.

"Our next one is July tenth, and it will be held at Mary Ellen Huyard's *haus*. I hope you'll be able to come so you can get to know the other ladies. It's hard to do so at worship service. So much preparation and cleanup." Marianne fumbled in her apron pocket, and Cora waited for her to pull something out, but she didn't.

"I hope to attend." Cora knew she wouldn't go. The thought of putting on a happy face for several hours when she didn't have to sounded awful. This conversation with Marianne was hard enough.

Marianne frowned and folded her hands in her lap. "Our Anna tells us that you lost a child recently."

Cora blinked, surprised at how Marianne just blurted it out. "Uh, *ya*. We did. Our *dochder*, Leah. She was twenty." She swallowed hard. "We miss her very much."

"I know. We are raising our granddaughter because her *daed* and *mamm*—our *sohn* and his *fraa*—were killed in a car accident."

Cora brought a hand to her chest. "I'm so sorry." She'd never thought to ask where Anna's parents were. "How long ago?"

"Fifteen years. They were traveling to Lancaster, and their driver apparently fell asleep. They veered into traffic coming the other way. It killed all three of them." Marianne's bottom lip trembled for a moment, but she blinked a few times, then smiled again. "It does get better, my dear. I know it doesn't seem like it now, but time lessens the hurt."

"Danki." Cora forced a smile as she thought about Leah, the problems with Eli, and the way her husband had abandoned them all emotionally. She'd love to have a friend to confide in, but she reminded herself that this woman, however kind, was the bishop's wife. "We are all healing as best we can."

"That's not what I hear." Marianne crossed one leg over the other and raised her chin. "Anna said there was a problem a few days ago—something with one of your boys. Is everything all right now?"

"*Ach, ya.*" Cora should have known that Jacob's date would say something. Couldn't her oldest son have chosen someone to go out with who wasn't the bishop's granddaughter? "Everything is fine." Her heart was beating hard in her chest. She'd have to ask the Lord's forgiveness for lying, but it wasn't safe to confide in this woman. "We had an incident with one of our younger *sohns*, but all is *gut* now." Her muscles strained from forcing herself to look happy.

Marianne stared at her long and hard, tapping a finger to her chin. Cora assumed she would go back to her husband and tell him about their fancy house and what a mess their family was. They'd left Middlefield to escape the memories and the pitying looks everyone gave them, but she supposed they'd just brought their problems with them. Her own husband was proof of that. Marianne started fumbling with something in her apron pocket again, and Cora was shocked when the older woman pulled out a slim cell phone.

"Do you know how to work one of these?" Marianne frowned. "It's an iPhone. I had a friend show me how to use it, but now I can't remember what she showed me."

Cora felt her brows lifting high above wide eyes. She blinked a few times and tried to mask her shock.

"I don't know." It was a much fancier phone than anyone in her family had. "I'll, uh, have a look if you'd like."

"*Ach, ya, ya.*" Marianne was quickly on her feet and sat down beside Cora. In a whisper, she said, "I'm not supposed to have this."

Cora pressed her lips together and tried not to smile—a genuine smile this time—then said, "I won't tell."

Marianne patted her on the leg but didn't say anything. Her

eyes were fixed on the phone. "Can you make the Internet work? I managed to get it to turn on." She shook her head, frowning. "But I can't remember what to do from there. I should have taken some notes."

Cora took the phone and looked at its sleek face. Her mobile phone didn't look anything like this fancy one. She studied the phone for a while and touched a few of the little squares on the screen. "This is it, I think," she finally said. "The one that says 'Safari.' You push that button to get to the Internet."

Marianne leaned much closer and squinted. "I forgot my reading glasses. But I see." She looked up and smiled. "Guess I didn't try that. *Danki.*"

Cora nodded and took a deep breath. "So why do you have a phone if it's not allowed? I mean, your husband . . ." Cora shrugged, unsure how to say it.

"Do you tell your husband every little thing?" Marianne didn't look up. She was busy fiddling with the phone.

"I suppose not," Cora finally said. *I haven't had much conversation with him at all since we moved here.*

"Do you know much about this Internet place?" Marianne put the phone down, and her eyes twinkled with excitement.

"I've heard of it. We have three *kinner* in their *rumschpringe.*" Cora wasn't about to tell Marianne that she'd even used the library computers back in Middlefield. Several times. The first time had been to research a rash Abe had on his arm. But then she'd learned from the librarian that she could e-mail her cousin in Iowa by using the Internet. She hadn't been guilty of using a computer since she'd moved to Paradise, but . . .

Marianne frowned, then handed the phone to Cora. "I've lost

my place again. One wrong move with this silly device and it gets a mind of its own."

Cora shrugged, keeping her eyes on the phone. "I don't know about this kind of phone." She touched the phone in several places. "But if you slide along this arrow, it seems to take you back to all the buttons. Then we just have to find the one that says 'Safari' again."

Marianne let out a heavy sigh. "I knew this would be too *gut* to be true. It's gonna take me a month of Sundays to figure this out."

Cora fumbled with the phone for a few more minutes while Marianne continued to sigh. Finally, Cora touched a place on the phone that pulled up a familiar-looking screen. She handed the phone to Marianne. "Here's the Internet."

Marianne leaned close to the phone, clapped her hands together like a small child, then latched onto the device. *"Ach. Gut."* She smiled at Cora. *"Danki."*

Cora spent the next hour with Marianne. Together they learned how to maneuver around the Internet on the phone. Then they discovered Amazon.com. "I think you can buy cows on the Internet," Marianne marveled.

Cora chuckled, something she hadn't done in ages. "I don't know about that, Marianne." Cora glanced up at her ballerina figurines on the mantel. How she'd love to have another one. There was also a new piece of Tupperware she'd been eyeing since before they'd moved from Middlefield. A neighbor had purchased it at a bridal Tupperware party—a hand-cranked device that was said to be faster than an electric or battery-operated mixer.

Cora suddenly realized she hadn't thought about Leah or the problems with John the whole time that she and Marianne were playing with the phone. What a wonderful distraction this lovely woman was. Her warm smile, gentle ways, and childlike enthusiasm brought a welcome breath of fresh air to Cora's household. And apparently she wasn't above keeping a few things from her husband.

Cora ran a finger down her cheek, a tinge of mischief building inside her. She'd spent months trying to be everything for everyone in her family, trying desperately to inject some sort of happiness into their lives, even though her own heart was far from mended. A wild thought seized her. "Do you think the Internet has books about ballerinas?"

Marianne smiled as she handed Cora the phone. "I think it has just about anything."

Cora still wasn't sure about purchasing cows. But as she took the phone from Marianne and began searching for "ballerinas," she felt lighter than she'd been in ages.

It was a guilty pleasure, true. But it was still pleasure.

7

FRIDAY AFTERNOON ANNA TOOK A DETOUR FROM HER bakery deliveries and tethered her buggy in front of the lumber-yard where Jacob worked. Anna knew her grandfather had made purchases from the local establishment, but Anna had never been inside. A bell chimed when she walked in, and she breathed in the aroma of freshly cut wood. A young *Englisch* woman sat behind a counter to her left.

"Can I help you?"

Anna smoothed the wrinkles from her black apron, pushed back a strand of wayward hair that had come loose from her *kapp*, and moved closer to the counter. "I'm looking for Jacob Hostetler." She dreaded having to tell Jacob that she couldn't go out with him Saturday night. *Mammi* had talked to *Daadi* but couldn't persuade him to relent. And as angry as she'd felt in the beginning, Anna couldn't bring herself to completely defy her grandfather.

The woman, dressed in a fitted white shirt, had long blond hair almost to her waist. She was very pretty, and Anna avoided her gaze, feeling suddenly self-conscious.

"He's on the clock. Can I help you with something?"

Anna bit her bottom lip, then turned to face the woman. The name *Glenda* was on her nametag, and the frown on her face suggested that dropping by wasn't appropriate. Anna didn't want to bother Jacob, but she wouldn't have another opportunity to talk to him. "I just need to talk to him for a few moments if he is able."

Glenda slowly stood up. "I'll go see if I can find him." Her voice was curt as she rounded the counter and gave Anna a thin-lipped smile.

Anna was wishing she hadn't come, but how else could she get a message to Jacob? A few moments later Glenda returned. "He's coming." She returned to the counter and sat down again. "Are you his girlfriend?"

Anna swallowed hard. *"Nee* . . . I mean no. I'm just a friend."

"Well, if I were Amish, I'd snap him right up." Glenda flung her hair over her shoulders and batted long dark eyelashes. "He's the hottest Amish guy I've ever seen."

No doubt about that. Anna was relieved to hear that Glenda had said, "If I were Amish."

Anna turned to her right when she heard footsteps. "I'm sorry to bother you at work," she said as Jacob walked closer.

He didn't even look toward Glenda, but instead his eyes met Anna's, and he smiled so broadly that Anna felt weak in the knees. "I can't wait until tomorrow night," he said in a whisper as he gently pulled her around the corner and away from Glenda. "What would you like to do?"

"I, uh . . ." Anna couldn't stop looking at his smile, his mouth. She'd come here to tell him she couldn't go, but the words weren't coming. "I . . . I don't know."

"Are we still on for four o'clock?" Jacob pushed back the rim of his hat, still smiling.

How can I not go? "Ya. I was just stopping by to make sure." Anna was racking her brain for a way to make this work. "Do you think you could pick me up at Emma's? I need to drop some things off at her *haus*, and it's closer for you."

Jacob shifted his weight and scratched his clean-shaven, perfect chin. "Are you sure your grandfather doesn't want me to pick you up properly?"

"*Nee*. It will be fine. He already met you once." She forced her guilt to the back of her mind, hoping her half smile was convincing enough.

"Okay, then. Think about what you want to do, and I'll see you at four."

Anna nodded as she took a few steps backward. "See you tomorrow."

Jacob gave a quick wave, then went back the same direction he'd come from. Anna walked over to where Glenda was sitting. "Thank you."

"Sure. Have fun Saturday night."

Glenda was smiling in a way that confused Anna—a mirthless smile that arched her eyebrows.

"Uh, thank you," Anna said again, then hurried out of the store.

Jacob punched the time clock, then stowed his card in its proper slot. He was thankful that he didn't have to work every weekend, and he was looking forward to spending time with Anna tomorrow night. He wished he could just snap his fingers and be sitting next to her in the buggy, maybe on their way to eat dinner or even to a movie.

Once on the road, the familiar dread seeped into his heart. He hated going home these days. Despite his mother's best efforts, it remained a place of great sadness. He wondered if that would ever change. It was the Amish way to trust that a person's passing was God's will. Jacob had always believed that—until the unthinkable happened to Leah. Now Jacob wondered if those who kept talking about God's will had ever really lost anyone close. But he thought about the One he needed to trust, the One who had given His only Son. The whole thing was so hard to figure out, even harder to live through.

He struggled through supper, trying to appear happy for his younger siblings, and he could tell his mother was doing the same thing. As usual, their father wasn't around.

Mary Jane was the first to scoot back her chair from the table, even though everyone had been done for a few minutes. "Do you want me to make a plate of food for *Daed*?" She picked up what was left of the chicken bundles from the center of the table and carried it to the counter. Jacob was surprised there were any left. The stromboli-type turnovers were filled with chicken, cream cheese, celery, onion, and lots of other ingredients that made them a family favorite. Jacob reached for the last piece of butter bread before Mary Jane took the basket from the table.

"Your father is a grown man," *Mamm* said. "If he wants supper, he can eat with the rest of us or come get his own plate." *Mamm* raised her chin, smiled, and left the room. Jacob heard her humming as she crossed into the living room, and he realized he'd stopped chewing, just as his siblings had stopped what they were doing.

Each one of them looked at Jacob as if he could explain what had just happened. Their mother had been bringing *Daed's* meals to their bedroom and catering to him in every way since they'd moved.

Jacob wanted to smile, to be proud of his mother, but a knot formed almost instantly in the pit of his stomach. Their father had always been the head of the household, and he'd made sure everyone knew it. He might not be tending to his family the way he should, but Jacob doubted he would tolerate disobedience from their mother. But as *Mamm* walked into their bedroom and slammed the door behind her, Jacob slowly rose from his chair and walked to the living room, all his siblings following.

They held their breath. Jacob could count on one hand the times he'd heard his parents bicker, at least in front of the *kinner*. Eli went so far as to press his ear against the door, and he nearly fell into their mother when she pulled the door open.

"Are my *kinner* eavesdropping?" *Mamm* tied the strings of her black bonnet. "I'm going out for a while. Your *daed* is in the bathtub. I'll be back before dark."

Mary Jane followed *Mamm* to the door. "Where are you going?"

"To the bishop's *haus*."

No one moved or said anything as their mother closed the door behind her.

"Why is she going to see the bishop?" Anna Mae peered out the window as *Mamm's* buggy headed down the driveway.

"I don't know." Jacob leaned over his sister's shoulder, watching the buggy round the corner. Did *Mamm* not know how strict the bishop was? Would his name come up during her visit?

He scratched his head and took a step back. "*Ach*, well, let's finish our chores and get bathed."

He glanced at the clock on the wall. Six o'clock. Surely *Mamm* wouldn't be gone long.

<hr>

Cora pulled up to Marianne's *haus*, glad she had accepted the other woman's invitation for coffee and dessert. She was a bit nervous about spending time with Marianne's husband, but she'd enjoyed her time with Marianne so much yesterday that she was willing to face Bishop Byler as well.

It had been a long time since Cora had met another woman as interesting as Marianne. Though old enough to be Cora's mother, she didn't act her age. And she certainly wasn't like the bishop's wife back home, a woman who let you know her standing and expected to be treated accordingly. Cora really looked forward to getting to know her better, even if that meant spending time with the stern-faced man who had forbidden their granddaughter to go out with Jacob on Saturday.

Cora had offered to explain what really happened—that the children's failure to attend the singing was her fault. But Marianne had said it would be best to let it lie, assuring Cora that she was working to get her husband to change his mind. Cora hoped that he would. Jacob was a good boy who had taken on the role of head of the household in her husband's absence. It was a heavy burden, and he deserved some happiness. Anna was a pretty girl, and Cora could see the attraction for Jacob. But she still wished he'd chosen someone who wasn't the bishop's granddaughter.

The bishop's *haus* was large and well tended, the flowerbeds immaculate, the shaded porch plain but still welcoming. Cora climbed the steps, thinking how good it felt to be out and about. Her stomach had knotted up a bit when she left John without bringing him his supper. But she was tired of tending to him like a child, as if his emotions were any more shredded than the rest of the family's.

She knocked on the door and jumped when a black-and-white cat scurried behind her. Seconds later Marianne answered.

"I'm so glad you could come to my home." Marianne pushed the screen door wide, and Cora breathed in the aroma of freshly percolated coffee as she stepped into the living room. A plain room with no décor and only simple furnishings. Cora was going to have to make some changes to her own home.

"*Wie bischt? Danki* for inviting me." She glanced around for any sign of the bishop or their granddaughter, Anna, but no one was around. Cora was still embarrassed that Anna had stayed outside during the ruckus with Eli, but better outside than to have seen such chaos.

"Sit, sit, my dear." Marianne motioned for Cora to take a seat on the couch. "I'll be right back with some *kaffi* and cake. Hope you like cherry crumb cake."

She hurried from the room. When she returned, Bishop Byler followed.

Cora stood up. "Good evening, Bishop."

He walked to where she was standing and shook her hand. "Nice to see you, Cora. Please, take your seat."

The bishop sat formally in one of the rocking chairs, as did his wife after she'd served everyone coffee and cake. Cora wanted so much to plead her case for Jacob, but Marianne had said it was best not to, so Cora sat quietly eating her cake, wishing it was just she and Marianne this evening.

"Where's Anna?" she asked when the silence grew awkward.

"She's bathing, but should be down shortly."

Bishop Byler was staring at Cora, and she wondered if perhaps something in her attire was somehow not right. She glanced at Marianne's dark blue dress and black apron, exactly the same as Cora was wearing. Cora and both her daughters had sewn new dresses right after they arrived in Paradise. They still needed more, but they had been anxious to adhere to the dress code here since it was a bit different from Ohio.

"Tell me of your travels here to Lancaster County. Did you come by bus or train?"

Cora swallowed hard. "*Nee*. We, uh, flew here by airplane while our things were transported in a large moving van."

Surprisingly, Bishop Byler just nodded. "It's a fine place to raise a family here in Paradise." He stroked the length of his gray beard. "I have not seen much of your husband around town, only briefly after worship. He must stay busy farming." He paused. "Or does he also work outside the home?"

"*Nee*. He only farms." Cora wished she hadn't come. She should have known that the bishop would ask questions. "We were fortunate the prior owners put in the crops before we arrived, but as you know, there is still always much to do."

"And your oldest boy helps with this?" Bishop Byler narrowed his eyebrows, and Cora suspected he already knew the answer to his question.

"*Nee*. He works at the lumberyard in town. And our middle son, Eli, works for Widow Kauffman, helping tend her animals." She paused, then smiled. "But our youngest, Abe, and my twin girls, Anna Mae and Mary Jane, stay home with me to take care of our household needs."

Bishop Byler frowned. "More and more of our young people are venturing out into the *Englisch* world. It wonders me what our community will be like when the next generation is in charge." He shook his head before taking a bite of cake.

"Isaac, many of the *kinner* are forced to work outside the home. You know that." Marianne smiled at Cora. "Times must change."

Cora thought of Marianne's new cell phone. They now shared a secret that was proof positive about how much things truly were changing. But Cora wasn't sure that was such a bad thing. They all wanted their children rooted in the Amish ways, but it seemed almost impossible not to alter their lifestyle at least a little.

They all turned toward the stairs when they heard footsteps. Anna appeared in the living room a few moments later, said hello, then excused herself and went back upstairs. Cora waited for Bishop Byler to mention something about Jacob asking Anna out, but he didn't. Instead, he began to rattle on about all the things in Paradise that he was unhappy about, the rules he planned to continue enforcing.

Cora again wondered why they hadn't checked out the bishop before they chose Paradise as their new home. This Bishop Byler was clearly a rigid man, and Cora could see why his wife had created a life of her own that he didn't know about. Maybe it was wrong—the deceit certainly was. But surely a person can only take so much. Cora thought about the ballerina music box she'd bought using Marianne's credit card, promising to pay her back with cash. She had planned to buy a book about ballerinas, but when she saw the music box, she instantly envisioned the lovely trinket on her night stand.

Cora was thankful when the bishop excused himself. But then Marianne started acting a little strange. She kept looking back toward the stairway and what appeared to be the basement door. Once she opened her mouth as if to say something, then apparently changed her mind. Finally, Marianne relaxed a little and started talking about the upcoming Sisters' Day. But now Cora found herself distracted, drifting back in time to the last Sisters' Day she'd attended with Leah in Middlefield.

"It's still very painful, I know." Marianne's voice brought Cora back to the present. "I'm sure you miss Leah every second of every day."

"Ya." She sighed. "Leah used to love Sisters' Day, and it's hard to think of going without her." Cora sat taller and raised her chin. "But I will go because my dochder would want me to. She'd want me to make new friends here."

Marianne glanced toward her basement door again, then looked back at Cora, a flush in her cheeks.

"Is everything okay?" Cora finally asked.

Once again she got the sense that Marianne wanted to tell her something but decided against it.

"Ya, ya. Everything is fine." Marianne glanced toward the basement door again, and Cora wasn't so sure.

Anna had wondered if Cora Hostetler's visit would sway her grandfather into letting her go out with Jacob. She'd stayed quietly at the top of the stairs and listened to the conversation, disappointed that the subject hadn't come up. She would have to stick to her original plan and say she was going to Emma's house. She didn't feel good about the lie, but her grandfather had pushed her to this by being so unreasonable.

It was late by the time she crawled under the covers, but she hadn't dozed off yet when she heard the basement door creak open. She knew *Mammi* went down there a lot, but usually not this late. She wondered if that's where the missing strawberries were. Maybe *Mammi* was planning something special with the fruit and didn't want Anna or her grandfather to know.

She tiptoed down the stairs, and once she got to the basement door, she pressed her ear against it and listened. She heard the door to *Mammi's* broom closet open, then click closed behind her. Other than that, it was so quiet that Anna could hear her grandfather gently snoring in her grandparents' downstairs bedroom, the light breeze coming through the open windows, the familiar creaking of their old farmhouse. She was just about to ease the door open and find out exactly what her grandmother was doing when she heard a loud sneeze outside. She got to the window in the living room just in time to see a small woman running from the garden.

Glancing back at the basement door, she knew it wasn't her grandmother, so she bolted out of the house and ran across the yard.

"Hey!" Anna chased after the woman in her bare feet and nightgown but couldn't catch her before she got lost in the high grass in the adjoining pasture. She stopped, caught her breath, and walked to her garden. In the dim light she walked down each row, then stopped when she got to her tomato plants. She leaned down, examining each one. All the tomatoes were gone, even the green ones.

She stared toward the pasture where the woman had fled. *Who is she? And why is she stealing my vegetables?* Sighing, she felt a tinge of guilt that she'd assumed her grandmother had snatched the strawberries.

What her grandmother did down in the basement was a mystery, but a stranger coming into the garden at night was even more bewildering. Anna scratched her cheek and thought for a moment. When no answer came to mind, she started back toward the house. She was almost to the white picket fence gate that surrounded the garden when she noticed something twinkling on the ground below her. She squatted down, stared at the item, and picked it up.

It was very pretty . . . and her only clue about the produce thief.

8

Jacob pulled up to the Lapps' *haus* at four o'clock exactly. Anna and Emma were in the garden, so he tethered Bolt and joined them.

"Look at this." Emma was pointing at something when he walked up. "I've been cleaned out of strawberries and tomatoes." She thrust her hands on her hips and shook her head.

Jacob's eyes drifted to Anna right away. He'd been looking forward to their date all week, and Anna looked beautiful.

"What's wrong?" he finally asked, forcing himself to pull his gaze from Anna.

Emma kicked at a tomato plant. "These were full of tomatoes yesterday. They would have been ready for picking soon."

"Apparently, we have a thief." Anna grinned as she spoke. "I've seen an old woman twice in my garden late at night. The first time she took all my strawberries, and last night she stole my tomatoes and the few strawberries that were left."

"Goodness." Emma's forehead scrunched. "Who would do that?"

Jacob shrugged. "Maybe she's hungry."

"That's what Anna said." Emma sighed, then looked back and forth between Anna and Jacob. "Oh well. I'll go tell *Mamm* what's going on. And you two have a *gut* time." She giggled before she turned and walked across the yard to her house, and Jacob smiled when he saw the flush in Anna's cheeks.

"Ready?"

"Sure."

Jacob followed Anna to the family buggy and helped her in. He'd be glad when he had a topless spring buggy, more traditional for courting. The newspaper said the evening was going to be clear, no rain, and seventy degrees. *Perfect.*

"I'm glad your grandfather changed his mind about letting you go out with me tonight." He pulled the reins and eased Bolt backward.

"Uh . . . what?" Anna raised her eyebrows.

"*Mei mamm* said that your grandmother told her that she was working on your grandfather, that he wasn't going to let you go out with me. I'm glad he changed his mind. I probably should have insisted that I pick you up at your *haus* so I could explain to him that it was my fault we didn't make it to the singing. I feel bad about that." He glanced to his right and smiled at her. "Your grandmother obviously swayed him." He paused. "And I'm glad."

"Uh, *ya.* She must have."

"We can do anything you want, but I was wondering if you wanted to go eat first and we can decide over supper."

Jacob waited for her to answer, but she was biting her lip and seemed lost in thought.

"Anna? You okay?"

"*Ya, ya.*" She turned to him and smiled. "I'm fine."

Jacob nodded, but he wasn't convinced. She was twirling the string of her prayer covering with one hand and fidgeting with something in her apron pocket with the other hand. Maybe she hadn't been looking forward to the date as much as he had.

A few minutes later they were turning onto Lincoln Highway. "What about pizza?" Jacob slowed the buggy, giving her time to answer.

"That sounds *gut*."

Jacob guided the horse into the parking lot of Paradiso's Pizzeria. Once he had the horse tied to one of the posts the restaurant kept for Amish patrons, he helped Anna out of the buggy. She was mighty quiet, and Jacob's stomach churned. Maybe this date wasn't such a good idea.

Anna knew she was blowing it with Jacob. Her mind was everywhere else but here. Jacob was the first person to ask her out on an official date, and she was having trouble enjoying herself already. She'd never lied to her grandparents, and the deceit was weighing heavily on her mind.

She reached into her pocket and fumbled with the item she'd found in her garden, wondering if she should show it to Jacob. She hadn't even shown it to Emma earlier. The silver chain was slightly tarnished and the clasp was broken, but the dainty locket with a tiny picture of a baby boy inside had still been on the chain when Anna found it in the garden.

Jacob asked what kind of pizza she liked, and she told him she liked all kinds. It was true. She even liked the little fishy things they sometimes put on pizzas. Taking a deep breath, she knew she needed to focus on her date, especially if she ever wanted Jacob to ask her out again. He ordered a large supreme pizza and two iced teas.

Once the waitress was gone, Anna decided to show him the locket. Maybe that would take her mind off lying to her grandparents. She'd told them she was going to Emma's, but not that Jacob would be picking her up there and taking her out.

"Look at this." Anna pulled the locket from her apron pocket and handed it to Jacob across the table. "I think the woman who was in my garden dropped it." She waited while Jacob studied it, then added, "And for some reason, that *boppli* in the picture looks familiar to me."

Jacob turned it over and brought it closer to his face. "There's an inscription on the back."

Anna sat taller. "Really? I guess I didn't look that close. Can you read it?"

Jacob squinted and moved the locket back, then closer again. "Barely. But it says . . . uh . . . it says 'To Grandma.'" He handed it back to her.

"Hmm." She paused, gazing at the locket and wondering about its owner. "I didn't get a *gut* look at the woman, but *grandma* is an *Englisch* word." She shrugged. "I'd like to return it, but . . ." She giggled. "I wonder if she'd return our strawberries in exchange for the locket."

Jacob chuckled. Anna looked at those kind eyes and dimples and wondered what in the world a man like him was doing out on a date with her. Then she remembered she'd started all this by asking him to the singing. But he'd followed up with this date. She gave her head a quick shake, forcing herself not to overanalyze . . . or to think about her grandparents.

"I, uh . . ." Jacob stopped when the waitress returned with their pizza. After she was gone, he said, "I just wanted to thank you for letting me talk to you about Leah the last time we were together. No one in *mei haus* mentions her name. It's almost like she never existed, so it felt *gut* to talk about her."

"I guess everyone handles grief differently, but I'm glad it made you feel better. I can't imagine how hard that must have been." Anna reached for a piece of pizza when Jacob did. Once it was on his plate, they both bowed their heads in silent prayer. Then Jacob waved his hand.

"Let's don't talk about that this time. I did most of the talking last time. What do you like to do? Any hobbies?"

Anna sighed. "Will I sound boring if I say no?"

Jacob shook his head as he chewed on his pizza, then said, "*Nee*. Not at all."

Anna swallowed her bite of pizza, then bit her bottom lip as she avoided his eyes. Then she looked up and said, "There is this one thing . . . something I would like to do." She shrugged. "I mean, I guess that's not a hobby, but just something . . ."

Jacob raised one eyebrow, his mouth full of pizza. He hurried to swallow. "What is it?"

Anna cast her eyes down to her plate as she felt her cheeks flushing. "I'd like to open my own bakery someday." She gazed up at Jacob, who was smiling. "*Daadi* would never allow it. He thinks women should tend to their husbands and homes. But *Mammi* has taught me to bake some of her special recipes. We sell them to all the nearby bakeries. I'd love to have my own place to sell our baked goods." She dropped her eyes as she shrugged again. "I mean, it's just a dream. The last thing Lancaster County probably needs is another bakery."

When she looked back up, Jacob had stopped chewing and

was just staring at her. Her heart started thumping in her chest. "What's wrong?"

"Nothing." He tipped his head to one side and smiled. "I think it's a nice dream. And sometimes dreams come true."

"Not this one, probably." Anna took another bite of pizza. "But I like to think about it."

"You never know. When you're out on your own—you know, married and all—you might be able to have your own bakery. That's what Leah always wanted."

Anna swallowed hard, hoping she hadn't upset Jacob. "I'm sorry."

"Don't be. Leah was the best cook in our family, even better than *Mamm*. She just had a knack for it. We'd always told her to open a bakery. Our *daed* especially wanted her to."

"So different from my grandfather." She shook her head, then took a sip of tea.

"*Ya*, there was a time when *mei daed* was the best father anyone could ever want." Jacob sighed. "But everything changed after Leah died."

"I'm sorry."

Jacob wiped his mouth with his napkin and shook his head. "*Nee*, I'm sorry. I really don't want every conversation we have turning to Leah." He sat taller. "So what would you like to do after this? I haven't been here long enough to have a suggestion."

Anna hadn't ever been on a date, so she wasn't an expert at making these types of decisions either, but her favorite place to run away to was the train tracks down behind the Kauffman place. Would Jacob find that entertaining? "I, uh . . ."

"I should probably tell you . . ." His face reddened. "I don't have a whole lot of money. I mean, I'm saving. I'm hoping to get a buggy soon." Smiling, he added, "I'm probably lousy date material."

Are you kidding me? Anna felt like the luckiest girl alive. "Well, there's this place I like to go. You might not like it, but it's tucked away in a valley. There's always a breeze blowing, and it's the perfect place to watch the sun set. And the train comes by every evening right before dark." She grinned. "I count the cars and wonder about what might be in them. I'm sure that sounds so dumb."

"I think it sounds *wunderbaar.*" Jacob laughed out loud as the waitress handed him their bill. "And it fits my budget."

Anna smiled as Jacob stood up and led her out of the restaurant to the buggy. And by the time they got to the train tracks, she was feeling almost comfortable. Jacob had spent the ride telling her about his life back in Middlefield. He and his brothers had always farmed the land with their father. This was his first time to work outside the home. A couple of times when he was talking, Anna wondered if he would mention Carolyn, the name she'd seen flash across his phone screen. But he never did.

"This is a nice place," he said as he parked the buggy underneath an oak tree.

They got out and walked toward the railroad tracks. "Lancaster is that way." Anna pointed to the west as she stood beside him in the plush green grass. Several trees formed a half circle thirty or forty yards from the tracks. On the other side of the tracks, green fields stretched for miles, and the farmhouses in the far distance looked like toy models.

"When does the train come?" Jacob reached into his pocket, and Anna heard coins jingling.

She studied the sun for a few moments. "About thirty minutes,

I think." Actually, she knew. She'd watched the sun set at this spot many times.

"Come on." Jacob grabbed her hand and pulled her toward the train tracks. She was pretty sure her hand was trembling.

Once they got to the tracks, Jacob reached into his pocket and pulled out two dimes. He handed her one and kept one for himself. Then he squatted at the edge of the tracks and placed his dime, tails up, on one of the rails. "Here, put yours beside mine."

Anna laid her dime on the track next to Jacob's. "Will it flatten them? Or will they fall off the track from the vibration when the train comes?"

"I guess we'll see." Jacob stood and again offered Anna his hand. "An old *Englisch* man told me once that if you make a wish and your coin is flattened, your wish will come true." He turned to her, smiling. "So we should make a wish."

Anna squeezed her eyes closed. *I wish that Jacob Hostetler could love me.*

"Did you make a wish?" Jacob stepped into the rail bed and peered to his left, then his right.

"*Ya.* Did you?"

He nodded. Anna wanted to ask him what he'd wished for, but then he might ask her, and she didn't want to have to lie to him again.

He reached for her hand once more, and together they walked back to the spot under the trees. Anna was sure she could spend the rest of her life just holding hands with Jacob. He had a strong, firm grip, and she wondered if her hands were as clammy as they felt. She was busy trying to slow her racing heart as they took a seat on a grassy spot beneath the trees.

"Did you have a girlfriend back in Middlefield?" Anna winced the moment the words slipped from her lips. Her mouth seemed to have a mind of its own.

Jacob frowned as he stretched his legs out in front of him and leaned back on his arms. "*Ya.* Her name was Carolyn."

Anna had never even held hands with a boy, and she wondered how far Jacob's relationship had gone with Carolyn. She'd probably never know, and she wasn't sure she wanted to. But her mouth took over again before her brain caught up.

"Was it serious?" She folded her legs underneath her and smoothed out her dress.

"I guess." Jacob turned to face Anna, his blue eyes flat and as unreadable as stone. "For her anyway," he added.

Anna felt sorry for the girl named Carolyn that she'd never met. She could imagine how it felt to fall for someone like Jacob, only to have him not return the affections. She needed to keep that thought in the forefront of her mind. But as Jacob reached for her hand and squeezed, ex-girlfriend Carolyn drifted from her mind.

"*Danki* for bringing me here. It's peaceful."

As he wrapped an arm around her and pulled her close, Anna almost panicked. How much did she really know about Jacob? How far had he gone with Carolyn? And how far would he expect her to go? Anna had never even been kissed. A wave of apprehension swept through her, but Jacob just stared straight ahead at the tracks in the distance.

After a while, he turned to her and said, "I hope you get your bakery." The warmth of his smile echoed in his voice, and Anna started to relax a little bit.

"*Danki.*" She pulled her gaze from his and focused on the grass in front of her. "It's a dream I've had for a long time." When he didn't say anything, she looked back up at him. "What's your dream?"

He eased his arm from around her and leaned back on both his palms, his expression tight. "I don't know anymore." He turned to her, and Anna wanted more than ever to ask him what he'd wished for when they put their dimes on the track.

"There must be something," she said softly. "If you could have anything you wanted, what would it be?"

Jacob's expression was somber, and it didn't take him long to answer. "Peace." He paused, sighing. "Peace for me and my family."

Anna's dream belonged to the physical world, and it touched her that Jacob's was of a spiritual nature. But she wondered what he used to dream, and if he'd ever tell her about it. Was it the same thing he'd wished for at the train track?

"I'll pray that you get your dream," she said softly, and Jacob's arm found its way back around her shoulder.

"*Danki.*" He sat taller and tapped her shoulder. "Hear it? The train's coming."

She leaned an ear forward, realizing she'd miscalculated . . . or the train was early. "I hear it."

A fluttering in the tree above their heads made Anna jump. "I guess the birds hear it too."

Minutes later the train whistle blew, and the lead car came into sight. Anna was tempted to put her fingers in her ears as she often did to block the sound, but when Jacob leaned close to her, she didn't.

"What's in the cars?" He was practically yelling, and Anna had to scoot away a little.

"What?"

Jacob got closer again, really yelling this time to be heard above the noise. "You said you like to guess what's in the cars!"

Anna smiled, then looked at the train. She tapped her finger to her chin. Most of the cars were red, but every third one was black. "I think the black ones have wheat, grain, and flour!" she hollered close to his ear.

"What about the red ones?"

She flinched a little as the whistle blew, then grinned. "Ice cream!"

Jacob laughed. "What kind of ice cream?"

"Chocolate, of course." She bumped him playfully with her shoulder.

He shook his head. "*Nee*, I think the black ones are filled with money. And the red ones are carrying pigs."

Anna laughed. "Money and pigs!"

They kept guessing for the next few minutes as the train continued past them and laughing at the randomness of their speculations. The caboose was just rumbling by when Anna saw movement out of the corner of her eye. She hadn't heard the buggy approaching until it was right up on them. They both stood up, and Anna was surprised to see Emma step out of the buggy.

"Big trouble, Anna!" Emma hurried toward them, shaking her head. "Your *daadi* came to *mei haus*—just for a visit, so he said. But then you weren't there!" She leaned over and put her hands on her knees. "I'm so sorry, Anna. *Mamm* told him that Jacob picked you up." She stood tall again. "He is really mad."

Anna couldn't even look at Jacob. She wasn't sure what was worse—that she'd lied to her grandparents, or that she'd lied to Jacob.

"What?" Jacob asked, frowning.

Emma took a few steps back. "I have to go. Just wanted you to know." She paused. "'Bye, Jacob." She said it like neither of them would ever see Jacob Hostetler again. And that might be true. For Anna, anyway.

"I'm sorry," she said as Jacob untied the horse from a nearby tree. "My grandfather was angry that we didn't go to the singing, even though I tried to explain. He just wouldn't listen, and I really wanted to go out with you."

Jacob's eyebrows were drawn into a frown. "You shouldn't have done this, Anna. Now how am I going to see you?"

There was such an urgency in his voice that everything else fell away for a moment. *He really wants to see me.*

"I'll make *Daadi* understand why I didn't tell him the complete truth." Anna knew that wouldn't be easy.

"You didn't exactly tell me the whole truth either." Jacob's smile softened the words as they climbed into the buggy.

"I know." Anna threw her head back and sighed. "I just wanted . . ." She stopped, knowing she'd already told him that she wanted to go out with him. This made her sound desperate.

"Anna, I really wanted to go out with you too, and I had a great time. Even though it got cut short." Jacob put the horse into a fast trot. "I think I should come in and talk to your grandfather when I drop you off."

"No!" Anna's grandfather had embarrassed her enough in front of Jacob. "We need to let him calm down first."

"What if he doesn't?"

Anna was sure he wouldn't. "He will."

When they pulled into Anna's driveway, she realized this was the end of their first real date—unless you counted the one she'd initiated, the singing they didn't go to. She held her breath, hoping and praying that her grandfather wasn't waiting at the door.

"Are you sure you don't want me to come in? I can explain what happened." Jacob stepped out of the buggy, but Anna was already hurrying toward the porch steps. She spun around.

"*Nee, nee.* It'll be fine. I'll talk to you soon."

Without waiting for a response, she climbed up the stairs two at a time, then paused and drew in a big gulp of air before she walked into the living room.

"You will never see that boy outside of worship service again. Do you hear me, Anna?" Her grandfather's face was crimson, his hands clenched at his side. Her grandmother stood nearby, head hanging. Anna was surprised by the anger that swept through her—not at *Daadi*, but at *Mammi*. She had the strongest desire to scream at her and say, "Why don't you tell *Daadi* what you do down there in the basement, *Mammi*?" Instead, she stood quietly as her grandfather told her repeatedly how disappointed he was in her. He ended by saying again that she would never again see Jacob.

She walked up the stairs, gritting her teeth. *I will too see him. I'll find a way.* She was a grown woman, and *Daadi* had to stop treating her like a child.

She couldn't help but wonder if Jacob would think she was worth the trouble. What had started out as a fake date to prove to others that she was dateable had landed her a real date that had been truly *wunderbaar* . . . until it went horribly wrong.

As tears burned in her throat, she wondered if the train would flatten their dimes.

And if her wish would come true.

9

LUCY TURNER HELPED HER MOTHER INTO THE BATH-
tub, not understanding how a woman her age could get so dirty.

"Let go of me. I can do this myself!" Momma shrugged loose
of Lucy's hold and eased her tiny, naked body into the water. Lucy
squatted beside the tub and longed for the mother who had raised
her. Alice Turner was a cantankerous woman these days, and to
Lucy she seemed like a stranger. Since the stroke, each day had
become a bitter battle, each moment a fight against the grief that
ripped through her. Her mother wasn't dead, but sometimes it felt
that way.

Two months ago Momma had been living at a wonderful
skilled nursing facility. But apparently punching another resident
in the face wasn't going to be tolerated, and Momma had been
kicked out. Lucy had no choice but to take her in until another
nursing home in the area had a room. Hopefully soon.

"Momma, what have you been doing? How'd you get so dirty?"
Lucy shook her head as she eyed the black streaks on her mother's
face and hands, then glanced at the old green dress on the floor
next to a pair of once-white tennis shoes. Momma insisted on
wearing it over and over. "You need to put on some fresh, clean
clothes too. You've got plenty in your closet."

"I don't like those clothes you bought." Momma shook her head so hard that strands of gray hair fell from the bun on her head.

"Momma, those clothes are fine." She paused, eyeing her mother's matted, gray mess. "We need to wash your hair too. I'll go get you a clean dress, okay?"

"Where is my Benjamin? Did you give him away?" Momma lathered soap onto a rag, then dabbed at her face.

"Of course I didn't give him away. He's asleep in his room." Lucy rubbed her forehead and wondered how bad things were going to get with her mother. It was like having another two-year-old, except this one was able to venture out on her own and roam the neighborhood. Lucy tried hard to keep up with her, but it felt like a lost cause.

"You should have never had a baby. You're a terrible mother. You're going straight to hell."

Lucy blinked a few times, surprised that her mother was still able to shock her. "Whatever, Momma." She scooped the dirty clothes into her arms and was almost out the door when her mother spoke up again.

"See, you don't even care. You're going to burn in the lake of fire for what you've done. That's what happens to whores."

"That's enough, Momma!" Lucy spun around. "You cannot talk to me like that in my own house!"

"But that's what you are. A whore. You slept with a married man, and now you have a bastard baby."

Tears burned Lucy's eyes. "Don't you dare call Benjamin—"

"Oh my! Oh no!"

Lucy sniffled, looking on as her mother put a hand to her

neck. "What is it, Momma?" She sighed, the smell of the faded green dress in her arms causing her to crinkle her nose as she sniffled again.

"My Benjamin necklace is gone! It's gone! It's gone."

"Momma, I'll get you another one." Lucy closed her eyes as her mother bounced up and down in the bathtub, sloshing water over the sides. *Please, Lord, give me strength.*

The prayer was utterly sincere, though the irony of the whole thing made her smile a little. Despite her religious ramblings, Momma outright refused to go to church with Lucy. But Lucy went without her. She was trying to spend the second half of her life making up for all the bad things she'd done the first half. First and foremost, she wanted to learn about God and do what her pastor talked about—develop a relationship with Him. Then maybe someday He would forgive her . . . and she could forgive herself.

Maybe.

Right now, she knew that most of what her mother said was true. *I am not a good person.*

Momma buried her face in her hands and cried, mumbling about how she'd lost the pendant Lucy had given her with a picture of Benjamin in it.

"Don't cry. I said I'll get you another one." Lucy was torn between comforting her and leaving the room. Leaving was a strong temptation. But she was never sure what her mother might do when Lucy wasn't around. Ever since Momma slipped out of the house this morning, Lucy had worried she'd get a call from someone.

She finally sat down on the commode and began to sing.

It was the only thing that calmed Momma sometimes. "Hush, little baby, don't say a word. Papa's gonna buy you a mocking-bird. If—"

Momma clapped her wet hands together. "Oh, I like this song."

Lucy dabbed at one eye and smiled. "I know you do, Momma." She swallowed hard and starting singing again.

Noah walked into the kitchen and wrapped his arms around his wife's waist, kissing her on the back of the neck.

"How many jars of strawberry jam are you going to make?"

Carley shrugged as she tightened the lid on a Mason jar. "I couldn't stand to see all these strawberries go to waste." She turned to face him. "No way we can eat them all." She grinned, leaned up on her toes, and kissed him on the mouth. "Tell your friend we have all the berries we need."

"I don't want to hurt her feelings."

Carley turned back around and continued tightening lids. "Didn't you say you thought she was homeless? Wonder where she got all these strawberries."

"I have no idea." Noah slid beside Carley at the counter. "Need some help?"

"Nope. I'm pretty much done."

They both turned when they heard footsteps coming into the kitchen. As usual, their twelve-year-old daughter had earbuds plugged in, and she headed straight for the pantry. For such a thin girl, she ate a lot. Noah could remember being like that when he was young—eating and eating and never gaining weight. But Jenna didn't get that from him; they didn't share the same genes.

Noah and Carley had adopted Jenna when she was six, and she was the love of both their lives.

"Hey!" Noah yelled, and Jenna removed one of the earbuds. "What's on your agenda today?"

"I dunno." She replaced the earbud and reached for a box of cookies on the shelf.

Noah turned to Carley. "What about you? As much as I hate that people aren't coming to the clinic, it gives us some extra time to spend together." He leaned his elbows on the counter and faced her. "I miss having you work at the clinic."

"I know, honey, but there just wasn't enough for me to do any-more, and don't you like coming home to dinner on the table and a clean house?"

Noah stood up and smiled. "Yes, I do." He narrowed his eyebrows as he peeked around the corner into the living room. "Are those new curtains?"

"Yeah. I bought them back in December when we thought David and Emily were coming for a visit. But then we found out they couldn't come, and I just never got around to hanging them until this morning."

"That David is a good kid. I appreciate that he was coming here to convince Bishop Byler what a great guy I am and that the bishop should let his district members use the clinic."

"I figured that was why he was coming, even though he said it was just for a visit." Carley carried two jars of jam to the pantry as Jenna walked away munching on a cookie. "But I can see why the doctor didn't want them traveling during that pregnancy. Twins make everything a little more complicated."

Noah reached over and pulled the picture of David and

Emily's infant twins from the refrigerator door. "Cute kids. Hard to believe David is old enough to have children and Lillian and Samuel are grandparents. Hopefully we'll get to see them all again soon." He placed the picture back beneath the magnet. "David was only fifteen when I gave him one of my kidneys." He sighed. "Time flies."

Carley was carrying more jars to the pantry when a knock sounded at the front door. "I'll get it," Noah said. He walked to the door in his socks, shorts, and gray T-shirt and was surprised to see Bishop Byler's granddaughter on the step.

"Hi, Anna. What brings you here?" Noah didn't care for the girl's grandfather, but Anna had always seemed like a sweet girl. He stepped back. "Do you want to come in?"

"*Nee, nee,* I won't be staying. I just wanted to ask you something." She reached into the pocket of her black apron and pulled out a chain and what looked to be a pendant. "Is this a picture of your nephew?"

Noah took the chain and flipped the pendant over. As he studied the baby in the picture, he thought about his nieces and nephews. Samuel and his wife, Lillian, had David, Anna, and Elizabeth—plus David's wife, Emily, and their twins. Katie Ann had Jonas. They all lived in Colorado. Here in Paradise, Mary Ellen had Linda, Luke, and Matthew. Rebecca had Miriam, Elam, Ben, and John. All of Noah's nieces and nephews were older than the baby in this picture. Some of them were adults.

"I guess it could be one of them, but that seems unlikely since all my siblings are Amish, and Amish folks don't pose for pictures." Noah handed the necklace back to her.

Anna bit her bottom lip, squeezed her eyes closed for a moment, then looked back up at him. "I think this is a picture of Benjamin Turner. He would be your nephew, right?"

Noah stiffened. His brother, Ivan, had died, but not before he impregnated two women—his wife, Katie Ann, and his mistress, Lucy Turner. Noah knew that Lucy lived nearby. One of his sisters—Mary Ellen—had even made an attempt to see Benjamin soon after he was born, but Lucy had made up some excuse. She rarely showed her face around town. Noah had often wondered if he should attempt to see his brother's child, no matter the circumstances, but he never had.

"I honestly don't know if that's my nephew," he finally said. "Why do you think it's Benjamin?"

Anna fumbled with the necklace. "Because Lucy Turner asked me to watch her *boppli* one time. She got my name from another *Englisch* woman I used to babysit for. Lucy just showed up at our house one day and asked me to keep Benjamin one afternoon. So I did." She paused, her cheeks red. "But *mei daadi* found out, and he didn't want me sitting for her anymore."

Noah wasn't surprised. In the Amish community, Lucy Turner wore a big scarlet *A*. Before Noah could say anything, Anna went on.

"Anyway, I found this in my garden. I think an old woman dropped it when she was stealing my strawberries." Anna grinned. "Odd. But I guess she was hungry. I think she may have taken some stuff from the Lapps' too."

Within seconds Noah had put two and two together. Alice Turner was related to Lucy Turner somehow. Mother, maybe?

Anna looked down at the necklace, then back at Noah. "Since Lucy brought Benjamin to me that day, I don't even know where she lives." She paused, pointing to the small picture in the pendant. "I remember him having the biggest dimples. See. He's just extra cute. I guess that's why I remember him."

Noah held out his hand. "I know where she lives, and I think I know who the owner of the necklace is too. I'll return it if you want me to."

Anna dropped the chain and pendant in Noah's hand. "That would be *gut. Danki.*"

Noah said "you're welcome" in his native dialect—Pennsylvania *Deitsch*. He smiled when she raised her eyebrows. "*Ya*, I still remember it."

Anna's cheeks reddened again, then she gave a small wave and turned to leave. But before Noah closed the door, she turned back. "Dr. Noah?"

He eased onto the porch. "Yeah?"

Anna gripped the sides of her dress. "I'm sorry about *Daadi*. I know everyone is hoping he'll change his mind about letting our people visit your clinic."

"There's nothing for you to be sorry about, Anna. You're not responsible for your grandfather's decisions."

"I know." She paused, staring at him. "He really is a *gut* man. He's just scared of the outside world."

Noah forced a smile. It was sweet of her to defend her grandfather, but Noah wasn't sure Bishop Byler's rules were really fueled by fear. He'd heard too many stories from other districts about bishops on power trips. "Take care, Anna. And thank you for bringing the necklace."

Anna smiled, then left in her buggy.

Noah walked back into the kitchen holding the necklace.

"What's that?" Carley leaned closer and peered at the pendant.

"Well . . ." Noah sighed. "I think I know where all the strawberries are coming from. And I think that is a picture of Benjamin Turner. Ivan's son."

"And your nephew." Carley smiled, but Noah had mixed emotions. He had promised to return the necklace. And part of him wanted to see his brother's son. But would that mean letting Lucy Turner into their lives?

10

IT WAS A FEW DAYS LATER WHEN ANNA WALKED INTO
the main entrance of the lumberyard. She was nervous about facing the girl at the cash register—Glenda—again, but she had
something for Jacob.

"He's on the clock." Glenda slung her hair over her shoulders
in an exaggerated motion and stood up. "But I'll go find him."

Anna shook her head. "*Nee*, that's all right. Can you just give this
to him when you see him?" She pushed a letter-size white envelope
toward the girl.

"Sure." Glenda put it to the side on top of a pile of papers, and
Anna couldn't help but wonder if Jacob would ever get it.

"*Danki.* Thank you."

Glenda just smiled and gave a little wave, so Anna left, looking all around her to make sure she hadn't been seen. So far she'd
abided by her grandfather's wishes to stay away from Jacob, but
she felt like there was something between them, and she needed to
know if he felt the same way.

By the time she got home, she was dripping with sweat. She
loved the summertime, the feel of the dewy grass between her
toes in the morning, the smell of honeysuckle in full bloom and
freshly cut hay, but this summer seemed unusually warm. When

she walked into the living room, all was quiet. She opened the basement door and walked down a few steps.

"*Mammi*, are you down there?" She stopped and waited, not sure if her grandmother could hear her. "*Mammi?*"

She walked down a few more steps, yelled again, then decided her grandmother must be somewhere else in the house. One of these days she was going to make *Mammi* show her what she was hiding down there, but every time she thought about it, she supposed she wouldn't want her grandmother snooping around in her room. There were probably quite a few things she wouldn't approve of—a couple of *Englisch* magazines and a tube or two of lip gloss, for starters. She'd never worn the lipstick anywhere except in her room, but she'd still be hard-pressed to explain it to her grandparents.

She walked from room to room, calling her grandmother's name. Finally, she heard the basement door open and walked back in that direction. Cora Hostetler came out of the basement first, followed by Anna's grandmother, who closed the door behind them. Anna wished she had known that Jacob's mother would be here. She could have given Jacob's envelope to her. But then her grandmother would have seen, so maybe it was best she delivered it to his work.

"Uh, Anna . . . *wie bischt?*" Cora was holding a small box wrapped in pink paper. "I must go." She gave a quick wave and scurried past Anna, turning to add, "*Gut* to see you."

Anna turned to face her grandmother—a grown woman who looked like she'd just been caught doing something naughty. Those two were up to something. And even though she knew she was taking advantage of her grandmother's secret, Anna decided this would be a good time to talk to *Mammi* about Jacob.

"Have you been able to convince *Daadi* to let me spend time with Jacob?"

"I'm working on it, dear." *Mammi* slid past her toward the kitchen, and Anna followed her.

"What were you and Cora doing in the basement?" Anna picked up a banana from the fruit bowl on the table and started peeling it.

Mammi opened the cabinet under the sink and pulled out her cleaning bucket. "*Ach*, nothing really. Just chatting."

"In the basement?" Anna took a bite of the banana and waited.

"Uh . . . *ya*."

"Did you tell Cora that *Daadi* has forbidden me to see Jacob?" Anna sat down at the table and took another bite of the fruit as her grandmother took inventory of the items in the bucket.

"*Ya*. Jacob told her what happened, and they both assumed there would be a problem with your grandfather." *Mammi* picked up the bucket and shook her head. "You should have known better than to not be truthful with him, Anna. I'm trying to talk to him, but I suspect it will be awhile before he agrees to let you spend time with Jacob."

Anna stood up, tossed the peel in the trash, and faced off with her grandmother. "Are you being truthful with *Daadi* about what you do down in the basement?" She slammed her hands to her hips. "What do you do down there, anyway?"

"Anna, I don't have time to get into this with you now. I've told you that it's my quiet place, and—"

"I know what you've told me. You also keep the door locked." Anna grinned. "But I know where the key is."

Mammi turned pale as the white wall behind her.

"Don't worry. I don't go in there." Anna shook her head. "I'm going to go tend to the garden." She took a few steps, then turned around. "Please keep trying to talk to *Daadi*. I really like Jacob, and unless *Daadi* wants me to live with you for the rest of my life, he's going to have to start giving me some freedom."

Her grandmother nodded, but Anna wasn't holding out much hope.

Jacob opened the envelope Anna had left and pulled out a flattened dime. Then he unfolded a white piece of paper and read her note.

Hope your wish came true. I'll be at the train tracks on Saturday at three o'clock. Anna.

Jacob's heart raced, even though he knew he shouldn't see Anna against her grandfather's will. He wondered briefly if he should go talk to Bishop Byler before Saturday, but he didn't want to risk not being able to see Anna, so maybe he would talk to the bishop after the next worship service.

He slid the note back in its envelope and tucked it into his pocket, then signaled Bolt to pick up the pace. He was glad he'd taken the family buggy to work today. The drive home gave him private time to think the situation out. Anna was proving to be much more than a distraction from his family problems. Thoughts of her kept him up at night.

It was nearing the supper hour when Jacob turned into his driveway. He was pleased to see the flowerbeds filled with colorful blooms. Maybe everyone was starting to heal after all.

"The flowers are pretty," he said to his sisters when he walked into the kitchen.

Mary Jane carried a loaf of bread to the table. "*Mamm* planted those earlier today."

Jacob nodded, then walked to the living room and hung his hat on the rack. He glanced around but didn't see his father or brothers. Or his mother.

"Where is everyone?" He pulled a pitcher of tea from the refrigerator.

Anna Mae leaned up against the kitchen counter. "Who knows where *Daed* is. Eli and Abe are at the creek. I told them to be home by supper."

Jacob sat down in one of the chairs at the table, hoping everyone's absence wouldn't hold up supper. "What about *Mamm*?"

"She said she had an errand to run." Anna Mae moved toward a pot on the stove. "She was walking, so she couldn't have gone very far."

Jacob mentally calculated how much more money he would need before he could buy his own buggy, then sighed. It was going to be awhile. But he could walk to the railroad tracks on Saturday if he had to. He got off work at two that day, so it wouldn't be a problem. He thought about the wish he'd made that day and smiled.

A few minutes later *Mamm* breezed into the kitchen, a smile on her face and a small pink box in one hand.

"Be right back to help you finish supper." *Mamm* was smiling, almost skipping, as she left the kitchen. Then Abe and Eli came in carting an ice chest full of fish and grinning from ear to ear. Even Anna Mae and Mary Jane were giggling among themselves about something. Jacob wasn't thrilled to hear Ben Raber's name mentioned. Ben hadn't been very nice to Anna the day Jacob met her. He hoped one of his sisters hadn't taken a liking to him. Still, it was nice to hear laughter in the house.

But as he looked around at people talking, smelling the aromas of supper, he couldn't help recalling a time when there were two more place settings at the table. Though time had offered a measure of healing, the pain was still there. Would his family ever be healthy again?

He strained his neck to see out the kitchen window, but there was no sign of *Daed*.

Again.

Noah drove to Lucy Turner's house to return the pendant Anna had brought to him. He dreaded facing her. She hadn't been very pleasant the few times he'd met her. But the longer Noah had stared at little Benjamin's picture, the more certain he was that Ivan would want the Stoltzfus family in his son's life. Noah wanted to be a part of that, even if it meant having to deal with Lucy.

He took a deep breath and knocked, then glanced around at the overgrown yard. His brother had built the house, but he'd still been married to Katie Ann when he died, so the house had technically belonged to her. But when Katie Ann moved to Colorado, she'd deeded the house to Lucy. Not many folks in Paradise could wrap their minds around that. Why would Katie Ann give her husband's mistress the house? But Noah had known Katie Ann a long time, and he assumed she had her reasons. A fresh start, perhaps. Noah wasn't even sure if Lucy understood just what Katie Ann had done for her.

Alice Turner opened the door, her hair tousled, but she

looked clean and wore a different dress? "Do you need more strawberries?"

Noah held up his palm toward her. "No. No I don't." He smiled. "How are you, Alice?"

"I think I'm okay." She scratched her chin. "Why are you here?"

Noah reached into his pocket and pulled out the pendant. "Is this yours?" He handed it to her, and right away her face lit up.

"My Benjamin necklace!" She turned and yelled over her shoulder, "Lucy! I have my Benjamin necklace back!" Pulling it to her chest, she squeezed her eyes tight for a few seconds, then looked back at Noah. "Thank you."

Noah nodded just as Lucy walked up beside Alice. She didn't look anything like the Lucy Noah remembered—bleached-blond hair, too much makeup, clothing a size too small. This new Lucy had short, dark hair and a freshly scrubbed face. She was dressed in simple blue jeans and a loose green T-shirt.

"Noah?" She asked as if she wasn't sure. They'd only been around each other a few times, and that was before Benjamin was born.

"Hi, Lucy. I brought Alice something I think she lost." He nodded toward the older woman.

"Momma, why don't you go check on Benjamin." Lucy gently pulled her mother inside, then stepped out onto the porch and closed the door behind her. "Thank you for returning her necklace. I have no idea where she lost it, but it's very important to her."

Noah shifted his weight, knowing he was about to get Alice in trouble, but Lucy should know what was going on. "Alice, I'm assuming, is your mother?" Lucy nodded. "I think she's been stealing strawberries from some of the Amish gardens. Anna Byler found the necklace in her garden after seeing an older woman there."

Lucy raised her chin, frowning. "So that makes Momma a thief?"

Noah shrugged. "Well, since she brought me a ton of strawberries, the strawberries were stolen by an older woman, and her necklace was on the scene . . . looks guilty to me."

Lucy rubbed her forehead, and Noah noticed the dark circles under her eyes. That, too, was a big change from the woman he remembered.

"I'll make this right," she said. "I'm not sure how yet, but I will. Who all did she steal from?"

"As far as I know, just the Bylers and maybe the Lapps." Noah paused. "I know both those families, and they would have probably just given her the strawberries. I guess I'm wondering what would make her steal them late at night."

Lucy glanced over her shoulder, then looked back at Noah. "Momma had a stroke awhile back. She hasn't really been right in the head since then."

Noah swallowed hard. "Is she okay in there with your baby . . . with Benjamin?"

"Oh yeah. She loves Benjamin with all her heart. I don't leave him alone with her, but she'd never do anything to put him in danger." She opened the door and stepped backward. "Thank you for bringing back her necklace, and again . . . please let the Bylers and the Lapps know I'll pay them for the strawberries. I'm not working much right now . . ." She pulled her eyes from his, paused for a few moments, then went on. "But as soon as I can, I'll make it right."

Noah shook his head. "I really don't think that's necessary. I just thought you should know what happened." He peered over her shoulder, and in the distance he could see Alice holding Benjamin. "Do you think maybe I could—"

"I'm sorry. I have to go. Thank you again." Lucy took a final step backward and closed the door.

Noah turned to leave but heard voices inside. He stopped and listened.

"None of them Stoltzfuses like you. I'm surprised that nice doctor even came over here to bring me my necklace back."

Noah moved in closer to catch what else Alice had to say, but Lucy spoke up next.

"Whether they like me or not, yes, it was nice of Dr. Noah to bring your necklace. But, Momma, you can't be going into other people's gardens and stealing fruit."

"Well, it ain't like you make any money for me to pay him, and he saved my life! Don't you think he deserved a little something for that effort?"

"Momma, I would have found a way to pay him. I told you that. Stealing is not the answer."

Noah listened as Alice began to cackle. "Well, ain't you the high and mighty one! You listen to me. You're not right in the eyes of the Lord, so I don't think you'd best be criticizing me."

"Momma, please don't start this again. You know I'm trying to live a better life! And God loves everyone."

Noah was now back up on the porch listening. His heart ached for Lucy, despite her past.

"God doesn't love you. No one loves you, Lucy Turner. Even my Benjamin will grow up not to love you. And he'll leave you as soon as he can."

Noah held his fist to the door, feeling an overwhelming urge to knock. Because maybe that would put an end to the old woman's vicious words. And because he wanted more than ever to meet his nephew.

But he pulled back his hand, eased down the porch steps, and walked to his car. He wondered if Lucy knew that there were medications for people like Alice, whether her problems stemmed solely from the stroke or involved something like depression or even Alzheimer's. Maybe he'd try to talk to Lucy at another time.

Cora placed the jewelry box on her nightstand and turned the knob until the delicate glass ballerina began to spin and music began to play. Though she didn't recognize the song, she felt transported to another place as the soft notes sounded and the dancer slowly spun on her pedestal. She didn't even look up when John walked out of their bathroom and into the bedroom, his hair wet and a white towel wrapped around him.

Marianne had been right about the joy of doing something just for yourself. Cora thought her new friend may have gone overboard, with that closet crammed full of items her husband would forbid. But Cora understood. Living with Bishop Byler couldn't be easy. Besides, women like them spent their lives tending to their husbands and children. Why couldn't they indulge themselves even a little?

"Where did you get that?"

Cora pulled her eyes from the ballerina, slid out of her slippers, then eased into bed without looking at her husband. "I bought it." She pulled the pins from her hair, found her brush in the drawer of the nightstand, and began running it the length of her hair. She glanced over at John when she heard the dresser drawer open, and her breath caught in her throat when she realized how thin he was. How had she not noticed? It had been less than a week since she stopped bringing him his meals to their bedroom. She'd hoped her bold action would send him back downstairs for meals with his family, but it hadn't. Had he lost that much weight in so short a time?

"Do you want me to bring you a plate of supper?" She glanced at the clock on the nightstand next to her new music box. It was almost nine o'clock, but she didn't like to think of her husband hungry, especially if it was her fault.

"Little late for supper, no?" He pulled on a pair of boxers and a white T-shirt, then went to his side of the bed.

"I can still get you something if you want." She stowed the brush back in the drawer. "I don't mind."

"*Nee.* No food." He climbed into bed and immediately pulled her close to him, his hands roaming her body in places that hadn't felt his touch in months. It should have been wonderful, but his aggressive actions were a far cry from what they'd shared for most of their married life. There was no tenderness, no kissing, no running his hands through her hair and whispering how much he loved her—all the things she'd been dreaming about for so long. Instead, it was mechanical, unemotional, and over quickly. And immediately afterward, he rolled over in the bed facing away from her.

Cora didn't move, just lay there on her back as warm tears pooled in the corners of her eyes. She turned her head to the side, hoping to get a glimpse of the ballerina, but all was dark.

She blinked her eyes once, and the tears spilled down her cheeks.

Marianne and Anna cleaned the breakfast dishes, then she helped Anna load the buggy with today's items for distribution. Once both husband and granddaughter were out the door, Marianne sat down at the kitchen table and stared at the half-eaten shoofly pie on the table. She cut her eyes toward her bottle of cinnamon tablets and frowned. She was out of the insulin pills, and she wasn't sure the cinnamon would keep her blood sugar under control if she ate that pie. But her mouth watered for a piece.

Anna had told her that Dr. Noah said she would have to go in for a visit before he'd refill her prescription. But since Isaac had put an end to all that, she didn't want to risk getting caught at Dr. Noah's. She leaned her head back and thought of the irony. She was well aware that she probably kept more things from her spouse than all the wives in the district—a terrible example to be setting as the bishop's wife.

She sat taller and shook her head, refusing to feel bad about her choices. And what about Cora? The woman had lit up the moment she saw the package with her ballerina music box. Such a small thing with such a big payoff.

Marianne just didn't believe the Lord would mind these little luxuries. Her husband would, but not the Lord.

She drummed her fingers on top of the oak table as she twisted her mouth back and forth.

Then she reached for the knife and cut herself a large slice of shoofly pie.

11

ANNA ARRIVED AT THE RAILROAD TRACKS WELL BEFORE three o'clock on Saturday. She'd told her grandparents she needed to use the buggy to deliver a batch of cookies to a bakery that was closed yesterday due to a family emergency. That much was true. She just hadn't told them where she was going after that.

She reached into her apron pocket and pulled out her flattened dime, rubbing it between her fingers as if it had some magical power. She sat down in the grass and leaned against the big oak tree, its canopy an umbrella from the fierce sun that shone this time of day. She drew her knees to her chest, her dark blue dress resting at her ankles, wrapped her hands around her legs, and rocked back and forth. She hoped Jacob would show up, even though she still wasn't sure they could be anything more than friends.

She straightened her legs out in front of her and leaned back. Maybe he wouldn't be able to use the family buggy to venture out today, although it wasn't too far for him to walk. Or maybe Glenda hadn't given him the envelope she'd left at the hardware store. Maybe he wasn't interested enough to come or brave enough to risk angering *Daadi* more.

Maybe, maybe, maybe.

Her stomach churned, partly from nervousness about Jacob,

but also from her conflicted feelings about betraying *Daadi*. He hadn't given her a chance to explain about Jacob, and he was making everyone in their district miserable. But he was still her grandfather. If only—

The sound of buggy wheels brought her to her feet. She smoothed the wrinkles from her apron and dabbed at her damp forehead, then smiled when she recognized Jacob's horse. She hurried to meet him.

"I wasn't sure if you'd be able to make it. Or if you'd gotten the message." Anna walked with him to the front of the buggy and waited while he tethered the horse. Then he turned to face her, and he was frowning.

"I have to talk to your *daadi*. I'm going to do that soon."

Anna stopped breathing for a few moments as she pictured that scenario.

Jacob's hand on her arm sent a chill through her despite the intense heat. "I don't feel right about sneaking around like this. I know he's forbidden you to see me."

Anna let out the breath she was holding, conscious of his hand still on her arm. "I don't feel *gut* about it either, but *Daadi* is being unreasonable. He's not being fair." She folded her arms across her chest, then regretted doing that because Jacob pulled back his hand.

He smiled, and Anna felt her knees going weak. "Come on." He reached for her hand, and together they walked to the oak tree and sat down on the grass. "No one was using the buggy, so I was able to bring it, but I would have walked here to see you. Anna . . ."

He let go of her hand and took off his hat, revealing a mass of gold-streaked hair. He ran his hand through it before he went on. "I've already told you that *mei* family is in a bad way." He paused, sighing, but then smiled. "I'm a mess too. But I really like you, and I'd like to date you. The right way, with your grandfather's blessing."

Anna swallowed hard. Despite her recent actions, family meant everything to her, and she could tell it was important to Jacob as well. That he wanted to do the honorable thing by talking to her grandfather made him even more attractive—and he was plenty attractive as it was. She wondered how many women he'd kissed, dated, spent time with. If Jacob ever kissed her, would she do it right?

"I told you. *Daadi* is unreasonable. He wouldn't listen to me when I tried to explain. He won't listen to anyone, really. That's why people in the district hide things from him. Even my grandmother does it." Anna turned to face him, cringing a little. Maybe she shouldn't have told on her grandmother. "I never want to live like them. Not telling the entire truth is still a lie, and they have so many lies between them."

Jacob cupped her cheek in his hand, and Anna stopped breathing again. "That's exactly why I have to talk to your grandfather. We're lying just by being here."

She knew he was right, but the feel of his touch reminded her that this small untruth was worth it. "Okay," she managed in a whisper as Jacob moved his hand. "But what if he still forbids us to see each other? Then what?"

He shrugged. "I'll figure it out."

"So how are things with your *daed*? Any better?"

Jacob had told her all about his father, the ways he'd been handling his grief about Leah. Or not handling it.

He rubbed his forehead. "He still stays to himself. And this week *Mamm* quit taking meals to him in their bedroom. I think she was trying to force him to be with the family at mealtime, but it didn't work. He just doesn't eat now, except for the lunch *Mamm* sends with him when he's tending the land."

Anna was quiet for a few moments. "*Daadi* would be a *gut* person for him to talk to."

"I'm not sure anyone can get through to him at this point. I feel the most sorry for *mei mamm*. And for Eli. He's twelve, and he really needs his *daed*."

Jacob leaned back against the tree and crossed his ankles. "Besides, you said your grandfather is unreasonable and unfair. What makes you think he could help my father?"

Anna sighed. "He knows how he feels. He lost his *sohn* and his *sohn's fraa*—my parents. And *Mammi* told me that he withdrew into himself for a long time after that. I know he's stubborn and strict, but he does love the Lord, and I know he wants to be a *gut* bishop. Maybe I should suggest that he pay your father a visit."

"Maybe." Jacob turned to face her. "Or maybe wait until after I talk to him about us."

Us. That sounded nice.

"If that goes well, I'll talk to your grandfather about *Daed*."

"I'm so sorry your family is going through this."

Jacob reached for her hand and squeezed. "Me too."

Anna reached into her pocket and pulled out her flattened dime. "Did you bring yours?"

"*Ya.*" He smiled as he produced his in the palm of his hand. "So what did you wish for?"

Anna shook her head. "Can't tell you. Then it won't come true."

Jacob sighed as he stretched his legs out and crossed his ankles. "Well then, I guess I can't tell you what I wished for either." He paused, leaning his face closer to her. "Maybe I'll just show you."

Anna's pulse quickened and her emotions whirled as she realized this was the moment she'd been waiting for. The feel of Jacob's lips on hers sent her stomach into a wild swirl. But after only a few seconds, she surprised herself and relaxed into the kiss, parting her lips as she shared an intimacy she'd only dreamed about. It was everything she'd hoped it would be, and as Jacob eased away, he kissed her tenderly on the cheek.

Anna couldn't take her eyes off him. Or his mouth. Without giving it much thought, she leaned up and kissed him again.

Maybe my wish is coming true.

Lucy carted Benjamin on her hip into Noah's clinic, hoping her little one would behave himself. She loved her son more than anything in the world, but there was merit to the entire "terrible twos" phrase she'd heard about.

She'd never been to Noah's clinic, and she wouldn't have ventured here today if she wasn't desperate. But she owed her regular doctor so much money, she didn't dare show her face at his office.

She walked up to the receptionist window and rang the bell. The foggy glass door slid open.

"I don't have an appointment, but I was wondering if Dr. Stoltzfus would have time to see us." Lucy repositioned Benjamin on her hip. "Benjamin is due for his shots, but he seems really congested too."

"Has he been here before?"

Lucy shook her head. "No. He usually goes to Dr. Bentson in Lancaster."

"Dr. Stoltzfus had an emergency. He should be back within

the hour. You're welcome to wait. There is one person in front
of you."

"That's fine. I'll wait."

The woman handed Lucy a clipboard. "Just fill this out, and
it will give us permission to get the records from Dr. Bentson.
And on the next page is all the other information we'll need about
Benjamin—his insurance and so forth."

Lucy hesitated. She didn't have insurance, and she wasn't
sure she wanted Noah's office contacting the other doctor.
What if he found out how behind she was in her payments to
Dr. Bentson?

But she took the clipboard. She'd just have to hope that Dr.
Bentson's rude receptionist wouldn't tell on her. *They'll probably be
glad to be rid of me.*

She glanced around the small waiting room. There were five
chairs against one wall, a large coffee table with magazines, and
five chairs on the opposite wall, where the other patient was sitting. She wore a long dark-green dress, a black apron, and one of
those white head coverings. Amish, obviously.

Lucy sat as far away from her as possible. She didn't know
many of the Amish folks, but she suspected most of them knew
her—and disapproved. It had been quite the scandal when everyone found out that Lucy was having an affair with Ivan Stoltzfus.
Lucy wanted to regret it—needed to regret it—but when she
looked at Benjamin, she just couldn't. If things had happened any
differently, she wouldn't have Benjamin, and he was all that kept
her going on most days.

She put Benjamin on a chair beside her and started filling out
the paperwork, but her son was quickly off the chair and running

around the room. *Not today, Benny. Please.* She didn't raise her head, but lifted her eyes toward the Amish woman. But she flipped through a magazine and paid the baby no mind.

Benny kept hopping around in his blue-checked shorts, navy T-shirt, and white tennis shoes. He was incredibly cute, actually, and Lucy silently thanked God for him. Again. But she also sent up a desperate prayer that he behave.

"Benjamin, come here," Lucy called softly. But he ignored her. He walked directly to the Amish woman and slammed both hands in the middle of her magazine. Lucy jumped up, still clutching the clipboard, and hurried to her son.

"I'm so sorry." Lucy reached for Benny's hand to ease him away, but Benjamin fell to the floor and screamed. She put the clipboard on the chair next to the Amish woman and picked up her wailing son. "I'm sorry," she said again as she walked back to her seat. Benjamin went limp in her arms, still screaming.

The woman was quickly on her feet, toting the clipboard Lucy had left behind.

"Here you go." She handed it to Lucy, then smiled. "I remember when my children were that age. Such a wonderful, fun age." The smile broadened. "But it can be challenging." She reached over and touched Benjamin on the arm. "Oh my. You have some lungs on you, no?"

"Please tell me the terrible twos won't go on into the threes and fours." Lucy bounced Benjamin on one knee.

The woman laughed. "They just change, and there are always challenges. But a child is the Lord's greatest blessing."

Lucy looked up at the woman just in time to see her expression shift to a much more solemn look, and Lucy wondered what she was thinking about. But then she reached out her hands. "I'd be happy to hold him while you finish your paperwork."

"Are you sure? He can be quite the handful." She didn't want to hurt the woman's feelings by telling her that Benny rarely went to strangers. And she was a little wary of speaking with an Amish woman. She usually avoided all of the Amish, never quite sure who might recognize her as the adulterous woman she was.

"I'm Cora, by the way." The other woman put her arms under Benny's and lifted him to her lap. To Lucy's surprise, Benjamin smiled and reached for one of the strings on the woman's white cap.

Lucy swallowed hard, knowing Cora might be handing Benjamin right back when she found out who she was. "I'm, uh . . . I'm Lucy. Lucy Turner."

Cora didn't turn her way as she bounced Benny on her knee. "Very nice to meet you, Lucy."

"You too." Cora smiled as she briefly glanced at Lucy, her head cocked to one side as Benjamin wrapped his fingers around the dangling string.

Lucy picked up the clipboard and finished filling out the paperwork, praying that Benjamin wouldn't rip the little cap from Cora's head, but Cora set him down on the floor in front of her and started playing patty-cake with him. Benjamin wasn't very good at it, but he was laughing, and so was Cora. "Such a little cutie." Cora cupped Benjamin's cheek. "Such a blessing."

Cora was a pretty woman, maybe ten years older than Lucy, in her early forties. Tiny lines feathered from the corners of big brown eyes that twinkled as she played with Benjamin. Watching Cora made Lucy miss her own mother that much more—the loving woman she used to be, not the angry, critical one she had become. Lucy assumed the love was still in there somewhere. She doted on Benjamin the best way she knew how. But when it came to Lucy, there was no love to be seen. She almost never spoke without getting a jab in at Lucy—that she was a terrible mother, an awful cook, a pitiful housekeeper—that part was a little bit true—and just a terrible person in general. It was a struggle for Lucy these days not to see herself as her mother did.

Before the stroke, Alice hadn't always agreed with Lucy's choices, especially her seeing a married man. And looking back, Lucy was sure the entire situation must have been painfully embarrassing for her mother. But she'd never degraded Lucy or talked ugly to her the way she did now.

"I'll be right back." Lucy stood up and took the clipboard to the receptionist, then went back to her seat. Cora had Benjamin in her lap now and was entertaining him with silly faces.

"How many children do you have," Lucy asked as she sat down.

Cora tickled Benjamin on his tummy. "I have six." Her face paled, and she bit her bottom lip. "Actually, I have five. My daughter died a year ago."

"I'm so sorry." Lucy gazed at Benjamin and couldn't imagine that kind of pain. "What was her name?"

Cora smiled again. "*Danki*—I mean, thank you—for asking. Her name was Leah. She was my oldest child."

Benjamin wiggled his way off Cora's lap. Both women watched as he picked up a magazine on the coffee table, sat down on the floor with it, and began flipping through it as if he were reading. Lucy couldn't help but smile. "Do you mind me asking, was she . . . sick or . . . ?"

Cora shook her head, eyes downcast. "*Nee*—no. She fell off the plow and hit her head." She looked up at Lucy and blinked a few times. "She died right away. We still miss her very much."

Lucy looked over at Benjamin. *Please, God, keep him safe.* She wasn't sure what else to say to the other woman. But she didn't need to say anything because Cora kept talking as if starved for conversation.

"That's why I'm here," she said, "to see Dr. Stoltzfus. I'm not supposed to be here. Our bishop has banned us from coming here." She waved a hand in the air and rolled her eyes. "Something about Dr. Stoltzfus being shunned a long time ago. But my husband really needs help, so I decided to take the risk."

Lucy wasn't following. If Cora's husband was sick, shouldn't he be the one at the doctor? Cora suddenly sprang to her feet and reached for Benjamin, who had stood up, tripped, and begun to fall before Lucy had time to register what had happened. Cora stood him up and handed him another magazine, which he began swinging around the room.

Cora sat down again and sighed. "I'm sorry. I'm talking too much and burdening you with my troubles. I'm just so anxious to get some help for my husband. We just moved here a month ago, and I was hoping the change would help him adjust to Leah's death, but he has only gotten worse."

Ah! They just moved here. That explained why an Amish woman was being so friendly to Lucy. But what a sad story she had to tell. Lucy recalled how she'd felt when Ivan died—the pain of losing him compounded by having to suffer silently on the sidelines. At the time she'd felt like she would never recover. But now that she had her own child, she was sure that losing a son or daughter had to be the worst thing that could ever happen to a person.

"Um . . . I'm wondering . . . what are you hoping Dr. Stoltzfus can do for your husband?"

Cora shrugged as she crossed her legs. "I don't know. I read in a magazine once that there are medications for people who are depressed, but I've heard there are herbal remedies too. Since Dr. Stoltzfus used to be Amish, I'm hoping he will be able to help me with one or the other." She paused. "I'm not sure why I'm telling you all this. You seem very nice."

Lucy couldn't help but smile at the unexpected compliment. She didn't have any friends, Amish or otherwise. When she wasn't working at the diner, she was tending to Benny and her mother, and the few friends she'd had before Benjamin was born had gone on living their single lives. This woman was kind, new to the area, and had her own problems. But she was Amish. How much could she and Lucy have in common? And would she even want to be friends with Lucy once she found out who she was and what everyone in the Amish community thought of her?

Her stomach lurched as she thought about having to face Ivan's brother. But she'd sensed when he returned the pendant that he wanted to see Benjamin. So maybe he would give her a discount or treat him for free, like he'd treated her mother.

If it had been Lucy who was sick, no way she would seek free medical attention. But this was for Benjamin, and she was willing to risk her pride for his sake. Even though he acted like he felt fine, Lucy could hear the rattle in Benny's chest.

"Cora Hostetler."

Both Lucy and Cora looked toward the opened door where a nurse was standing. Noah must have returned through a back entrance.

Cora stood up. "It was nice talking to you." She smiled before she walked to where the nurse waited.

"You too." Lucy wished their visit could have been longer. She picked up Benjamin, who had toddled back to her. He snuggled up close, and she rocked him in her lap, rehearsing what she would say to Noah. Should she ask him about her mother? Maybe there was a drug that Mom could take, a nice pill or something. She grinned at the thought, even though there wasn't anything remotely funny about the situation.

Twenty minutes later Cora returned to the waiting room. She went straight to the window and apparently settled her bill, not even glancing at Lucy and Benjamin, who had finally fallen asleep. When the nurse called her name, Lucy carefully eased him onto her shoulder and moved in that direction. Cora was closing a small wallet and stuffed it in her purse. Lucy hesitated, wanting to ask if she'd gotten some help for her husband. But she knew enough about the Amish people to know that they didn't normally seek friendships with outsiders. There were exceptions to that, of course, but Lucy couldn't imagine why Cora would want to be friends with a woman she just met in the doctor's waiting room.

She'd been hoping Cora might ask her for coffee or want to chat more. But when Cora just gave a quick wave in her direction, Lucy walked through the open door and down the hallway.

She heard the front door close behind her, doubting she'd ever see the woman again.

12

NOAH STOPPED ABRUPTLY WHEN HE WALKED INTO THE examining room, wishing he'd taken a look at the name on the chart before he rushed into the room. "Lucy." He gazed at Benjamin, swallowing hard as he thought about Ivan.

"Hi, Dr. Stoltzfus." Lucy was bouncing Benjamin on her knee. "He needs his shots, and he's congested."

"Most people just call me Dr. Noah. Or Noah." He inched toward them and held his hands out. "May I?"

Lucy lifted Benjamin into Noah's arms. When he dropped the pendant off, she'd made it clear she didn't want him to see Benjamin, so he wondered what brought her here now. Surely she had a regular pediatrician. He glanced at the file he'd set down on the chair beside them. *Dr. Bentson.* Hmm.

Noah set the little boy on the examining table as Lucy walked to her son's side. After asking Lucy a few questions and examining Benjamin, Noah diagnosed his nephew with a mild case of bronchitis, crediting Lucy for bringing him in early. Gloria came into the room and gave Benjamin his shots, and Noah was surprised at how well he did, barely a whimper.

Noah couldn't take his eyes off of Benjamin, and his heart ached, remembering his brother. Ivan would have been so proud of this beautiful child. Would little Benjamin ever meet his half-brother, Jonas, who lived in Colorado with Katie Ann and her new husband? Noah hadn't had an opportunity to meet little Jonas, but Benjamin was right here in Paradise, in his office. He made a few notes on the baby's chart as Lucy picked him up, balancing him on her hip. "He's a handsome boy."

"Thank you." She avoided Noah's eyes but glowed as she looked at her son.

"How is your mother doing?" Noah wasn't ready for them to leave just yet. He certainly didn't have any other patients waiting. He'd been surprised to have two this morning, both of them first-timers.

Lucy shrugged. "I'm sorry for any trouble she's caused for you and those Amish families. Ever since the stroke . . ." She shifted the baby on her hip and looked up. "Do you think, I mean, are there medications for that sort of thing?"

"Does she have a regular doctor? She only came to see me for an ear infection."

Lucy shook her head. "No. Not really. We don't have insurance, and well . . ." She looked away.

Noah rubbed his chin as he took a deep breath. "I'd be happy to see your mother if you want to bring her in, and we can work something out about payment." He paused. "Listen, we're having a family get-together in a couple of weeks to celebrate my daughter's birthday. Would you and Benjamin like to come? I'm sure everyone would like to meet him. It will be both my sisters—Rebecca and Mary Ellen—and their families." He hesitated, then added, "And of course your mother is invited." He said it to be polite, but he hoped Lucy wouldn't bring Alice. It would be hard enough for his family to be around Lucy.

Was he betraying Katie Ann by inviting the woman who had wrecked her marriage? It felt that way. But Katie Ann and Jonas were far away. Lucy and Benjamin were right here, and no matter what, Benjamin was Ivan's son.

"Oh, I don't think . . ." Lucy hung her head and shook it, then looked back up. "Thank you for asking, but I'm not sure that would be such a good idea."

"My family isn't even supposed to sit down and dine with me since I've been shunned." Noah gave her what he hoped was a reassuring smile. "None of us are perfect. We've all made mistakes. But Benjamin has lots of cousins that I know would love to meet him." He grabbed his prescription pad from the counter and wrote down his address, phone number, and the date and time. "Here. I hope you and Benjamin will come. And your mother." He smiled as she took the piece of paper. "My sisters are great cooks. And my wife, Carley, doesn't do so bad either."

Finally, Lucy smiled. "Thank you for asking us." She picked up her son, a diaper bag slung over her shoulder, and walked toward the door. "And thank you for seeing Benjamin on such short notice."

Noah's heart was heavy. "I was happy to. I hope to see you both at the party."

Lucy just smiled. Noah was fairly certain that they wouldn't be there. He hurried around the corner and gave instructions to the receptionist to tell Lucy that Noah would bill her for the visit. After Lucy left, Noah revised those instructions. "Today's visit was no charge. Don't send her a bill."

He walked to the window facing the parking lot and watched Lucy loading Benjamin into his car seat. They'd all despised Lucy for getting in between Katie Ann and Ivan, but Noah knew it took two to play that game. His brother was just as guilty. And no matter the circumstances, Ivan would want the family to accept Lucy and Benjamin into their lives.

But would Lucy allow that? Noah was pretty sure her choice to come to his clinic was more about money than family. That was okay. He'd still gotten to see Benjamin and to extend the invitation to Lucy.

The ball was in her court now.

───────

Lucy was glad that she didn't have to come up with the money for the doctor visit today. She'd get paid on Friday, and hopefully she'd have enough then to pay at least half of whatever the bill was. She couldn't believe that Noah had invited her and Benjamin to a family gathering. She knew it had nothing to do with her, that it was all about Benjamin, but she was still surprised.

No way was she going to put herself through that, though. She could already picture the peering, accusing eyes of Ivan and Noah's sisters, Rebecca and Mary Ellen.

Lucy knew she judged herself plenty without help from everyone else. But her pastor had said that the Lord forgives everyone, that anyone could have a relationship with Him. She was trying hard to believe that—to live a better life—even though her mother kept trying to derail her at every turn.

Speaking of judgment . . . Lucy shuddered at the idea of having her mother in the same room with Noah's family.

Lost in her thoughts, she almost didn't see the Amish woman walking on the side of the road. Once past her, she saw in her rearview mirror that it was the woman from the clinic. Cora, that was her name. They were still on the back road that led to Noah's clinic, and there wasn't any traffic. She backed up until she was beside Cora and rolled down the window.

"Can I give you a ride?"

"*Ya.* That would be great. It's hotter than I thought it would be this time of day." Cora opened the car door and got in. "It's not very far. I was happy to walk to the clinic this morning, but this afternoon heat is oppressive." She paused, smiling. "My daughters took the family buggy early this morning to go to town."

"I'm happy to give you a ride anytime. I'll give you my phone number. Just call me, and if I'm not working, I can take you wherever you need to go."

"That's so nice of you."

They were quiet for a few moments while Benjamin happily chattered from his car seat in the back. Cora twisted around and put a hand out toward Benny. "He's such a joy. I didn't ask—is Benjamin your only child?"

Lucy swallowed hard, knowing this would probably put an end to her potential friendship with Cora. "Yes, he is." She paused, not wanting to lie, but not wanting to be completely truthful either. "I'm not married, though. Benjamin's father died."

"Oh my. I'm so sorry." Cora turned back around, then looked at Lucy. "How long ago?"

Lucy knew she needed to change the subject before she was either forced to lie or forced to tell the truth. "He died when I was pregnant with Benjamin."

Cora shook her head. "So sad. He never got to see this beautiful child." She pointed to her left. "Turn in here. That's our place."

Lucy pulled into the driveway. There was a large white farmhouse and a big barn. Like most of the Amish homesteads, it was very well kept. Two young boys stood near the barn. They stared at the car as she eased to a stop.

"That's Abe and Eli, my two youngest." Cora opened the car door. "And I have twin girls, Anna Mae and Mary Jane, and then my oldest son, Jacob." She stepped out of the car. "Thank you so much for the ride." Cora started to close the door but then pulled it wide, narrowing her eyebrows. "Uh . . . would you and Benjamin like to come in? Maybe have some coffee or iced tea? I made a raspberry swirl cheesecake early this morning."

"We'd love to." Lucy couldn't put the car in Park quickly enough. It would be so nice to have a friend who didn't know about her past and couldn't judge her. Someone who could get to know her for the person she was trying to be.

"Wonderful!" Cora opened the rear door and began fumbling with Benjamin's car seat while Lucy grabbed the diaper bag. Before they had the car doors closed, the two young boys had run up to their mom.

"Eli, Abe, say hello to Mrs. Turner. And this is her boy, Benjamin." Cora adjusted Benjamin on her hip. "Isn't he a handsome fellow?"

Both the boys said hello, then asked if they could come into the house for a while to rest since they'd finished most of their chores.

"I think that's a fine idea." Cora smiled. "And go down into the basement and fetch some of those old toys I have boxed up. There are some building blocks and a few other things that will entertain Benjamin."

"Please don't go to any trouble," Lucy said as she followed Cora into the house.

"No trouble at all. It's been a long time since we've had a little one around. I thought about giving these things away when we moved, but I just couldn't."

The house was stuffy even with the windows opened, but Lucy didn't mind. She couldn't remember the last time she'd felt so welcomed—and by a woman who was surely still grieving the loss of her daughter.

Cora asked Lucy to follow her into the kitchen, where she started coffee brewing on top of the stove. A few minutes later Cora's boys had unloaded toys onto the living room floor and taken Benjamin in there to play with the blocks. Lucy followed and watched them for a minute, then returned to the kitchen. It felt so . . . normal—her son being entertained by someone else's children, having coffee and cake with another mother.

Cora placed a piece of cheesecake in front of Lucy, then sat down across the table from her. "The coffee will be ready shortly." She paused. "Or would you prefer iced tea?"

"Coffee is just fine. Thank you." She hesitated, not wanting to overstep. "Was Dr. Stoltzfus able to help you?"

Cora put her elbows on the large table and rested her chin in her hands. "He referred us to a counselor in Lancaster, and he said he can't give John any medications without seeing him in his office. I asked him about herbal remedies, but the only thing he suggested was B-12. He said it's a natural antidepressant, but I think John needs more than a vitamin."

"Maybe your husband just needs time." Lucy bit into the cool, creamy dessert and shut her eyes, savoring the sweetness.

"Maybe." Cora shrugged. "Not many people around here know—what ails my John, that is. Only one person, really." She chuckled. "Ironically, it's the bishop's wife. Do you know Marianne Byler?"

Lucy leaned to the side and glanced around the corner into the living room—to check on Benjamin but also to give herself time to ponder how she should answer. Lucy certainly knew *about* the Bylers, and she had a pretty good idea what they would think of her. "I know that the new bishop is named Byler," she said, "but I've never met either of them."

"Marianne is wonderful. She's the only woman I've felt close to since we moved here. Of course, much of that is my own fault because I haven't wanted to be social. But being around Marianne just makes a person happy. She's—I guess you could say she's playful. She has a childlike attitude that just makes you want to be around her. I'll introduce you sometime. You'd love her."

Lucy bit her bottom lip, forcing a smile.

"*Ach*, coffee is ready." Cora got up and returned with two cups of coffee, then brought over sugar and cream.

Lucy loaded her cup with both. "Thank you."

For the next hour, they drank coffee and chatted—about the flowers Cora had finally gotten around to planting, about her family back in Ohio, about her hopes for her children. She talked a lot about how they were all trying to heal. And about Leah.

In return, Lucy told Cora all about her mother. Cora kept a stern expression throughout this part of the conversation. Then, when Lucy was done, Cora reached over and touched her hand.

"You shouldn't have to live like that, Lucy. I understand that your mother has an illness, but it must be so hard for you."

Lucy opened her mouth to tell Cora about her new walk with Christ, but fear stopped her. Telling about this new path would mean revealing the old one too, and Lucy wasn't ready for that to happen. She was enjoying her fledgling friendship with Cora too much.

"She's my mother," she simply said. "I do the best I can with her." She looked at her watch. "Speaking of . . . I've left Mom alone for hours today. I guess I better go check on her." She stood up and reached for her coffee cup and plate.

"Oh, leave that. I'll get it later." Cora stood up too, and they walked into the living room. Abe and Eli were still entertaining Benjamin, and Lucy wished she had the boys around more often. She hadn't seen her baby boy this content in a long time.

Lucy squatted down, thanked the boys for playing with Benjamin, then started to help them pick up the toys.

"Lucy, just leave that. Eli and Abe will get it all cleaned up." Cora picked up Benjamin. "You come back to see us soon." She kissed him on the forehead and handed him to Lucy.

"Thank you so much. This has been great." Lucy smiled, then felt compelled to give Cora a hug, even though she knew the Amish weren't typically affectionate with outsiders. Cora hesitated, but then she returned the embrace.

"You and Benjamin come back any time." Cora walked Lucy to the door. Lucy stepped out on the porch, then turned suddenly.

"Oh, I was going to leave you my phone number in case you need a ride somewhere."

"That's right." Cora smiled and clapped her hands together gently. "Wait right here."

She hurried back to the kitchen and returned with a piece of paper and pen. "I don't know how much longer I'll have my cell phone number. The bishop here doesn't allow them. But if I have to give mine up, I'll go to a neighboring shanty to phone you."

Lucy had been in Lancaster County long enough to know what a shanty was. Usually several families shared a telephone that was located away from their houses in a structure similar to a phone booth. Lucy wrote her phone number down on the paper and handed it back to Cora. Then she was on her way, feeling better than she had in a long time. She actually had a friend.

For now.

Cora told Eli and Abe to go finish their chores while she got supper started. But once her applesauce pork loin was in the oven, she sat down at the kitchen table and dabbed her forehead with a wet rag. She was surprised Lucy hadn't said anything about how hot it was in the house. The *Englisch* woman was surely used to air-conditioning. Anna Mae and Mary Jane had come home shortly after Lucy left and gone upstairs to finish a sewing project and to strip the beds. Jacob would be home any minute, and she assumed John would come straight from the barn and go upstairs.

As their typical evening routine settled in around her, she felt a stab of longing for the way things used to be. Chatting with Lucy had been a welcome change, even though Cora had never meant to share so much. She hadn't even told Marianne about John. But Lucy had appeared sympathetic and hadn't seemed to judge her. Cora hoped to spend more time with Lucy and hopefully introduce her to Marianne. Maybe she would invite them both over for tea sometime. Cora knew she needed to get friendly with the other members of the district, but she dreaded having to keep retelling the story about why her family had moved here. She'd even backed out of attending Sisters' Day, though Marianne had urged her to come.

She looked up when John walked in the door. He crossed over to the refrigerator and poured himself a glass of iced tea.

"I made one of your favorites, applesauce pork loin, and I've got a fresh loaf of butter bread." She recalled their night of intimacy— or lack thereof—and wondered if their marriage would ever be right again. "Mary Jane and Anna Mae said they spent time with some of the girls in our district today, and Abe and Eli helped me watch a new friend's little boy." Cora stood up and walked to the oven, realizing she hadn't set the timer. "Maybe the *kinner* are finally starting to get settled here, no?"

"*Ya*, I hope so."

Cora smiled. It wasn't much, but it was the most positive response she'd gotten from John in a while. She moved closer and touched his arm. "Please eat with the family, John. Please."

"I'm not hungry, Cora." He walked to the rack by the kitchen door and hung his hat there.

"Even with your hat, your nose and cheeks are sunburned. There's some ointment in the cabinet in our bathroom."

Her husband nodded before he left the kitchen.

Cora just stood there by the sink, wondering how much longer she could live like this. *But what can I do?*

Back in Middlefield, she would have sought help from the bishop. But things were already strained between her family and Bishop Byler since the bishop had forbidden Jacob from spending time with his granddaughter. Marianne said she was been working on her husband, but Bishop Byler's strict ways were well known in the district.

But there had to be someone who could help them.

For the umpteenth time, Cora begged the Lord to put joy back into their lives.

13

JACOB HADN'T HEARD FROM ANNA SINCE THEIR SECRET meeting by the train tracks. She hadn't even been at worship service on Sunday. He'd wanted to talk to Bishop Byler then, but a thunderstorm had rolled in during the noon meal, so everyone had packed up and left early.

He'd gone to sleep every night for the past week with Anna on his mind instead of Leah. Anna was helping him heal, even if she didn't realize it. He'd overheard her grandmother say on Sunday that she wasn't feeling well, but he was curious why she hadn't stopped by the lumberyard this past week. Had she been sick all week?

As he pulled into the Bylers' driveway, his stomach churned. It was almost the supper hour, so Bishop Byler would most likely be home. He pushed back the rim of his hat, stood taller, and knocked on the door.

"*Wie bischt*, Marianne? I came by to check on Anna, to see if she's okay." Jacob swallowed hard, nervous but relieved that Anna's grandmother was the one who answered the door.

"Hello, Jacob." Marianne pushed the screen door open. "Come in, come in." She smiled, and Jacob tentatively stepped over the threshold. All the windows were open, but the house was stifling hot, just like his house. Jacob was sure that if he could change one thing about their lifestyle, it would be to use electricity during the summer months.

Marianne motioned for him to sit down on the couch. "Anna is resting, but she is all right. She's been battling an awful case of poison ivy." She paused, frowning. "On her face."

Jacob raised his eyebrows. "Oh no."

Marianne sat down on the couch beside him. She scrunched her face into a scowl. "I'm not sure how that poor girl got that stuff on her face, but she's all blistered up." She leaned closer and whispered, "I don't reckon she wants anyone to see her like that. I made all the bakery deliveries for her this week, and she wouldn't even go to Sisters' Day with me."

Jacob couldn't imagine that anything could take away from Anna's beauty. "Will you let her know that I stopped by to check on her?"

Marianne nodded. "She'll be glad to know that." She patted him on the leg. "But no need for you to run off. This will give us a chance to chat. Do you want some *kaffi*, or maybe a glass of iced *tee*?"

"*Nee. Danki*, though." Jacob wondered where the bishop was. Both buggies were out front. He looked to his left, then to his right, half expecting Bishop Byler to be lurking somewhere nearby.

"Isaac isn't here, dear." Marianne smiled. "Deacon Lantz picked him up, and they are out making a few rounds."

Jacob had heard about Bishop Byler's rounds. The man went from house to house making recommendations, as he called them, for people to clean up their act. He wondered if his house was on the route today.

"I was hoping to talk to Bishop Byler." He paused. Marianne

smiled again, so he went on. "About Anna. I know we both made a couple of unwise choices, but I'd like a chance to prove myself to him. I care for Anna, and I'd like to get to know her better."

This was so much easier than having to face the bishop. Maybe Marianne would convince him to allow Jacob to date Anna. According to Jacob's mother, she was already working to change her husband's mind.

"Anna seems to care a great deal for you too. And *ya*, unfortunately you two got off on a bad foot with Isaac. But he will come around."

When? Jacob ran the back of his hand across his forehead. "I hope so."

"He will." Marianne clasped her hands in her lap. "Now, tell me about your family. How is everyone doing? When the storm hit, everyone left so quickly, I didn't have a chance to chat much with the ladies."

"I think things are getting better." Jacob avoided Marianne's eyes, knowing that wasn't entirely true. His father wasn't any better. If anything, he was worse.

"Goodness me, child. You are dripping with sweat. You wait here. I'm going to go get you some iced *tee* and a cold rag." Marianne stood up, then walked around the corner.

Jacob couldn't help looking behind him toward the stairs. He wished he could see Anna. He didn't care what her face looked like.

Anna held her breath, listening from the top of the staircase. She'd missed seeing Jacob this week, but hadn't been able to get word to him about why. She fumbled with the compact mirror in her apron pocket, then pulled it out and held it close to her face. *Ugh*. No matter how many times she looked at the red, blistering bumps, they didn't get any less hideous. Her right cheek was covered, her eye was swollen, and even her upper lip was affected. *Mammi* had taken her to the herbal doctor earlier in the week, and the ointment helped the itching, but her face still looked awful. No way she was going to show herself. She was sure she'd gotten the rash while working in the garden, and probably wiped sweat from her face, spreading it there. She had a tiny spot on her hand, but nothing like what was on her cheek.

"Here you are." Her grandmother was back in the living room. Jacob thanked her for the iced tea. Anna sat down at the top of the stairs, pulled her knees to her chest, and kept listening.

Mammi asked Jacob how he liked his job, how they were all adjusting to the area, and if he would be seeking baptism in the fall.

"I'm ready to be baptized," he said. "But I . . . well . . . we just moved here, and . . ."

"You want to be sure that this is where you want to settle." *Mammi's* soft voice was harder to hear. "That's understandable."

"I feel strong in my faith and am ready to commit."

"That's *gut*. So many times, when there is a tragedy, folks turn away from God. He is our strength, though, the One to count on during troubled times."

Anna wondered if Jacob's mother, Cora, had shared with *Mammi* about her husband. According to Jacob, his father had little to do with the family these days because he wasn't able to cope with Leah's death. She leaned forward when she heard Jacob's voice again.

"It's near the supper hour, so I should probably go."

"No rush, dear. I'm just planning to warm up some leftover soup."

From where she was sitting, Anna could see downstairs, out the living room window, and she slammed a hand to her chest when she saw Deacon Lantz's buggy coming up the drive. *Daadi* was home. She silently prayed that he would be nice to Jacob. A few minutes later she heard the door open and her grandfather's heavy boots crossing into the living room.

"Jacob stopped by to check on Anna. Wasn't that nice?" *Mammi's* voice was overly cheerful, like she was trying to sell something. Anna hoped her *daadi* was in the mood for buying.

Anna listened for a response, but her grandfather must have nodded. Or maybe not. Jacob spoke up next.

"Bishop Byler, I was hoping I could talk to you about dating Anna. I know we made some bad choices, but—"

"You did not take Anna where you said you would. In turn, Anna lied to us, saying she was going to Emma's and not out with you. This was the first time Anna has lied to us, and that doesn't bode well for you, Jacob Hostetler."

Anna held her breath again, knowing she *had* lied to her grandparents before that. Little white lies—but lies nonetheless. Like when her grandmother had knitted her some gloves. They were silly looking, but Anna had assured her that she loved them.

But the lie about going to Emma's, then going out with Jacob—she had to admit that was the worst lie she had ever told. She could almost feel the Lord frowning down on her, but she lost the thought when she heard Jacob's voice.

"Sir, my mother was having a problem at our *haus*, a problem with my little *bruder*. It was an emergency, and I had to go help. That's why Anna and I didn't make it to the singing."

Despite the situation, Anna could feel herself glowing. Jacob was standing up to her grandfather because he wanted to date her. She reached up and touched her cheek, knowing she shouldn't. She was pretty sure Jacob would change his mind if he saw her right now.

"Bishop Byler, I am trustworthy, and I won't disappoint you again if you'll let me court Anna properly."

Court. It was an old-fashioned word, and it melted Anna's heart to hear Jacob use it. But the warmth didn't last long.

"Nee." Daadi's voice was gruff. "I don't think so."

Anna gritted her teeth. *Mammi, speak up.*

"Bishop Byler, respectfully, Anna is a grown woman." Jacob's voice had risen, and Anna squeezed her eyes closed, knowing this wasn't the way to win her grandfather's approval. Even though Jacob was right.

"I am going to bathe now. The answer is no. Please give my best to your family."

Anna listened as her grandfather's steps led to his bedroom and the door closed. She felt almost thankful—that could have gone a lot worse. But what was it going to take for her grandfather to see what a good person Jacob was?

"Give him time," *Mammi* was saying softly. "He fears for Anna—that's what it is. I've told him he can't keep her under his roof forever. The girl has to live her own life. I think he'll see that eventually."

"Please tell Anna I came by to check on her." Jacob paused and whispered something Anna couldn't hear. A few moments later she heard the front door close behind him.

"You can come downstairs now, Anna."

Anna cringed, then slowly made her way down the stairs. "How'd you know I was there?" she asked when she hit the landing.

"I can smell that ointment you have on your face."

"Really?" She reached up and dabbed at one of the welts.

"Quit touching it. Or it's going to spread." *Mammi* walked to the kitchen, and Anna followed. She sat down at the kitchen table as her grandmother pulled out a tub of leftover chicken soup from the refrigerator.

"*Daadi* is going to have to change his mind about Jacob, because I *am* going to see him. Jacob is right. I'm a grown woman."

Mammi put the container on the counter, turned around and leaned back. "I don't like that kind of talk."

"*Mammi*, you know I love *Daadi*, but he isn't being fair. I don't think it would matter who I dated. He just doesn't want me to have my own life."

"That is why I don't want you dating that boy." Anna turned around to see her grandfather scooting into the kitchen in his socks. "He brings out this behavior. You didn't use to talk like this."

"Behavior?" Anna shook her head. "*Daadi*, I'm not a child. And I know you're scared for me to go out on my own, that something will happen to me. But you've raised me well, and you can trust me to make my own decisions."

"He isn't *gut* enough for you, *mei maedel.*"

Anna sighed. "*Daadi*, I love you. But you're never going to think anyone is *gut* enough for me. You don't even know Jacob."

"Neither do you." Her grandfather took his seat at the head of the table.

"I'm trying to get to know him. Please, *Daadi*, just give him a chance." She grinned. "He's been the only one brave enough to come face you."

Daadi frowned as he reached for his glass of tea. "He was disrespectful."

"That's enough. No arguing at the supper table." *Mammi* put the pot of soup on the table, and Anna got up to get the bread, jams, and chowchow. Then she pushed her grandmother's bottle of cinnamon pills near her spot so she wouldn't forget to take them. *Mammi* had said the pills were keeping her glucose under control and that she didn't need the insulin anymore. Anna hoped that was true. She'd seen her testing her blood sugar just the other day.

They were quiet during the meal. After *Daadi* pushed back his chair and left the room, her grandmother handed her an envelope. "Jacob left this for you."

"*Danki, Mammi.*" Anna started clearing the table as fast as she could.

"I'll clean up." Her grandmother waved a hand in the air. "Go on with you. I know you're anxious to read that letter."

Anna kissed her grandmother on the cheek, then darted upstairs. She'd barely closed her bedroom door when she tore open the envelope.

Dear Anna,

It's been a long week not seeing you, and I can't stop thinking about you. I overheard your grandmother talking to someone at worship service, and she said you aren't feeling well.

As I write this, I'm planning to go to your house to check on you and also to see your daadi. I'm hoping I can get him to change his mind about us seeing each other.

Everything at my haus is better, except for mei daed. Eli made friends with a boy about his age—Johnnie King—and they have been running around together between chores. Mamm really likes your grandmother, and she also has another new friend named Lucy.

Lucy? Anna blinked. That wasn't a common name, especially in their community. Could he be referring to Lucy Turner? That seemed unlikely.

Everyone is trying to get on with their lives. I don't know what to do about Daed though. Can you maybe include some extra prayers for him? I'm mad at him a lot because he's not doing right by his family, but I still pray for him every day.

Anyway, I'm writing this in case I don't get to see you, and I wanted you to know that I'm thinking about you. And our kisses.

Hope to see you soon.

Jacob

Anna smiled, reread the letter, then put it in the drawer of her nightstand. She pulled out the small compact mirror again and held it to her face. She was still a long way from being presentable. Just the same, she would make her deliveries next week. Her grandmother had been gracious to do it, but Anna could tell the long hours in the hot buggy were taking their toll. *Mammi* had come home exhausted, even though Anna had tried to take up the slack with the cooking and cleaning.

She placed the mirror on the nightstand and lay back on the bed, smiling.

Jacob misses me.

Lucy slipped Benjamin's shoes on him, then double-checked the diaper bag to make sure she had everything she'd need for an afternoon.

"I don't understand why I can't babysit my own grandson. Think how much money you'd save if you let me keep him while you're at work instead of taking him to that day care." Mom flung herself on the couch and grunted. "And I can keep him this afternoon while you go play with your new friend."

Lucy picked up her son and the diaper bag. "We've had this conversation before, Mom." She found her purse and keys. "Please don't go anywhere while I'm gone. I'll take you wherever you need to go when I get home."

"I'm a prisoner here."

"You are not a prisoner." Lucy took a deep breath. "But you can't be doing things like stealing strawberries from people's gardens."

"You need to put some makeup on. You look awful."

Lucy closed her eyes, took a deep breath, then looked back at her mother. "I'm going to Cora's house, and she doesn't wear any makeup, so I think it's okay for me not to. Besides, you know I don't wear much makeup anymore."

"That doesn't mean you shouldn't. How're you gonna find another man looking all pale and homely?"

The last thing Lucy needed or wanted was another man. She had her hands full with her mother and Benjamin, and she didn't feel very lovable these days anyway.

"I'm going," she said firmly and headed toward the front door. "And remember not to cook anything while I'm gone. There's plenty of cold stuff in the fridge."

The only answer was a string of curses.

Tears filled Lucy's eyes as she closed the door behind her. This was not good for Benjamin, living in this environment. It wasn't good for Lucy either, and it couldn't be good for Mom. It wasn't just Mom's attitude. She had forgotten to turn the stove off twice this week, and who knew what would happen if she took it in her head to go wandering again. Lucy made a mental note to check back with those assisted-living facilities to see where her mother was on the waiting lists.

Lucy worried about Mom as she buckled Benny into his car seat. But by the time she pulled into Cora's driveway, she had made up her mind not to let her mother upset her. It had been a long time since someone invited her over for a visit, and Lucy wanted to enjoy it. She liked Cora. Cora saw Lucy the way Lucy wanted to see herself. Since Cora didn't know her past, there was no judgment. *Not yet, anyway.*

Cora met Lucy at the car and quickly opened the back door to unbuckle Benjamin from his car seat. "This little one brings a bright light wherever he goes." She pulled him from the seat and set him down on the grass. "I made some chocolate chip cookies especially for you, Benjamin." Cora latched onto his hand, then finally looked up at Lucy. "I'm so glad you both came. Eli and Abe have been looking forward to seeing Benjamin."

Lucy couldn't help but smile as they climbed the steps and crossed the threshold. Cora's house was always so warm and inviting. Today it was almost *too* warm, but Cora had the windows open, and Lucy had dressed herself and Benjamin in light clothing. She knew that wearing shorts would be offensive to Cora, so she'd chosen a pair of white Capri pants, a loose brown blouse, and sandals for herself. Benjamin wore a pair of short, striped overalls, and Cora was going on about how adorable he looked.

Lucy got Benjamin settled in the middle of the living room floor, where Abe and Eli had already spread out toys. Then Cora motioned for Lucy to come to the kitchen—far enough from the children that they could talk privately, but close enough for Lucy to keep an eye on Benny.

They sat down at the kitchen table. After a few minutes of small talk, they dove into a more serious conversation about what was heaviest on Lucy's heart. Her mom.

"I just don't know what to do with her." Lucy shook her head, then took a sip of coffee. "She's unbearable to be around sometimes." She paused, sighing. "And just *mean*."

"Has she always been like this?" Cora's voice was sympathetic, and Lucy could see the concern in her expression.

"No, not at all. Just since the stroke." She shrugged. "And she's my mother, so I do my best to take care of her. She and my father divorced when I was about Benjamin's age, so Mom raised me by herself. And we weren't well off at all, but I never wanted for anything." She blew on her coffee, then took another sip. "But I'm hoping to get her into a nice care facility soon. She's on several waiting lists."

She let out a deep breath and took a sip of her coffee. It felt good to have someone to talk to—about some things, anyway. It would be a long time before Lucy shared the story of Benjamin's father and her role in destroying Ivan's marriage.

"I can understand how you want to take care of her, but it's a shame that the stroke left her in such a bad way." Cora glanced into the living room. "How is she with Benjamin?"

"Oh, she's crazy about Benjamin and sweet to him, but she talks so ugly to me in front of him. It's not a good environment for him. And of course I don't trust her to watch Benjamin alone. And I'm getting worried about leaving her in the house by herself."

Cora leaned back against her chair, biting her bottom lip for a few moments. "Are there medications that can help her?"

Lucy shrugged. "I don't think so. I don't remember her being on anything for her temperament when she was at the last care facility."

As soon as the words were out of her mouth, Lucy wished she hadn't said them. And Cora responded just as Lucy expected. "Oh. What happened to that arrangement?"

Lucy swallowed hard. "She, uh . . . she assaulted another resident, so they basically threw her out."

Cora covered her mouth with one hand, her eyes round.

"It was awful. I got a call while I was at work that Mom had words with another woman." Lucy shook her head. "And then she punched her in the face."

"Oh dear."

"So she can't go back there. But I'm going to have to do something—if not for my sake, for Benjamin's."

After a bit more conversation, they both admitted that they

didn't know what the answer to Lucy's problem was, so Cora moved on to what was heaviest on her heart. Her husband.

Lucy lent a sympathetic ear, thinking how much worse Cora's problems were than her own and marveling that she kept such a cheerful disposition. Cora's daughter had died, and her husband had mentally checked out, blaming himself. Lucy wished there was something she could do to ease her new friend's pain.

As Cora went on talking, Lucy looked at the woman across the table from her. An Amish woman with no makeup, all the traditional clothing, and a faith in God stronger than anything Lucy would probably ever know. It was an unlikely friendship, and Lucy felt a mixture of joy and regret. Once Cora found out who Lucy really was, the friendship would surely be over.

"I would really like for you to meet my friend Marianne. She's the bishop's wife. I think I told you about her." Cora smiled. "Such a lovely, fun person. Can you go with me to her house for a visit next week?"

Lucy sighed. Her friendship with Cora was going to end sooner than she thought. But why avoid the inevitable? Cora was a good person. Lucy wasn't. It was a simple fact, and no matter how normal Lucy felt around Cora, their friendship couldn't last.

Marianne Byler knew exactly who Lucy was. She and her husband had always lived in Lancaster County. Marianne knew that Lucy was the adulterer who had wrecked Ivan and Katie Ann's marriage. Soon Cora would know it too.

They set the date for the following Thursday.

14

BY THURSDAY MORNING ANNA'S FACE WAS FINALLY looking better. She'd made her bakery deliveries all week, but she'd hurried in and hurried out, and she hadn't stopped to see Jacob at his job. This morning she planned to go by and see him.

She grabbed her lunch pail from the refrigerator, slipped on her shoes, which waited by the front door, and was opening the screen when her grandmother called her name, rushing into the room. "Where are you going?"

Anna let out a small grunt. "The same places I go every day, *Mammi* . . . to make deliveries. I've already loaded the buggy."

Her grandmother tapped a finger to her chin. "Oh."

Anna closed the screen and walked back into the room. "Are you okay?"

Mammi smiled. "Of course, dear. I just . . . oh, I don't know. Guess I got confused for a minute."

Anna squinted at her grandmother. "I think you need to go see Dr. Noah and get your prescription refilled. I'm not sure the cinnamon pills are controlling your blood sugar. Do you check it regularly?"

"*Ya*, dear. I check it." *Mammi* pressed her palms together in front of her. "Today is Thursday. Cora and Lucy are coming for a visit. See, I'm fine."

Anna had been surprised to hear that Cora and Lucy Turner had become friends. That seemed like a strange friendship. Everyone in their district knew what Lucy had done, and Cora seemed like such a nice person.

"Does *Daadi* know you are entertaining Lucy today?" Anna couldn't keep the irritation out of her voice. Her grandfather still wouldn't agree to let her see Jacob.

Mammi raised her chin. "*Nee*, I haven't mentioned it."

Anna shook her head. "That's as *gut* as lying, *Mammi*—just like whatever you do down in your room in the basement." She cringed a little inside, knowing she would be doing the same thing by visiting Jacob today.

"Mind your tongue, Anna. I don't lie to your grandfather."

"*Nee*, you just don't tell him the entire truth." Anna turned to leave, mumbling, "I'm never going to live like the two of you." *Not after I'm married, anyway.*

Her grandmother said something, but Anna didn't hear. She was out the door and hurrying to hitch the horse. She couldn't wait to see Jacob.

Marianne sank down on the couch and sighed. Anna was right. What had started as a fairly innocent hobby many years ago had turned into a wall-to-wall hoard of objects her husband would disapprove of. Looking back, she wished she had stood up to Isaac about his silly rules early in their marriage. Marianne felt confident that nothing she was doing compromised her faith or love of the Lord, but lately the secrets had been weighing heavily on her.

She was a little anxious about her upcoming visit with Cora and Lucy Turner. She'd been surprised to hear that Cora and Lucy had become friends. What a scandal it had been when everyone found out Ivan Stoltzfus had cheated on his wife with Lucy. It wasn't Marianne's place to judge, and she doubted that Ivan was an innocent victim. But being around Lucy would still be a bit awkward, especially if Isaac found out. He had insisted that Anna not babysit for Lucy. What would he say about having Lucy in their home?

And why was Isaac being so stubborn about Anna and Jacob? If he didn't ease up a little, their granddaughter would become more defiant, and his rigid attitude might affect Marianne and Cora's friendship as well. Poor Cora had been through enough, and she was trying desperately to put her family back together, no thanks to that husband of hers. Marianne would like to give John Hostetler a swift kick in the behind. It was the man's place to run his household, and he wasn't doing that.

Marianne stood up when she heard a car coming up the driveway. She waited at the door while Cora and Lucy got out of the car. She hadn't realized that Lucy would be bringing her *boppli*. Ivan's *sohn*. But it had been a long time since Marianne had a little one in the house. Nothing like a small child to ease any tension and light up a room.

As Cora and Lucy grew near, Marianne wasn't sure she would have recognized Lucy. She was a bit heavier than Marianne remembered, she didn't have on any makeup, and her hair was a different color. The cute little one on her hip was smiling ear to ear.

"Wie bischt? I have a fresh shoofly pie on the table and hot *kaffi* ready." She reached over and touched the child on the arm. "And who is this handsome fellow?" He really was a cutie. Marianne remembered Anna telling her how adorable Lucy's little one was.

"This is Benjamin." Lucy glowed when she said the boy's name, but she also avoided looking at Marianne. The girl was bound to be nervous. Marianne doubted Lucy made very many visits to their people these days.

"Well, I bet I have some snacks for him too." Marianne touched his cheek. "How does that sound, Benjamin?"

"Danki, Marianne." Cora reached her arms out and took Benjamin from Lucy. "I've been eager for you to meet Lucy. You two have become my dearest friends, so it seemed fit you should meet." She snuggled her face into Benjamin's tummy. "Isn't that right, Benjamin?"

Marianne found herself avoiding Lucy's eyes as well. *"Ya,* I think Lucy and I might have met a long time ago." She finally looked up, and Lucy was pale. Did Cora know about Lucy's past? Marianne wasn't about to spill the beans. That was up to Lucy. "It's nice to see you again, Lucy. Please, let's all go into the kitchen." Marianne went into the pantry and pulled out a booster chair she kept on hand for when they hosted worship service or Sisters' Day.

Soon they were seated with coffee and pie, and Benjamin entertained them by making faces as he nibbled on crackers and cookies. He was a precious boy, and it was refreshing to have a little one around. After a while, Marianne asked Cora how things were at home. She worried a lot about Cora and her family. It was a sin—worrying—but Cora had a lot to deal with.

"Everyone is doing *gut*." She paused, glanced at Lucy. "Except John. I've told Lucy about my husband."

Cora spent the next half hour talking about how her husband had quit being both a husband and father after their daughter died. Marianne recalled how Isaac acted after their son and daughter-in-law died. She thought he could help, if only John would agree to let him pay a visit.

Marianne was still processing everything Cora was saying when Cora changed the subject.

"Lucy is having troubles at home also." Cora patted Lucy's hand. "Her mother is ill and giving her a hard time."

Marianne finished chewing a piece of pie—pie she knew she shouldn't be having—then swallowed and asked, "What's the matter with her?"

Lucy wiped some crumbs from Benjamin's mouth with her hand and finished her own mouthful of pie, then she lifted the little boy from the booster chair and put him in her lap. He had been rubbing his eyes and now leaned his head against his mother's chest. "She had a stroke awhile back and was in a nursing home. But she sort of . . . uh . . . got kicked out." She shrugged. "She's difficult."

"And mean to Lucy," Cora added.

Lucy's face turned red. "I don't think she can help it. But it's hard."

"You're a good daughter to tend to her, but I'm sure it's a struggle." Marianne stood up to clear their plates.

"I do the best I can." Lucy smiled as she lifted her plate to Marianne. "Thank you. That was very good."

"You're welcome, dear." Marianne put the dishes in the sink, refilled their coffee cups, then sat back down. Her heart was heavy for both Cora and Lucy. Cora was solid in her faith, and things were hard enough for her. But what about Lucy? A relationship with the Lord would surely help Lucy with her mother.

Marianne sat taller and smiled as she glanced back and forth between the two women. They'd prayed silently before eating the pie, but this situation seemed to call for additional blessings. Both women bowed their heads when Marianne did.

"Dear heavenly Father, we ask for Your blessing for both John and Lucy's mother . . ." Marianne lifted her head, cleared her throat, and raised an eyebrow at Lucy.

"Alice." Lucy barely raised her head.

". . . for John and Alice. May You guide them both through these troubled times, and also their families. *Aamen*."

"Thank you, Marianne," Lucy said as she kissed Benjamin on the forehead.

"Of course, dear." Marianne gazed at the small child in Lucy's lap, remembering when Anna was that age. "I wish my granddaughter was here to visit with us, but she's out making our deliveries to the bakeries."

"Are you having any luck convincing your husband to let Jacob and Anna date?" Cora turned to Lucy. "Bishop Byler isn't fond of the idea of our *kinner* dating. They had a rocky start, and now he isn't very trusting of my son." She shook her head. "And that's a shame. Jacob is such a *gut* boy. He's really filled in as head of the household since John has gone into seclusion."

Marianne reached over and snatched a cookie from the plate on the table as guilty pleasure flowed through her. "He will come around." Although Marianne wasn't sure that was true. "He's very protective of Anna. And I know that's because our son and daughter-in-law were killed. If Isaac had his way, Anna would never ride in a car, and that's just not realistic. He's so afraid of something happening to her, but I fear he's going to push her away. And I've tried to explain this to him, but he doesn't listen. Besides, Anna is of age to make her own choices."

"Lucy's husband died before he had a chance to meet this sweet little fellow." Cora took a deep breath and let it out slowly. "I guess that loss is part of life, but it's still so hard, no matter how strong our faith."

Marianne pressed her lips together, watching Lucy and wondering if she would correct Cora's mistake. Benjamin's father had never been Lucy's husband.

Lucy glanced sideways to Marianne and stared at her for a few moments as if she was waiting for Marianne to offer up the truth. Then Lucy stood up, cradling Benjamin in her arms.

"Is it okay if I lay him on your couch? And can you point me toward the bathroom, please?"

"Of course, dear. Do you need a pillow? It's too warm for a blanket."

"No, but thank you."

"Bathroom is the first door on the right past the staircase." Marianne waited until Lucy was out of earshot before she turned to Cora. "Is Lucy a spiritual woman? Does she have a relationship with God? She seemed to feel *gut* about the prayer earlier."

"Based on the little bit she's told me, I think she is finding her way." Cora paused. "She told me she attends church. But she seems a bit lost and in need of a friend." She glanced at Benjamin on the couch. "I can tell that she's a very *gut mudder*."

Marianne smiled. "You're a nice person, befriending the *Englisch* woman. I think you are right . . . about her needing a friend."

Cora twirled a strand of hair that had come loose from her *kapp.* "I was worried about moving here and making new friends. And honestly, I just didn't think I had the energy for it." She smiled. "You made it easy to be friends with you, and I felt the same way about Lucy."

Marianne didn't think she and Lucy Turner were anything alike. But the moment she had the thought, she wondered if she was unconsciously judging Lucy. "You're a *gut* person, Cora. And the Lord is going to see you through this with your husband. Isaac will come around too. Who knows, maybe one day we will be sharing your grandchild and my great-grandchild."

Cora pointed a finger at Marianne. "Then you better get your husband convinced of what a great catch Jacob is."

Lucy walked back into the room but didn't sit down. Her bottom lip was trembling.

"What is it, dear? What's the matter?" Marianne sat taller, but Cora was quickly up and beside Lucy.

"What's wrong?" Cora touched Lucy on the arm.

Lucy pressed her lips together for a few minutes, her eyes to the ground. "I haven't been completely honest with you, Cora. I like being around you, our visits, and I don't have any real friends, and . . ."

She glanced over at Marianne, clearly aware that Marianne knew what she was about to confess. *Bless Lucy's heart for coming clean with her new friend.*

"Now, now . . ." Cora eased Lucy back over to the table. "Sit. And tell us what has you troubled." She rubbed Lucy's back gently.

"You can tell us anything. We've both shared about our husbands and the problems we're having."

"I've never been married." Lucy shifted her weight in the chair. "I didn't lie. Benjamin's father *did* die. I was just never married to him."

Cora was quiet for a few moments, then put her hand on Lucy's. "We all make mistakes, Lucy. God forgives us, and you have beautiful little Benjamin. And despite the way it happened, I'm sure you loved Benjamin's father."

Lucy glanced at Marianne and blinked a few times before turning back to Cora. "Benjamin's father was Ivan Stoltzfus, a well-known Amish man in this district. He—he . . . was married." She took a deep breath. "To someone else, a woman named Katie Ann. Ivan left Katie Ann, and I lived with Ivan until he was killed in an accident."

Cora withdrew her hand abruptly. "You cheated . . . with a married man?" Her voice had taken on an icy edge.

"I know I should regret it, but . . . like you said, I have Benjamin now, so how can he be a mistake? And I did love Ivan. Very much." Lucy forced a smile, but Cora didn't return it. She sat frozen, her eyes accusing.

"Did you know he was married when the affair started?" Cora's voice was heavy with accusation as she stared at Lucy.

Lucy grabbed a napkin from the table and dabbed at her eyes. "Yes, I did. I know it was wrong, but I loved Ivan, and he said he loved me. We were building a life together when he was killed."

Marianne wasn't sure about that last part. She'd heard rumors that Ivan was planning to reconcile with his wife at the time of his death. But no need to rub salt in Lucy's wound. Cora seemed to be doing a fair job of that.

Cora stood up quickly from the table. "Excuse me while I use the bathroom."

Once Cora was out of the room, Marianne said, "Lucy, you did the right thing, painful as it was. Real friends are truthful with each other, and to continue to let Cora assume something that isn't true . . . well, that wouldn't have been right." Marianne tensed, knowing she wasn't being exactly truthful with Isaac.

"I pray every single day, asking God to forgive what I did." Lucy blinked back tears.

Marianne thought for a few moments. "Lucy, you don't have to ask God for forgiveness every single day. The Lord forgave you the first time you asked Him. To continue to ask Him every day is like saying you don't trust Him. You mustn't carry the burdens of the past. *Ya*, we have choices to make, but we also can't see God's plan for us."

"Thank you, Marianne. Thank you for saying that. I'm trying so hard to live a good life, to be a good mother to Benjamin. I'm trying to take care of my mother, even though she says the most awful things to me. And I'm establishing a relationship with God. Every day I feel closer to Him."

Marianne smiled. "A daughter of the promise."

Lucy sniffled. "What?"

"You're on your way to becoming a daughter of the promise. A daughter of the promise is someone who is on a spiritual journey and discovers new meaning to the words *faith, hope,* and *love.*"

Lucy gave a wobbly smile. "I like that."

"I guess we need to be going." Cora strode into the kitchen

carrying her purse. She must have retrieved it from the living room. "*Danki* for a lovely time, Marianne."

Marianne looked at the clock on her oven. "It's so early. Are you sure you need to go so soon?"

"*Ya, ya.* I have much to do at home." She walked toward the living room, where Benjamin still slept on the couch.

Marianne followed her. "Sure you want to wake him?"

"I'll get the diaper bag." Cora scooped up the bag, not waiting for Lucy to get Benjamin as she moved toward the door. Lucy hurriedly picked up the little boy, who wiggled and groaned in her arms, still half asleep.

"Thank you, Marianne, for having me in your home, for the pie, coffee, and conversation." Lucy balanced Benjamin on her hip as the boy rubbed his eyes.

Marianne touched her on the arm. "Continue on your journey, dear. And I will pray for you."

Lucy leaned over and hugged Marianne. "Thank you."

Marianne walked Lucy to the door and waved. Cora was already in the car. It didn't take a brilliant woman to see that this visit hadn't ended well. But Marianne had meant what she said. She would keep Lucy and Benjamin—and Cora too—in her prayers.

The tension in the car was suffocating. Lucy had tried to talk to Cora but received only clipped responses. Not once did Cora look at Lucy, and she didn't lean over the seat to play with Benjamin the way she had done in the past.

How stupid she'd been to think she and Cora could really be friends. Lucy knew how the Amish lived, which was a much better life than Lucy had lived. But she'd hoped that Cora would understand and realize that she was working toward a better life. Surrounding herself with good people like Cora had been part of the plan. Lucy thought about the school shootings that had happened years ago nearby. The Amish community had forgiven the gunman, a man who had killed their children. Yet Cora couldn't forgive Lucy for having an affair with a married man?

Maybe she just needs time.

Lucy pulled to a stop in Cora's driveway. "Thank you for taking me to meet Marianne. You were right. She's a very dear person. I do think our paths have crossed before, but only briefly." Lucy waited for Cora to goggle over Benjamin the way she usually did. But she didn't even look in the backseat.

"*Ya*, Marianne is special. 'Bye, now." Cora closed the door firmly and hurried to the house. She didn't look back.

Once Lucy was on the road, she let the tears pour freely. She'd lost Cora as a friend, just as she'd expected, and now she was on her way home to face her mother. *God, I'm trying. I'm really trying. Please give me some guidance.*

Benjamin had fallen back asleep in his car seat, so she carried him inside and settled him in his crib to finish his nap. She dried her tears as best she could before she walked back into the living room to find her mother was standing with one hand on her hip.

"So how was your visit with your new friends?"

Lucy wished there was an ounce of sincerity in the question. "Fine."

"That bishop's wife knows who you are, right? Surprised she even let you in her house."

Lucy walked to the couch, sat down, and put her feet on the coffee table. "Marianne was very nice."

"That's how those Amish are. Nice to your face, and they act all holy, but they're just as hateful as anybody else behind your back."

Lucy silently prayed for patience as her mother kept up the harangue. "I guarantee that woman didn't want you there, and she's probably telling everybody about it right—"

"Shut up, Mother! Just shut up!"

"Now, there's the Lucy I know. Welcome back." Her mother cackled, and Lucy resisted the urge to scream at her again. She was trying for a new life, and that life didn't include yelling at her mother, no matter how justified. *I am becoming a daughter of the promise, a daughter of the promise, a daughter of the promise . . .*

Lucy laid her head back against the couch and closed her eyes, but as her mother's footsteps grew closer, she braced herself.

"I'm all you got. You know that, right? Just me and Benjamin."

Lucy didn't open her eyes. "Yes, Mom."

"Good. As long as you realize. Nobody 'round here's ever gonna accept you, especially them Amish people."

"Yes, Mom."

Lucy fought to swallow past the knot in her throat. Maybe her mother was right.

15

ANNA PULLED HER BUGGY INTO THE LUMBERYARD PARK-
ing lot around the time Jacob was due to get off work. She tethered
her horse and stood leaning against her buggy. If she squinted, she
could see through the glass window and into the store. A tinge of
jealousy nipped at her when she saw Jacob standing at the counter,
talking to Glenda. She recalled Glenda's comment to her awhile
back. *"Well, if I were Amish, I'd snap him right up."*

She smoothed the wrinkles in her dress and fumbled with the
cherry-flavored lip gloss in her pocket, wondering if Jacob would
kiss her again and also pondering what they could do to get her
grandfather's blessing. She felt bad sneaking around like this, and
she knew Jacob did too. He might decide to quit seeing her if she
didn't get *Daadi's* approval soon.

Her stomach churned as she watched Jacob and Glenda laughing together. What were they talking about? Jealousy was a bad
thing, but it had crawled under her skin just the same. She pulled
out the small watch she kept in her apron pocket since jewelry was
forbidden. She would give Jacob five more minutes, but then she
would need to head home.

Twenty minutes later she still hadn't been able to bring herself
to leave. Another buggy pulled into the parking lot, and finally

Jacob walked out of the store. Anna was irked that they'd lost precious time together while he'd been inside with Glenda.

"*Wie bischt?* How long have you been out here?" Jacob stopped in front of her, then glanced to his left at the other buggy. "Mary Jane is here to pick me up."

"Not too long." Anna managed a smile, though she was still feeling a little miffed.

"I missed you. I'm glad to see you're better, but I would have been happy to see you even with poison ivy on your face." He winked at her, and all was forgiven. She wanted to run into his arms, but his sister's eyes were on them.

"When can I see you?" he asked. "Things didn't go well with your *daadi* when I was there. I'm not sure what to do."

Anna shrugged. "I don't know. I could come by and pick you up for lunch tomorrow."

He hesitated. "Uh, *ya*. It won't solve the problem with your grandfather, but I'd love to have lunch with you." Pushing back the rim of his hat, he added, "I don't like deceiving him, though."

"Me either. I'll keep trying to figure out what to do."

"All right. Now, I have to go. Mary Jane's waiting." He leaned down and, to her surprise, kissed her on the lips with his sister watching. "I miss you."

"I'll see you tomorrow for lunch." She gave him a quick wave as he headed for the only other buggy in the parking lot. Mary Jane took off as soon as he climbed in, so Anna set to untethering her horse.

"I saw you out here in the parking lot. Why didn't you just come in the store?"

Anna turned to see Glenda standing a few feet away, her long blond hair pulled into a side braid. Her pink lip gloss looked to be about the same color as what Anna had in her pocket, although Anna had never worn hers. Glenda wore a short blue-jean skirt, a tight blue T-shirt, and white flip-flops. She looked fantastic.

Anne could feel herself blushing. "I, uh, didn't want to bother Jacob at work." *If you saw me out here, why didn't you tell Jacob?*

"Oh, he'd been off the clock for about thirty minutes. We were just talking." Glenda dabbed at her forehead. "I'm so sick of this heat."

Anna nodded. "*Ya*, it's hot for sure."

Glenda adjusted the white purse on her shoulder and took a step closer to Anna. "Listen, I'm having a party a week from Saturday. I know how it is for you—for Amish, I mean. You're allowed to party until you're baptized. So I asked Jacob if he wanted to come to the party." She grinned, batting her eyelashes. "And to bring you, of course." She brushed a strand of wayward hair from her face. "Hope to see you both there. I live on the street back behind Beiler's Bed and Breakfast. My house is the blue two-story house with white shutters. Jacob knows which one. Gotta run now."

"Thanks. Sounds *gut*." Anna gave a quick wave before Glenda walked off, then she got in her buggy, knowing full well that she'd only been invited because Glenda wanted Jacob at her party. Gritting her teeth, she backed up the buggy, disgusted at her jealousy. Why should she care about an *Englisch* party, anyway?

But as she picked up speed, she thought about it again. Going to the party—assuming that her grandfather allowed her to go in the first place—would give her a chance to be with Jacob. But that would make it yet another deception. Would it be a lie if she just didn't mention that Jacob would be at the party?

"You are not to see that boy." Her grandfather's words echoed in her head. She decided she'd talk with Jacob tomorrow at lunch. He'd mention the party to her then, and they could put their heads together about whether to go or not.

She decided to go by Emma's on the way home. Maybe her friend could help her figure the whole thing out.

Cora pulled her nightgown over her head, then removed the pins from her hair. John was already in bed, his back to her, when she sat down and took her brush from the nightstand. As she ran it the length of her hair, she fought the urge to smack him over the head with it. She was itching to pick a fight over the decade-old topic that had reared its ugly head while she was with Marianne and Lucy today.

She hadn't thought about John's affair in years. A woman just like Lucy had seduced him into a three-month dalliance that almost destroyed their marriage. Luckily, John had come to his senses and ended it. Cora had done her best to forgive, but it was hard to forget what that woman had done to her. And Lucy had done the very same thing to another Amish woman! She didn't need someone like that in her life. If nothing else, Lucy was a reminder of John's bad judgment and betrayal.

John started snoring, and without even thinking, Cora gave him a sharp jab in the back.

"Hey!" He rolled over, and in the dim light of the lantern, she could see the scowl on his face.

"You're snoring," she said as she stowed her brush back in the drawer.

"Ya, well. You didn't have to poke me so hard." He rolled back

over, and Cora threw back the sheet. It was too warm to sleep with
any type of covering. Not that she could sleep anyway. She didn't
snuff out the lantern, and as she lay there on her back, her blood
was boiling. She was sick and tired of John's attitude, angry that
Lucy's confession had brought up bad memories of the worst time
in her marriage. Most of all, she missed her oldest daughter.

She got out of bed, grabbed her pillow and lantern, and went
downstairs to the small mudroom where she'd set up her sewing
table and supplies and the old recliner where she sometimes did
her mending. She snuffed out the lantern and set it on the table.
Curling up in the recliner, she thought about all the time she'd
spent with all her girls around that table. Especially Leah, who
had done most of the mending and sewing.

"I miss you, my sweet girl." Cora reclined in the chair and buried her head in the pillow.

Marianne placed an order on her iPhone for two Christian novels
she'd found online. It had taken her three tries to enter her credit
card number correctly on the little thing, even using her magnify-
ing glass. When she was done, she sat back in her chair and eyed
her collection. Isaac would have a heart attack if he knew how much
stuff she had and what she'd spent on it over the years. Enough to
buy a small house, most likely.

She picked up one of the crystal glasses from a set of eight she'd
ordered a few years ago. Much too luxurious for Isaac's taste, but
Marianne dreamed of setting them out for supper one night when
they were having guests. She put the glass back on the shelf and
picked up a decorative serving bowl. Mary Ellen Stoltzfus had used

one almost exactly like it when she invited Marianne and Isaac for supper a few years back. Isaac had said it was much too fancy, with tiny flowers etched into the fine china. Marianne had thought it was just beautiful.

She set the dish down and leaned back in her comfy chair, staring at her things with the familiar mixture of comfort and guilt and thinking back over the day.

She thought about Anna. Marianne knew she was going to have to stand up to Isaac. Anna was going to see that boy with or without their permission, and that would only cause more problems down the line.

Then she recalled the visit with Cora and Lucy. Marianne was still surprised at Cora's quick switch from kindness to being cold and judgmental. It seemed so out of character.

Marianne eyed her things. *Maybe I'll pay Lucy a visit and give her a gift.*

Anna pulled up at the lumberyard, unsure whether to go in or to wait for Jacob to come out. She could see Glenda through the plate-glass window. Sighing, she decided to go in.

Glenda closed a magazine she was reading when Anna pulled in. "I'll buzz Jacob and let him know you're here. He told me you were picking him up for lunch."

"Thanks." Anna fought the nasty little bug of jealousy burrowing into her skin. Again. She wondered how often Jacob and Glenda talked, and how often Anna's name came up.

Jacob rounded the corner a few moments later. He stopped at a time clock on the wall behind Glenda, punched out, then turned to Anna. "Ready?"

They decided to walk to the deli down the street. As Jacob
opened the door to the restaurant, they both scanned the room to
see if there was anyone they knew. But Anna wasn't very worried.
"My grandparents wouldn't be in here," she said, "and I think *Daadi*
is the only one we have to worry about."

They both ordered from the counter. Jacob got a ham and
cheese sandwich, and Anna chose chicken salad. As they ate, they
made small talk. Anna was waiting for Jacob to mention Glenda's
party. She was already plotting how she would get out of the house.
Using Emma as an excuse wasn't going to work again—not that it
had worked that well before. And though she and Emma had spent
an hour yesterday discussing strategies, they hadn't been able to
resolve her dilemma. What she really wanted was to be able to see
Jacob with *Daadi's* approval. But until she had that, she was willing
to do what was necessary.

Jacob said nothing about the party, but something was on his
mind. Anna could sense it in his bleak expression and the way he
was pushing the same chip around on his plate.

"Are you okay?" She lightly touched his hand, wishing more
than ever that they could find some time by themselves.

"*Ach, ya.* I guess." He finally picked up the chip and ate it. "I
just . . ."

Anna spoke softly. "What is it, Jacob?"

"I heard *mei mudder* crying last night. She was in her sewing
room, and I'd gotten up to get a drink." He paused. "I almost
went in to check on her, but I didn't. Sometimes I need to just be
by myself and grieve about Leah, and maybe she does too." He
paused, rubbed his chin. "Only thing is, I'm not sure that's all
that's going on. I think my parents are really having problems."

"Like marital problems?" Anna kept her eyes on him as she took a sip of tea. It was twelve fifteen, and lots of people were bustling around them, ordering food and getting seated.

"*Ya. Daed* isn't any better. Still keeps to himself. And *Mamm* tries to carry on for the rest of us, but it's really taking a toll on her."

"I still wish your *daed*—or your *mamm*—would talk to *Daadi.* He is so sympathetic about the loss of a loved one. I've heard him talk to others when they are grieving." She sighed. "I know he's strict, but he truly is the most compassionate man I know. Everything he does, he does out of love for God and his belief that we are straying too far into the *Englisch* world."

The Englisch *world. What about Glenda's party?*

"I think *Mamm* confides in your grandmother. They've been spending time together."

Anna was quiet for a few moments. "You know . . . I'm just going to have to stand up to my grandfather. I'm eighteen, and I should have the freedoms that go along with my *rumschpringe.* I have to get him to understand that I am old enough to make my own choices. I won't be living there forever." She let out a nervous chuckle. "I hope not, anyway."

"He is protective because he loves you." Jacob smiled before he finished the last little bite of his sandwich.

"I know he does, but he doesn't realize that sometimes he just pushes people away—or forces them to keep secrets from him. I know my grandmother does—especially in that broom closet down in the basement where she goes all the time. It's more like a small room. She's hiding things down there that she doesn't want *Daadi* to see."

"Like what?" Jacob grinned.

Anna shrugged, smiling herself. "I don't know. She keeps it locked, but there is a key up on top of the door molding. I've been tempted to go in there, but it's her private space, so I don't. She doesn't think I know, but she orders things and UPS brings them."

Jacob laughed aloud. "Your *daadi* wouldn't like that."

"*Nee*, he wouldn't. To him, that's just another connection to the outside world that threatens our way of life."

"What do you think she orders?" Jacob wiped his mouth. Anna watched him in frustration. Lunch was coming to an end with no mention at all of Glenda's party.

"Oh, probably quilting supplies, cinnamon pills for her diabetes, canning jars . . ." She shrugged. "Things that would ordinarily require a trip to town in the buggy. I guess she's figured out that ordering is a lot more convenient, especially in this heat or in the cold winter months." She grinned as she lifted up one finger. "However, I think she also splurges on some things *Daadi* wouldn't agree with even if she purchased them in town."

Jacob chuckled. "It's kind of funny."

"*Ya*. I know."

He glanced at the clock behind the deli counter. "I guess I better get back to work."

Anna stood up when he did, and he waited for her to go in front of him. She was starting to think that he'd forgotten about the party. Or maybe he just assumed she couldn't go.

"I'm glad the weekend is almost here," she said as they walked to the lumberyard.

"Me too. I'm off tomorrow. But I promised *Mamm* that I would repair the fence, so that will take up most of my day." He paused, then looked her way. "I'd rather be hanging out with you."

"Maybe tomorrow evening when you're done?" She slowed down as they got to the entrance of the lumberyard and took a deep breath. "Or next Saturday?"

But he didn't take the hint. Instead, he turned to face her, put his hands in his pockets, and rocked back on his heels a couple of times. "What about your grandfather? I don't want you sneaking out to spend time with me. It's bad enough that we're meeting for lunch like this. As much as I want to be with you, I don't want you getting in more trouble. And I don't like lying."

Anna hung her head. "I know."

Jacob gently lifted her chin and glanced quickly to his left. "I want to kiss you, but I can see Glenda and one of the guys I work with. They're watching us."

Anna felt her face flush, wishing he'd kiss her anyway. But he winked at her, then gave a quick wave and left.

She walked to her buggy, looking back only once. Jacob was standing in front of the counter talking to Glenda. She swallowed back a lump in her throat. No mention of the party, and she had to consider that maybe Jacob didn't want her going, that he'd rather spend time with Glenda.

As she flicked the reins, she wondered when she'd become this jealous person. Knowing it was wrong was one thing, but controlling the emotion was becoming a challenge.

She drove off, looking through the plate glass once more. Jacob was still there, talking and smiling. Anna decided right then and there that she was going to that party, even if Jacob never said a word about it.

After all, Glenda had invited her too.

16

NOAH PEERED OUT THE WINDOW OF HIS LIVING ROOM. Everyone had arrived for Jenna's party—everyone except Lucy and Benjamin. Maybe it was too late to make them a part of the family. Perhaps too much time had gone by or there had been too much pain.

"I knew she wouldn't come." His sister Mary Ellen eased up beside him. "I tried a long time ago to get to know her a little bit. I don't think she wants to be part of the family." She paused. "And I have to admit I have mixed emotions about the whole thing."

Noah turned to face his sister while everyone else was busying themselves in the kitchen, the women preparing snacks, the men nibbling. "No matter what happened, Benjamin is our nephew, and Ivan would want us to make sure he's okay. He would want us to make a place for him in our lives."

"What do you think Katie Ann would say?" Mary Ellen turned to face him, hands on her hips. "Do you think she might be hurt that we invited Lucy to a family gathering?"

"Katie Ann is happily married to Eli in Colorado. She has Jonas, plus Eli's children and grandchildren. Every time I talk to Katie Ann on the phone, she sounds very happy. I don't think she'd have a problem with us getting to know our nephew." He sighed. "But I'll ask her next time we talk."

"So maybe you should have asked her *before* you invited Lucy?" Mary Ellen's words were softened by her gentle teasing tone.

Noah shrugged, peering out the window again. "Well, it doesn't look like she's coming anyway."

"*Nee*, it doesn't." No matter what she'd said, he could tell she was disappointed.

Noah scratched his forehead. "Aren't you worried about getting caught here? You and Rebecca both. What if the bishop were to find out that you come to our house?"

Mary Ellen grunted. "That new bishop, Bishop Byler, is simply unreasonable." She shook her head. "You were shunned a long time ago, then reestablished into the community when Bishop Ebersol was still alive. Bishop Byler is hurting his district by reinstating the shunning." She pointed a finger at him. "He better be careful. He'll start running people off. No doubt he means well, but he needs to follow the lead of his district members, and almost no one agrees with the decisions he's making."

"I do miss all the Amish folks coming into the clinic. They made up the bulk of my clients. Not to mention that we've had to dip into our savings to keep operating."

Mary Ellen looked up toward the air-conditioning vent above their heads, closed her eyes, and smiled. "I think I'll spend the rest of the summer right here in the air-conditioning."

Noah chuckled. "You'd be shunned for sure then."

"And it might just be worth it." She stood there enjoying the cool air for a few more moments, then sighed. "Guess I better go help with the food. But you let me know when you talk to Katie

Ann and what her feelings are about including Lucy in our lives."
She paused, frowning. "Although, since Lucy didn't show up, I'm
thinking it probably won't be an issue."

Noah followed her into the kitchen, thinking the same thing.

———

Lucy cleaned up her mother's vomit from the kitchen floor, thankful that Benjamin was still napping.

"I'm sorry." Mom covered her face with her hands and wept
like a small child.

Lucy had already cleaned up her mother's face and helped her
get into fresh clothes. "It's okay, Mom. Go sit down on the couch,
and I'll go get you some crackers."

She wiped up the last of the mess as her mother shuffled into
the living room. She wasn't sure what was worse—when her mother
was cussing her and calling her a worthless person, or when she was
out of her mind and sick, like today. Twice she'd asked Lucy who
she was, and once she'd asked if she could go to the post office to
catch a train to Harrisburg. So far, her mother's behavior had been
blamed on the stroke, but Lucy couldn't help but wonder if she had
Alzheimer's.

She tossed the soiled paper towels into the trash can, then followed up with damp rags. Once she was done, she cleaned herself up and went to check on her mother. She was sleeping on the
couch. *Thank goodness.* She'd heard back from one of the facilities that
her mother was third on their waiting list. But that could mean two
weeks or two months.

She sat down on the chair across from the couch. Her mother's
matted hair needed washing, but Lucy had put it off for a couple

of days because Mom threw such a fit about it. She leaned her head back and closed her eyes, hoping Benjamin and Mom would sleep for a while longer. As weary as she felt, it was probably just as well that she hadn't made it to Noah's. She didn't have the strength to face that family today.

Was it really supposed to be this hard? As much as she worked and prayed and tried to live a better life, she just couldn't seem to catch a break. Maybe she would have to spend the rest of her life making up for all the mistakes she'd made so far. Was that how it worked—for every bad year, you had to serve a good year? If that was the case, she had a long way to go.

But then she thought about what Marianne had said, about being a daughter of the promise. That sounded like heaven to her . . . a spiritual journey, discovering new meaning to *faith, hope, and love*. With each step on this new path, she did feel like she was one step closer to finding true peace. But some days it seemed like one step forward, two steps back.

She closed her eyes and prayed.

Jacob sat on the front porch steps, waiting for his father to come up the walk. *Daed's* routine rarely varied these days. He'd come in after a long day working in the barn or the fields. He'd hang his hat and wash up. Then he would sit silently at the table while everyone else ate and perhaps eat a bite or two himself before disappearing into his room. He must be getting pretty hungry now that *Mamm* had quit taking him food in the bedroom. He never ate a complete meal.

Sitting with *Daed* at the supper table was like being with a stranger. His eyes were empty, his attention elsewhere. And Jacob's emotions were all over the place about that. Sometimes he was so angry with his father he wanted to punch him. Other times he just wanted to cry . . . or wrap his arms around him. It was like there had been two deaths in the family.

"Wie bischt?" Jacob raised a hand to his forehead to block the setting sun. "Can I talk to you before you go in?"

His father kept walking, stopping in front of him. "Jacob, I'm tired and hungry. Are you and the other *kinner* okay?"

Jacob stood up from the step he was sitting on and swallowed hard. *"Ya,* I think everyone is okay. But . . ." He knew he was about to cross a line he'd never gotten near. "But it's *Mamm.* I hear her crying a lot still."

Daed stood there a minute, his eyes cast down, then walked up the steps past Jacob. Just when Jacob was sure there would be no more conversation, his father reached for the screen door handle and turned around. A breeze stirred beneath the rafters on the porch, and Jacob waited, his hair blowing gently.

"These things take time. It will take time for healing."

"I know, but . . ." Jacob took a few steps toward his father, but *Daed* went in the house and closed the door behind him.

Jacob stayed on the porch, a sense of hopelessness filling his heart. Maybe he should have made plans to go to Glenda's party after all. Glenda had even invited Anna. But Jacob knew what kind of party it would be, and he hadn't wanted Anna at something like that. And then there was the issue of her grandfather.

He finally walked inside, wanting nothing more than to just go upstairs and be alone. But he was hungry too, and he wasn't going to abandon his family the way his father had.

Anna sat at home on Saturday night, as she did most nights, but tonight she kept picturing Jacob at Glenda's party. Unless maybe he didn't go.

She'd changed her mind about going to the party herself. For one thing, she wasn't sure how she'd have gotten out of the house, though she would have found a way if she wanted to badly enough. But her main reason for staying was that *Mammi* had acted odd at supper, and Anna had reservations about leaving the house. Several times *Mammi* had gotten confused, and she'd tripped once and almost fallen down in the kitchen. Anna suspected her blood sugar was off, but when she questioned her grandmother about it, *Mammi* said all was well and that she'd been checking it. She hadn't mentioned anything to Anna about her expired prescription, so Anna knew *Mammi* was trying to control her glucose level with just her diet and the cinnamon pills.

The evening breeze felt wonderful coming through the open window, but as much as Anna tried to sleep, she couldn't stop thinking about Jacob. She was starting to wonder if fighting to see him was a good idea. To her recollection, she'd never been jealous about anyone—not even Emma, who was gorgeous and seemed perfect in every way. Jacob was the first guy to show a real interest in her—the only one to have ever kissed her. And she liked that he was willing to stand up to her grandfather. But could she be on God's path and have these crazy feelings of jealousy? She was pondering that question when a loud knock sounded at her door. Before she could answer, her grandfather pushed the door open.

"I can't find your *mammi*." He held up his lantern with a shaky hand. "I got up to get a drink of water. She wasn't in the bed, so I figured she must be doing the same thing. But I can't find her anywhere." His voice cracked as he spoke, and in that moment, Anna was sure she'd never seen her grandfather more vulnerable.

She sat up in bed. "*Daadi,* I'm sure she's in the basement. You know how she likes to go down there for meditation and prayer."

His tired eyes widened. "At this hour? It's nearly eleven o'clock."

Anna glanced at the battery-operated clock on her nightstand. She'd been so lost in her thoughts she hadn't realized it was so late. She swung her legs over the side of the bed, reached for her robe, and picked up her lantern.

"I'll go down there and make sure she's okay."

"What does she do down there that she can't do in the main *haus?*" Daadi stepped aside so Anna could go by him.

"I told you. Meditate and pray." She turned around before she got to the stairs. "Come on, *Daadi.* Let me help you down the stairs." Her grandfather rarely came up the main stairs, and it was impossible for him to navigate the steep basement steps.

"*Nee.* I will take *mei* time and be fine. You hurry now and go check on your *mammi.* I don't think these knees will make it down to the basement." He groaned as he took the first step downward, and Anna didn't move at first until she saw that he had mastered a couple of steps and seemed to be doing okay.

She darted down the stairs, hurried to the basement door, and carefully made her way down the steps, holding the lantern with one hand and grasping the handrail with the other. These stairs were steep—her grandmother had no business going up and down them all the time.

When she got to the door of the broom closet, she knocked. *"Mammi,* are you in there?"

She waited a few moments, then yelled louder. *"Mammi?"*

Her stomach churned as she turned the knob, jiggling it when it didn't open. She reached above the door and found the key, which meant *Mammi* most likely wasn't in there. Anna put the key in the lock anyway.

She pushed the door open and lifted the lantern above her head, then gasped and brought her free hand to her chest. She'd suspected *Mammi* had more going on down here than just prayer, but she wasn't at all prepared for what she saw. Dishes, glasses, serving pieces, clothes, lotions, a radio?

She took a few steps into the room. Magazines, books, trinkets. *Jewelry?* She opened up a black box and lifted a silver chain, an angel pendant dangling from it.

"Is she down there?"

Anna jumped at the sound of her grandfather's voice. She wanted to stay, to keep looking at what appeared to be thousands of dollars worth of hidden treasures her grandmother must have been collecting for a long time. *And for what?*

She yelled over her shoulder, *"Nee!* She's not down here. I'm coming back up." She forced herself to refocus on the fact that *Mammi* was missing, but she couldn't peel her eyes away from the sleek cell phone sitting in her grandmother's chair. She walked closer and picked it up, then quickly put it back down.

Her heart thumped in her chest as she closed the door, locked it, and put the key back. Had her grandmother lost her mind?

When she reached the top of the narrow steps, her grandfather was waiting, his face tight with worry.

"We'll find her. She couldn't have gone far." Anna hurried past him, then out the front door. *"Mammi!"*

She checked the barn, the old outhouse, the garden, and the woodshed. After catching her breath, she yelled again, as loudly as she could, *"Mammi!"*

Her grandfather crossed the yard to where she was standing, toting his lantern. Anna saw his lip tremble. "Where could she be?"

Anna swallowed hard and tried to think. If her grandmother wasn't right in the mind, she could be anywhere. "I . . . I don't know, *Daadi.*"

"What do we do?" He shook his head, his brow furrowed. For a man of such power in their community, he looked absolutely helpless, waiting for his granddaughter to make a decision.

She made it. "We call on members of the community to help us look for her."

"I will go hitch the buggy up, then start making rounds."

"Daadi, we don't have time to start going *haus* to *haus* for help. She might be hurt. Just wait here, and I'll be right back."

"Where are you going?" he called after her, but Anna didn't answer. She had quite a few phone numbers written down since most of the district members had cell phones. *Or they used to.* There was a phone shanty nearby, so they could use that.

Then Anna remembered the phone in the basement. *Mammi* might get onto her later for blowing her secret, but this was an emergency. She headed straight for the basement. Once she had the phone, she went upstairs to her room and got her phone list. By the time she got back downstairs, her grandfather was pacing the living room.

"Where did you go? Should we call the *Englisch* police?"

Anna was surprised to hear him make the suggestion, since he'd always said that involving the *Englisch* in their lives should be a last resort. But even with her phone list, by the time everyone hitched up their buggies and started to look for *Mammi* . . .

She pulled the phone from her robe pocket.

"Anna, you have a portable phone?" *Daadi* stood taller, frowning.

She fumbled with the phone. She'd used others before, but this one was different. *How do you turn it on? Is it charged?*

"*Ya, Daadi.* And I'm going to call the sheriff's office." Pausing, she let out a heavy sigh. "As soon as I can figure out how to use it."

"When did you get a phone? You know that it—"

"*Daadi!*" She'd never used such a tone of voice with her grandfather. "*Mammi* is missing. Do you really want to talk about the phone now?" She finally managed to dial 911 and hit call.

She was waiting for it to start ringing when her grandmother walked through the front door and into the living room. She was carrying a black-and-white kitten under one arm. Anna quickly hit End.

"Where have you been?" She took a few steps toward her, but her grandfather moved even faster and wrapped his arms around *Mammi* and the cat. "*Mei fraa,* I have been so worried." He eased away, grasping Anna's grandmother by both arms. "Are you all right?"

Mammi frowned. "What in the world are you two doing up at this hour?" She shook loose of *Daadi's* hold. "Of course I'm all right."

Anna walked up to her grandmother and gave the kitten a quick scratch behind the ears. "*Daadi* woke up to get a drink, and then he couldn't find you. He was worried." She tucked her long hair behind her ears. "We were outside calling you. Didn't you hear us?"

"*Ya*, I heard you. And I yelled back, asking for someone to help me, but no one came. I even shined the flashlight I was using, but I guess you didn't see it. I was pretty far out." She put the kitten down on the couch. "I couldn't sleep because I kept hearing a faint crying, so finally I got up to see what it was. After a while, I realized that the sound was coming from back behind the *haus* in the back pasture, so I went out to investigate."

She leaned down and stroked the kitten's head before he darted off the couch and across the room. "This little fellow was caught in your coyote trap. But I don't think he was in there too long before I found him." She shook her head, frowning. "You know I don't like those traps, Isaac."

"*Ya*, well . . . you don't like them coyotes killing the cows either."

"Anyway . . ." *Mammi* brushed cat hair from her blue robe. "I could hear you yelling, and I yelled back, but I guess since I was on the other side of the *haus* with the wind blowing to the south, you didn't hear me." She raised her eyebrows and pressed her thin lips together when she saw the mobile phone in Anna's hand.

"I was just getting ready to call for help." Anna lifted the phone.

"*Ya*, and we will speak in the morning about why you have this portable phone," her grandfather said in a gruff voice.

"Isaac, about the phone . . ." Her grandmother scratched her cheek.

"Let's go to bed, *Mammi*. *Daadi* said we'll talk in the morning." Anna linked her arm through her grandmother's and led her to the bedroom.

"What about this cat?" her grandfather bellowed.

Anna turned around and saw him staring at the kitten, hands on his hips. "Just put him outside, *Daadi*. If he's still there in the morning, I'll tend to him." She kept walking with her grand-mother until they were all the way into the bedroom.

"You went down to the basement." *Mammi* scowled.

Anna helped her grandmother out of her robe and into bed. "Tomorrow we will be talking about more than just this phone."

17

CORA GOT OUT OF HER BUGGY AT MARIANNE'S, TETH-ered her horse, and stood staring at her friend's house, wondering if she could trust Marianne to keep her secret. She couldn't talk to her children, and there was no way she was going to talk to her husband.

She shuffled to the porch and walked up the steps. While she waited for Marianne to answer, she counted in her head. It had been weeks since she'd spent any significant time with her friend apart from brief hellos at church. This past Sunday they hadn't even had that.

"Cora, *wie bischt?* I've missed you. I was going to check on you folks when none of you were at worship on Sunday." Marianne stepped aside and motioned for Cora to come in. "Have you been ill? Is one of the *kinner* sick?"

Cora shook her head. "*Nee.* I just wasn't feeling well, and after some arguing, I gave in and told the children they could stay home as well. John had already said he wasn't going." She hung her head for a moment. "*Mei* family played hooky, I guess."

"I won't tell." Marianne grinned as she gently put a hand on Cora's arm. "Come with me to the kitchen. I have a batch of oat-meal raisin cookies in the oven that I'm bound to forget about if I'm not nearby."

"Those are John's favorite," Cora mumbled as she followed Marianne into the hot kitchen and pulled out a chair from the kitchen table.

"We will send him some home, then." Marianne turned to face her, still smiling. Cora knew that's why she liked coming here. Marianne always seemed happy. She was married to the gruffest man around, yet her demeanor was always one of good cheer.

"I don't think John deserves any cookies," Cora said, then chuckled. "I know. That's awful of me to say."

Marianne pulled a pan of cookies from the oven and put them on a cooling rack before joining Cora at the table. "Then maybe we will send him just *one*. You know . . . to torture him."

Cora chuckled. It felt good to laugh a little. "*Ya*, we should do that."

"I'm glad you came by. I've missed our visits." Marianne eased herself down into a chair, then locked her hands together atop the table and leaned toward Cora. "And I wanted to talk to you about Lucy Turner."

Cora should have suspected this, but she'd been preoccupied with other matters. She waited for her friend to go on.

"It took a lot for Lucy to tell you the truth about . . . about her situation. The girl really seems to be trying to make a *gut* life for her and Benjamin."

Cora humphed. "She's hardly a *girl*. I'm guessing she's in her midthirties. And she knew what she was doing when she seduced another woman's husband." Cora swallowed hard. Though John's infidelity had occurred years ago, recollections of it were still fresh in her mind.

Marianne chewed her bottom lip. "You don't know that's how it happened, Cora. Maybe Ivan pursued her."

Cora shrugged. "Does it really matter?"

"Maybe. Maybe not. But Cora . . ." Marianne reached over and touched her hand. "You know it's not our place to judge. And before you knew about this, you and Lucy were becoming *gut* friends. I think Lucy needs friends. It sounds like she has her hands full trying to take care of her *mudder.*"

"That's all fine and *gut*. But it's not my job to minister to an *Englisch* woman, someone who's clearly used bad judgment in the past. That doesn't mean I'm judging her. Only God can do that."

"Exactly."

They were quiet for a few moments before Cora spoke up again. This wasn't the conversation she wanted to have with Marianne. But her friend had managed to make her feel guilty— and for what? "I think you're judging me because you think I'm judging Lucy."

Marianne didn't say anything, just raised an eyebrow.

"I'm free to choose who I want to be friends with." Cora lifted her chin.

"*Ya*. You are."

Cora slouched back in the chair. Despite her resolve, she was blinking back tears.

"Maybe you should give Lucy another chance. Seems a shame to just disregard the friendship so easily."

Cora squeezed her eyes shut, then sniffled as she opened them. "Look, I didn't come here to talk about Lucy. I—I have something else on my mind, and . . ." She put her elbows on the table and rested her forehead in her hands.

"What is it, dear?" Marianne's voice was soft and sympathetic, as Cora knew it would be.

Might as well spit it out. "I'm pregnant." Cora shook her head. "I'm forty-three years old. I have six—five—*kinner*, and now I'm pregnant again."

Marianne's eyes lit up. "Oh my. I didn't realize that you and your husband, uh . . . I mean, I thought you were having so many problems . . . But, Cora, this is good news. A—"

"I don't want this *boppli*." Cora almost jumped as she heard the words clip across her tongue. Until now, she'd never said aloud what she was feeling. "A *boppli* cannot replace Leah. And as for John . . ." She took a deep breath. "Nothing has changed. It was one time. Just that one time, and . . ." She leaned her head back on her shoulders as she felt a headache brewing. Had she really expected any other reaction from Marianne?

"Of course you want the *boppli*." Marianne smiled. "But you weren't expecting this, so it has caught you off guard. Have you told John?"

Cora shook her head. Marianne was wrong, but why bother arguing? "*Nee*, I haven't told him."

"Honey, I know this little one won't replace Leah—of course not. But a child is such a gift, and the Lord has seen fit to bless you with another one. You must share this news with your husband. Maybe it will ease his suffering in some way."

Cora didn't care about John's suffering at the moment. She flattened her palms across her belly, knowing what was ahead for her. The morning sickness, the weariness and mood swings, the difficulty of being pregnant at her age. And then, to bring an infant child into their sad, lonely house—she didn't think she could bear it. But Marianne wasn't going to understand that, so Cora changed the subject.

"I have something else to talk to you about. I don't want to get Anna in trouble, but Jacob told me he and Anna eat lunch together most days."

Marianne shifted her weight in the chair, then folded her hands in front of her again. "Anna hasn't said anything, but I figured she was seeing Jacob while she was on her route."

"Well, I think it's a shame those two can't spend more time together. Jacob seems to care about Anna a great deal. Have you had any luck talking to your husband?"

"Not yet. But I'm sure he will come around."

"You keep saying that, Marianne. But when? Jacob is a fine boy. He would make a *gut* husband. Your husband isn't giving him a chance."

"I will talk to Isaac again." Marianne pulled her eyes from Cora's, and Cora didn't think she would talk to her husband at all. Cora felt anger building—about Lucy Turner, John, the pregnancy, the bishop's strict ways. About everything. It was time to leave before she said something that would cost her the only real friend she'd made since she moved here.

"I better go." She stood up and smoothed the wrinkles from her apron. "I just came to tell you about the *boppli*. And about Jacob and Anna. I really hope you can do something to convince Bishop Byler to allow them to date."

Marianne stood too and touched her on the arm. "I will talk to him, I promise. And, Cora . . . I will be praying for you and your little one. This pregnancy really is a gift. You will see that when you adjust to the idea."

I hope so. Cora summoned a weak smile. "I will see you soon."

Marianne followed Cora through the living room to the front door. "I'm having Lucy and Benjamin over on Thursday for lunch. It's Lucy's day off. I'd like for you to come too." Marianne smiled. "That little Benjamin just brightens any room he's in."

Cora tensed. "Thursday isn't *gut* for me, Marianne. But *danki* for asking." She walked out the front door without looking back. Marianne was wonderful, but if her new friend was going to keep meeting with Lucy, Cora needed to pull back from her friendship with Marianne.

Cora had no intention of being friends with an adulterous woman. And she couldn't believe Marianne was pushing for it.

Marianne's heart filled with sadness as she watched Cora head down the driveway. She'd been polite enough, but Marianne could see the tension in her face and hear the discord in her voice. *The woman needs her husband.*

As for Lucy, she couldn't force Cora to accept the younger woman. And Marianne certainly didn't condone what Lucy had done, but something deep within tugged at Marianne to help her. Marianne had always believed that when the Lord calls on us, we have to respond. And she'd meant what she said about Benjamin. There was nothing like a child to brighten a room, and Marianne missed having little ones around the house. She couldn't wait for great-grandchildren.

That thought brought Anna and Jacob to mind. She was going to have to do something extreme to get Isaac to loosen up before

he ran everyone in their district off—but mostly before he pushed
Anna away.

It was all too much to think about this early in the morning,
so Marianne decided to seek comfort the only way she knew how
these days. She headed to the basement, savoring the underground
coolness, and unlocked her special room.

She'd confessed to Isaac about the cell phone, saying she kept
it only for emergencies, and so far he hadn't pressured her to give
it up. But he still didn't know anything about the other items in
the basement room, and Anna hadn't told him. She and Marianne
seemed to have fallen into a kind of unspoken agreement—*I won't
tell on you if you won't tell on me.* Marianne had been pretty sure that
Anna was seeing Jacob. Otherwise, she would have been pushing harder to get Isaac to relent. Instead, apparently, the girl
had taken matters into her own hands. Marianne couldn't really
blame her.

She glanced around at all her things, knowing she wasn't in a
position to judge anyone about deception. As she sank down in her
comfy chair, she eyed all the boxes, one in particular. There was
no reason in the world for her to have a box full of jewelry that she
was never going to wear. *I'm such a silly old woman.*

She shook her head as she retrieved the box and placed it in her
lap. She fingered through the necklaces, earrings, and bracelets.
Some of the items had cost a considerable amount of money. She
probably had thousands of dollars' worth of jewelry in here—all
because she'd needed to feel somehow in control of her own life.

But harboring such luxuries was weighing more and more
heavily on Marianne these days. While many of the things she'd
collected would look lovely around her home—dishes, curtains,

knickknacks—so many others had been a total waste of money, not to mention setting up a habit of deception.

She put the box of jewelry back on the shelf and reached for her new pink sweater. Even on this hot August day, its softness felt good to her. As she wrapped it around her shoulders, she wondered how she'd allowed herself to get to this point. Anna had been shocked to see this room. This was not setting a good example for her granddaughter.

She put the sweater back in its place when she heard a noise upstairs. It was much too early for Anna to be home yet, so she trudged back up the narrow steps. When she opened the basement door, she heard someone beating on the front door.

"I'm coming!" Compared to the basement, the main floor of the house felt like a sauna. She wiped at her forehead as she moved through the hot living room, surprised to see Lucy Turner standing on the other side of the screen with Benjamin in her arms. Marianne's new kitty, whom she'd named Patches, was rubbing up against Lucy's legs.

"Marianne, I'm so sorry to bother you." Lucy shifted Benjamin to her other hip.

"No bother, dear. Come in." She pushed the screen door wide so Lucy and Benjamin could come in. She couldn't help but feel a bit relieved that Lucy hadn't bumped into Cora. Cora didn't try to hide her feelings, and Lucy would have left feeling bad.

"I'm sorry to ask you this, but is there any way you could keep Benjamin for me today? I'm already late for work, but my day care won't take Benjamin because he has a low-grade fever. I told them he's just teething, but they're sticking to their policy. I can't leave him with my mother, and my backup sitter moved last week."

Marianne swallowed hard. As much as she would love to keep Benjamin, she knew Isaac would be home before Lucy returned. She didn't think anyone was ready for *that* confrontation. Plus, she was feeling a little tired this afternoon—the heat, no doubt. She'd be happy when fall arrived.

"I completely understand if you can't," Lucy was saying. "I just don't trust many people to keep him, and he seems to like you so much."

Marianne felt the compliment from head to toe. "Of course I'll keep this lad." She held out her arms. "I've got a full day of baking planned, and I bet I know someone who would like to help." She recalled how Anna used to love to sit in the middle of the floor licking the spoons and bowls when Marianne was baking.

Lucy pulled the diaper bag from her shoulder. "Marianne, I owe you lunch, dinner, or something . . ." She paused. "Or I'm happy to pay you."

Marianne shook her head. "No need, dear. Little Benjamin and I will have a *gut* time."

"I would have asked Cora, but . . ." Lucy shrugged, and no further explanation was necessary.

"I'm happy to have some company today."

Lucy leaned over and kissed Benjamin on the cheek. "I love you, Benny. Be a good boy, and I'll see you this afternoon." She looked at Marianne. "I should be here by five thirty."

"That will be just fine." Marianne stood Benjamin on the floor beside her. She wasn't used to carrying a young one around, and her back was already feeling it. She latched onto his small hand and looked back at Lucy. "We will see you this afternoon."

Lucy thanked Marianne again, gave a quick wave, then hurried to her car.

Marianne walked Benjamin into the living room, glad he hadn't cried when his mother left. She squatted down in front of him. "Looks like it's just you and me, Benjamin. How about we go make some whoopee pies?" She brushed back a strand of light brown hair that had fallen across his face, and he rewarded her with a happy smile. *Such a precious child!* But her heart flipped in her chest, knowing Isaac would not be happy that she was associating with Lucy Turner.

Anna breathed lightly between parted lips as Jacob pulled her closer and kissed her again. For weeks, they'd met daily for lunch at the deli, followed by a stroll around the corner to the alley in back of the restaurant. A delivery man had caught them kissing there once, but only once, and they had never seen any other Amish people around the deli. Anna thought it was because the prices were higher there than at other cafés and restaurants in the area. Whatever the reason, they were lucky to have a place where they could meet and even spend a little time alone.

Anna was in love with Jacob. He was everything she wanted in a spouse—kind, tender, generous, and devoted to family. It didn't hurt that he was so handsome. Everything about him called to her, and she was sure he was the man she would marry, but Jacob hadn't shared his feelings with her. Although their passion had surely soared, sometimes to a point where Anna had to back away, Jacob had never told her that he loved her. That was bothersome, but he seemed to "talk" to her in other ways, and she wondered if that counted. The way he gazed into her eyes, ran his thumb down her cheek, told her how pretty she was. And most of all, the way he encouraged her dreams, often telling her that she would have her bakery one day.

"Am I going to see you tomorrow? Same time?" Jacob's breath smelled of the peppermint she'd seen him pop into his mouth on the way out of the café. His mouth covered hers again before she could answer, and her stomach swirled the way it did every time she was close to him.

She eased away. "*Ya*, I will be here tomorrow."

Frowning, he asked, "Is it time for me to try again with your grandfather?"

Anna didn't want to spoil the moment, but their sneaking around hovered over them like a dark cloud. "I don't know."

Jacob shook his head. "We've got to make things right." Then he grinned. "But I can't stay away from you."

She playfully slapped him on the arm. "*Daadi* knows I'll leave home someday." As soon as she said it, she wondered if it sounded like she intended to leave with Jacob. They'd never discussed such a thing. Was he thinking it too?

He kissed her gently. "Well, he's going to have to come around, before I just show up and whisk you away."

Anna's knees went weak, and she could feel herself blushing. *I'll go anywhere with you.*

He teasingly tipped his hat, bowing slightly. "See you tomorrow, Miss Anna."

She grabbed each side of her blue dress and curtsied. "See you then, Mr. Jacob." She turned to head back to the street where her buggy was parked. When they arrived at the sidewalk, Jacob headed in the other direction toward the lumberyard.

Anna unhitched the horse for the trip home, glad she'd gotten all her deliveries done for the day. Though she passed the lumberyard as usual, she didn't bother to look in the window. Anna didn't worry much about Glenda these days, since Jacob had mentioned on several occasions that Glenda's new boyfriend was a really nice guy. And it helped that Jacob hadn't gone to Glenda's party either. He hadn't even mentioned it to Anna because he knew there would be alcohol and activities they wouldn't be comfortable with.

It was a good thing the horse knew the way home, because Anna kept drifting off into daydreams about Jacob. But as she pulled her buggy up to her house, she was startled awake by a strange sound coming from the house. It sounded like a wailing child.

She jumped from the buggy and ran for the door without taking the horse to the barn. The closer she got to the house, the louder the cries, and when she burst through the front door, she found little Benjamin Turner sitting in the middle of the floor with a glass of spilt milk. He was red in the face, screaming.

Anna glanced around but didn't see Lucy or her grandmother. She picked up Benjamin and bounced him on her hip. "There, there, little guy. Where is everyone?"

She walked into the kitchen and noticed a burned batch of cookies on top of the stove and a carton of milk on the counter. "*Mammi?*"

Anna walked from room to room as panic spread over her. Benjamin just kept screaming at the top of his small lungs. Finally, she walked into her grandparents' bathroom.

"*Mammi!*" Her grandmother lay sprawled out on the wooden floor.

Anna set Benjamin down and rushed to *Mammi's* side. She

shook her, but she didn't move. Anna's mind raced with panic as she wondered what to do.

Mammi's cell phone!

She picked up Benjamin and carried him with her to the basement to get the phone. Thank goodness it still had a charge! Once upstairs, she dialed 911.

"It's my grandmother . . ."

Benjamin had stopped crying by now, but Anna had started.

Please, Lord, don't take Mammi. *Not today.*

18

LUCY STOOD OFF TO ONE SIDE IN THE WAITING ROOM at the hospital. If she hadn't been completely sure of how Cora felt before, she was now. She had nodded curtly at Lucy when she arrived but otherwise ignored her and Benjamin. Now Cora and other members of the Amish community huddled together across the room. Anna Byler was there with a man Lucy believed to be her grandfather, the bishop. The others Lucy didn't recognize, though she was certain they recognized her.

She pulled Benjamin closer to her as she continually thanked God that he was all right. So many things could have happened to him today. But they didn't. Lucy felt sure that the Lord had been in that house with both her son and Marianne.

The doctor had already come out and said that Marianne was stable. Her blood sugar had gotten so high that she'd passed out. Until today Lucy had no idea that Marianne was diabetic. She'd definitely seen her eat sweets.

Lucy swallowed nervously as Bishop Byler left the group and walked toward her. Lucy could feel his eyes on her, but she kept her focus on Benjamin, who stood next to her playing with some cars Lucy had found in the diaper bag.

"The boy is *gut?*"

Lucy looked up into Bishop Byler's tired eyes as he stooped in front of her. "Yes. He's fine."

Bishop Byler nodded, but didn't say anything.

"Is Marianne going to be okay?" Lucy took a deep breath and held it.

"*Ya, ya.*" Bishop Byler took off his hat, revealing a bald spot in the middle of his head, then he ran his hand the length of his gray beard. "She will be very upset about this. About putting the child in danger."

Lucy had gotten over her panic once she'd seen that Benjamin was okay. "She couldn't help it, though, if she was ill." She smiled. "And Benjamin is fine."

Bishop Byler's frowned, his eyebrows drawn together. Lucy could tell that he was very worried about what had happened.

"Does she keep the boy often?" The bishop put his black hat back on.

Lucy shook her head. "No. This was the first time. My day care couldn't keep him, so I asked Marianne if she could help me just for today."

"She is a *gut* woman," he said in a shaky voice.

Anna walked up. "Hi, Lucy." Then she squatted down and said hello to Benjamin. When she stood back up, she said, "*Daadi,* do you know Lucy Turner?"

Lucy cringed at the mention of her full name. If the bishop didn't already know, he would surely recognize her name now and assume her to be the seductress they all thought her to be.

But Bishop Byler simply nodded. "I am glad the boy is well." He turned and walked away. Anna stayed.

"*Mammi* is going to be beside herself, knowing she put poor Benjamin in danger."

"That's what your grandfather said, but Benjamin is fine, so she needn't worry."

"I'd be happy to sit with Benjamin again sometime. I'm usually gone most of the day making deliveries to the bakeries, but if it's a Saturday or something."

"Thank you, Anna. I appreciate that." Lucy was pretty sure it would never happen, but it was kind of Anna to offer.

She glanced down at her son, who was happily entertaining himself on the floor. "I guess I should get Benjamin home before he starts getting cranky. It's about time for his nap." She leaned down and picked up Benny's cars, then scooped him into her arms. "Please tell your grandmother that I will come visit, as soon as I have some time off from work. And, Anna . . . please tell her everything is all right. I like your grandmother very much, and I know she will feel badly about this, but I'm just happy she's okay. I don't blame her at all."

"I'll tell her." Anna touched the baby on the arm. "'Bye, Benjamin."

Lucy started to leave the room, but she turned around before she pushed open the glass door. Cora was staring at her, and they locked eyes for a few seconds before Cora looked away.

Lucy headed to her car, holding Benjamin extra close, praying for Marianne.

And trying to rid herself of the sadness she felt about her relationship with Cora.

Cora excused herself right after supper, unsure if her meat loaf was going to stay down. She told the girls she wasn't feeling well, so Mary Jane and Anna Mae set to cleaning the kitchen by themselves, saying they would check on her later.

"Nee, nee. I'll be fine. *Danki* for taking care of the kitchen, and please make sure the boys do their Bible study. Abe will try to weasel out of it." She kissed each of the girls on the cheek, unsure where her two youngest boys had run off to. Jacob had already excused himself to go check on one of their goats, which was due to kid any day.

John was in the bathroom. She heard his bathwater running when she walked into their bedroom. She hoped he wouldn't take too long. Her stomach was still queasy, and she didn't want to lose her supper while he was in there. She kicked off her shoes, sat down on the bed, and laid her head back, dangling her socked feet over the side.

As she rested her hands on her belly, she thought about the life growing inside her, and guilt flooded through her like poison. How could any mother not want her own child? But her guilt about not wanting the *boppli* was compounded by resentment. No other child could replace Leah. But people would say that. They would think that's what she was trying to do. And it wasn't true. It was just the opposite.

She closed her eyes and thought about how she'd treated Lucy today, recalling the look in Lucy's eyes before she left the waiting room. Marianne was right about Lucy needing a friend, but Cora couldn't be that person. She had too many bad memories about John and Stella Parks, the *Yankee* woman John befriended at the auction barn.

Stella had always been friendly to Cora when she went to auctions with John. About ten years Cora's junior, the woman had been responsible for assigning everyone an auction number and collecting the money. Cora probably wouldn't have known anything was going on between the two of them if John hadn't crumpled up one day and made a full confession.

Cora had made him suffer miserably for his actions, but that had been ten years ago, and now she rarely thought of it until something reminded her—like Lucy's confession. Now she couldn't look at Lucy without thinking of Stella. That type of woman didn't change, and Lucy represented everything Cora despised. But if she were honest with herself, she missed Lucy and Benjamin, and in hindsight she wished Lucy had never shared her past. Then they could still be friends.

John stepped out of the bathroom just as Cora was sitting up. Her nausea had passed, thankfully, but her pent-up resentments toward John were bubbling to the surface. And now she was carrying his child. Should she tell him? Would he be one of those people who thought this *boppli* could replace Leah? Or would he instantly resent this unborn child the way Cora did?

The minute that last thought crossed her mind, she laid her hands protectively across her tummy. It wasn't the child's fault he or she was coming into their messed-up lives. She rubbed her belly, trying to muster up some sort of positive feelings about her situation. *He or she.* For the first time, she found herself wondering if the *boppli* she was carrying would be a boy or a girl.

"What's wrong with you? You look pale." John stood in front of her, a white towel wrapped around his waist, his grayish-brown beard dotting the wooden floor with droplets of water.

It was the first time in a very long while that he'd showed some sort of interest in her well-being, and Cora worried she might burst into tears. Maybe she should tell him now. He would figure it out eventually.

"I'm fine. My stomach was just a bit upset during supper." She stood up, walked to her dresser, and pulled out fresh nightclothes. "Maybe a hot bath will help."

Cora turned to face him, knowing she must have a blank look on her face. She wasn't sure what to say. Was this a real conversation? "Maybe," she said softly, her eyes still on him, a tiny bit of hope in her heart. Could it be that her husband was returning to her?

But then he walked around her to his side of the bed and pulled back the sheet. He slipped beneath the light cover, reached for his reading glasses, and picked up a book. And he was gone from her again.

Cora walked to the bathroom, closed the door, sat down on the commode, and wept quietly. When she was done, she stood up, lifted the lid, and vomited.

In between her heaves, she listened to see if John might be coming to check on her.

He never did.

⸺⸺⸺

Noah dropped Jenna off at school since Carley had an early eye doctor's appointment in Lancaster.

"Have a good day, sweetie."

"You too, Dad." Jenna pulled her backpack from the floorboard, opened the door, and blew him a kiss. "See you tonight."

Noah smiled. Jenna had been blowing him kisses for as long as he could remember. It was their thing, and he hoped she'd keep doing it for a while. He couldn't believe how fast she was growing up.

As he left the school and crossed Lincoln Highway, he thought about Benjamin. The child was already two years old. Ivan would be very upset with his siblings for not getting to know their nephew, even though Benjamin had been born out of wedlock.

Noah picked up his cell phone as he pulled into the clinic parking lot and dialed Katie Ann's number. She answered on the third ring.

"How is my favorite sister-in-law?"

Katie Ann chuckled. "You best not let Lillian hear that." She paused. "How are you, Noah? How are Carley, Jenna, and everyone else?"

"Fit as a fiddle. We're all doing good and sure wish you would come for a visit sometime."

"*Ach*, I know. I miss all of you, but planes and trains go both ways. I would love for you and Carley and Jenna to come here to meet Eli, his children, and all our grandchildren. And of course Jonas is growing like a weed."

Noah felt a little stab of guilt. It would be much easier for them to go see Katie Ann and Samuel and their families in Colorado than it would be for them all to come here. He felt bad that he hadn't made it happen.

"We were really looking forward to seeing Emily and David, but we certainly understood why the doctor didn't want Emily traveling."

"Oh, Noah, you should see those twins of theirs—Rose and Lena. They're so precious, and you can definitely tell they are Stoltzfuses."

"I hope to see all of you soon." He paused, thinking of a good way to broach the subject of Lucy, then decided there wasn't one. "I need to talk to you about something."

"Uh-oh. Is something wrong?"

"No. Nothing's wrong. I just . . . well, I need to talk to you about Lucy Turner."

Silence.

"Katie Ann, are you still there?"

"*Ya*, I'm here. What about her?"

Noah knew that Katie Ann was happily married, but he suspected that the mention of Lucy still stung. "Her son, Benjamin— he's two now. I guess you know that. Anyway, Carley and I feel like Ivan would want us to get to know his son, but we don't want to do anything that will upset you. I guess we'd kind of feel like we were betraying you if we befriended Lucy against your wishes. And Lucy and Benjamin are a package deal."

After another silence, Katie Ann asked, "How do Mary Ellen and Rebecca feel about it?"

Noah remembered his recent conversation with Mary Ellen. "They're worried about your feelings too."

"The past is the past, Noah. I agree that Ivan would want Benjamin to know his family, and I'm sure that Jonas and Benjamin will want to meet someday." She paused, and Noah heard a long sigh. "I'm happy, Noah. I really am. I have a wonderful life. If I lived there, I wouldn't want to be around Lucy all the time. Just bad memories for me. But I'm not there, and all of you are. You should get to know Ivan's son." Another silence. "Ivan's other son," she added.

Noah knew that Ivan had been secretly planning to get back together with Katie Ann. He had built the house where Lucy lived now in the hopes of reuniting with his wife. Noah wasn't supposed to know that. The attorney who had handled Ivan's estate had accidentally let it slip, assuming that Noah knew. The amazing part had been that Katie Ann had just signed over the house to

Lucy. She'd been anxious to start her life in Colorado and to cut her ties here. Noah didn't think Lucy knew that Ivan had basically cut her out of his life even before he died.

"If it's really all right with you. We wouldn't—"

"Noah, it's fine. It really is. Please assure Mary Ellen and Rebecca that I'm okay with it. I appreciate you all feeling a sense of loyalty, but I suspect Lucy might not have the type of family we do. I think Benjamin should at least be introduced to our way of life. I'm not saying he'll grow up and want to join the Amish community, but I think it's important that he understands our core values and faith."

"You're an amazing woman, Katie Ann."

"And don't you forget it." She laughed. "Come see us soon, Noah."

"I sure hope to. It's not like I have patients beating down my door these days."

"It's so sad that the bishop has banned everyone from seeing you. That's why David had hoped to visit last year, to maybe help with that."

Noah smiled as he thought about his nephew wanting to battle the bishop on Noah's behalf. "He's a good kid, that David."

Katie Ann chuckled. "Hardly a kid anymore."

"True. Well, Katie Ann . . . give everyone our love, and all of you take care."

Noah hung up the phone and got out of the car, glancing around at the empty parking lot. Only Francine's car was there. He sighed as he walked into the building.

"Anything scheduled for today?" He stopped at the small window. Francine shook her head.

"Sorry, Dr. Stoltzfus."

Noah nodded, then headed down the hall to his office. It was only a few minutes later when Francine walked in. Noah sat down in his chair and motioned for Francine to sit down.

"Dr. Stoltzfus, you know how much I've loved working here, right?"

Noah caught her use of the past tense—*loved* working here—right away. "Yes," he said softly, waiting for the "but."

"But I've accepted another job in Lancaster, and I'll be starting right after Labor Day. It's just that I'm a people person, you know, and . . ." She shrugged.

Noah forced a smile. ". . . and there aren't many people here."

"Yeah. Do you hate me?"

Noah rubbed his forehead for a moment, then looked up at her. "Of course not, Francine. I understand."

"Are you going to try to find someone else quickly so that I can train them?"

Noah thought for a few moments. Carley used to work in his front office. But Carley had quit to stay home with Jenna when she was younger, and she'd just never gone back to work. Maybe she'd want to fill in part-time while Jenna was in school. Or maybe he and Gloria, his nurse, could just function without a receptionist for a while. That would certainly help the clinic balance sheet, which was rapidly tilting out of balance. So far their savings had kept them out of real trouble. But he couldn't continue the way he was going.

"I'm not sure what I'm going to do. I'll figure something out."

"I'm really sorry. I hope that mean old bishop guy changes his mind. All those Amish people really loved you." Francine shook her head. "It's just a real shame."

Noah nodded. He wished the old man would change his mind too. "Well, you never know what the future holds."

"True." Francine got up. "Okay. Well, let me know if you need anything."

Noah watched as the door closed behind Francine. He hated to see her go, but he could certainly see why she'd want to.

Noah scrounged around in his desk until he found Lucy's phone number, the number he'd asked Alice for the day she came to his office. Lucy didn't answer, so Noah left a message, unsure if he'd reached a cell phone or home phone.

"Hi, Lucy. This is Noah Stoltzfus. Could you please give me a call when you have a few minutes to talk?" He rattled off his phone number and hung up. He doubted she'd call, but at least he was trying.

"Why is Ivan's brother calling you, and why didn't you answer the phone?"

Lucy listened to the message again, but she didn't write the number down before she hit Delete on the answering machine. "I think they want to get to know Benjamin, and I'm not sure I'm ready for that."

Mom snorted. "Yeah, and they can't get to know little Benny without having to be around his mother."

Lucy bit her tongue, walked to where Benjamin was playing, and gave him the cracker she'd had in her hand when the phone rang. *I am a good person. I love God. I'm a good mother. I'm going to be a daughter of the promise.*

Lucy put her hands on her hips. "I'm going to scramble some eggs for Benjamin and me. Do you want some?"

Her mother plopped her bare feet up on the coffee table, and Lucy cringed at how black they were on the bottom. She noticed her mother was wearing the same blue pants and white blouse she'd had on yesterday. Only the blouse wasn't very white anymore.

"Ain't you got work? Or did they fire you?"

Lucy took a deep breath. "I'm off today because they needed me to work Saturday. And I'm off tomorrow too because that's my regular day off. Do you want any eggs or not?"

"No. I think you might try to poison me."

Lucy laughed. "Mom, if I wanted to poison you, don't you think I'd have already done it?" She picked up Benjamin and took him with her to the kitchen, but not before turning around to catch the look of surprise on her mother's face. Mom's jaw hung low, and Lucy just shook her head.

Dear Lord, give me strength.

19

MARIANNE SAT AT THE KITCHEN TABLE, FEELING LIKE A small child as her husband reprimanded her. She'd sent Anna out early this morning, fearful this was coming. She was actually a bit surprised that Isaac hadn't started chewing on her last night when they got home from the hospital. Surprised, but thankful. She'd been mighty tired. The folks at the hospital had wanted her to stay overnight, but she'd insisted on coming home to her own bed. She'd finally won that argument, but it had worn her out. This morning she felt stronger, though she could have skipped the argument with Isaac.

"Why would you not take your insulin pills?" he was saying. "I have always said to seek out homeopathic remedies first, but if your health is at risk, I would never expect you not to take medications prescribed by the *Englisch* doctors."

Marianne sat taller, raised her chin. "The only doctor I've gone to for years is Noah Stoltzfus, and he wouldn't refill my prescription without a visit to him because it had been so long."

Isaac pulled out a chair and sat down across from her at the kitchen table. "There are other doctors. I would have made sure we got a driver to take you to Lancaster . . . or even Philadelphia or Pittsburg or Harrisburg. Dr. Stoltzfus is not the only doctor there is."

"He's the only doctor I trust." Marianne folded her arms across her chest. "Everyone around here likes him, and I'm sure I'm not the only one not taking care of my medical needs because I don't want a new doctor."

Isaac hung his head, sighing heavily. "*Mei lieb.* You know why we can't use Dr. Stoltzfus. He's been shunned. He took his vows, broke them, and even wrote a book defaming his family."

"Oh pooh, Isaac!"

Her husband's eyes widened as his mouth fell open.

"Noah is a *gut* man, and his whole reason for opening a clinic in the heart of our district was to give back to our people. He has more than made up for any mistakes he's made, and his family has forgiven him." She pointed a finger at her husband. "Besides, he's cheaper than anyone around. He's a *gut* doctor, and I'm not going to anyone else." She gave her head a taut nod, grunting just a tad.

"You're behaving like a child, Marianne." Isaac shook his head. "I try and try and try to make our people see the dangers of becoming too involved in the world of the *Englisch*. We're already forced to do business with them because we can no longer make a living just tending our land. Our young people are exposed to things that would have curled our grandparents' toes."

He leaned back, frowning. "All those electrical gadgets they have these days. That rock music, the television shows and movies—all the outside influences that past generations haven't had to deal with. It's all very dangerous, Marianne."

"You tell me exactly what is dangerous about using a skid loader? Why must elderly men use a push mower for dozens of acres when a riding lawn mower is much safer for their hearts? And is it so bad to have a cell phone for emergencies? What would have happened if I hadn't had a phone in the basement for Anna to call for help?"

He didn't reply, so she went on. "You have to choose your battles, to listen to people and be reasonable instead of just forbidding everything. As it is, half the district thinks you're abusing your power. I hear things, Isaac, when folks don't know I'm listening."

"I have nothing but the best interest of this community in my heart, and I prayerfully ask the Lord's guidance in all that I do. We must not veer so far from our ways that we will never be what we were again." He paused and stared at her. "And when did you decide it was all right to talk to me like this?"

"Today. Something awful could have happened to that sweet Benjamin—and all because I haven't felt like standing up to you about Dr. Stoltzfus. I'm going to go see him, Isaac. So I guess if you want to shun anyone, you had better start with your own *fraa*!

"And another thing." Marianne stood up from the table, slamming her palms down. "Jacob Hostetler is a good boy. And it's just your own stubbornness that makes you forbid Anna from seeing him. And if you're not careful, you'll push her so far away that we'll never see her. So you think about all of this, Isaac Byler. You just better think!" She turned and marched out of the kitchen.

She didn't turn around when Isaac called her name. Instead, she opened the basement door and started down the stairs. Isaac might need to clean up his act, but Marianne knew she had some housekeeping of her own to do.

Jacob finished his potato soup and half a ham sandwich, but Anna was picking at her salad. "Not hungry?" he finally asked.

"Still just a little worried about my grandmother." She picked up her napkin and dabbed at her mouth. "She scared us all by letting her blood sugar get high enough for her to pass out, and I shiver to think what could have happened to the *boppli* who was in her care at the time." She shook her head. "And all because she wouldn't go against my grandfather and get her prescription filled."

Jacob pushed his empty dishes to the end of the table when the waitress walked up. "But she hides all that stuff in the basement, right?"

"*Ya.* She does. It's very childish, but maybe years of living with my grandfather pushed her to do some silly things."

"Anna, I have to get straight with him. I love meeting you for lunch every day, but I want us to be able to do some other things, and I want to have you over for supper. I want my family to know and love you as much as I do."

Jacob felt the heat rushing up his face as he realized what he'd said. He'd known he loved Anna for a long time, but this wasn't exactly the way he'd planned to tell her. Still, her smile told him he'd waded into safe waters. "I do, you know." He reached for her hand. "Love you, that is. And I want everyone to know."

Her face was as red as the checks on the tablecloth. "Really?" she asked softly.

"*Ya.* Really." Jacob was waiting to hear how she felt about him when a thump on his shoulder caused him to jump and look to his left.

Bishop Byler.

"Anna, go home." The bishop glared at Jacob, who tried to stand but bumped his knee on the table. There wasn't enough room to stand and face Bishop Byler, so he was forced to sit there while

Anna hurried away. Jacob was surprised when the bishop slid into her spot. He pushed Anna's plate out of the way and leaned forward. "We have a situation."

"Yes, sir." Jacob sat as tall as he could and tried to keep his voice level. "I love your granddaughter, and she . . ." He paused, unsure if he should say that Anna loved him. She hadn't had time to tell him how she felt.

"Did I tell you no kissing?"

"*Ya.*"

"Have you kissed *mei maedel*?"

"*Ya.*"

"More than once?"

"*Ya.*"

The bishop took off his hat and scratched his head for a few moments before he put it back on. "You have both been untruthful about your plans in the past. And now this . . ." He waved his arm around. "I'm guessing these lunches have been going on for a while."

"Yes, sir." Jacob held his breath, worried he would never see Anna again. Bishop Byler would surely see to that.

"You will come for supper on Saturday."

Jacob blinked. Had he heard right?

"I will allow you to see Anna. But . . ." The bishop pointed a long finger at Jacob. "There will be no more of this kissing." He leaned closer, his scowl so intense that Jacob shivered. "There hasn't been anything more than kissing, has there?"

Even if there had been—which there hadn't—Jacob was pretty sure that at that moment he would have lied. "*Nee.* Only kissing, sir."

Bishop Byler pounded a fist on the table. "No more. No more kissing until you are married."

Jacob swallowed hard. He'd fantasized a hundred times about making Anna his wife, but he'd assumed her grandfather would never allow it. "Okay," he said hesitantly.

"I am serious. You may court Anna, but no more of this sneaking around. And no more kissing!"

Jacob glanced around the restaurant as he wondered how many people heard the bishop's booming voice. He lay in bed every night counting the hours until he could kiss Anna again. Was this a promise he could keep? "But we've already kissed, so I'd think that—"

Bishop Byler hit the table again. "Promise me now. No more kissing until your wedding."

Jacob liked the sound of that so much that he nodded. "Yes, sir. No kissing until we are married."

"We will publish the news soon enough."

Jacob swallowed hard. Maybe he should actually ask Anna to marry him before any more plans were made. But he just smiled and said, "Yes, sir."

Anna finished her deliveries and got home around four o'clock. Her eyes were swollen from crying, and she'd wondered all afternoon what her grandfather must have said to Jacob. She'd probably never be able to see Jacob again. And he'd said he loved her.

Distraught as she was, her own worries moved to the back of her mind when she walked into the living room. It was not the same room she'd left that morning. Lacy white curtains had replaced the green shades that had covered the windows, the mantel was lined with angel figurines, and there was a large decorative bowl filled with potpourri in the middle of the coffee table.

"Mammi?" Anna called softly as she walked into the kitchen. Her eyes widened when she saw the table set with fine china she'd never seen before, along with gold-rimmed tea glasses and fancy cloth napkins. A beautiful serving bowl etched with tiny flowers sat in the center of the table.

Anna's eyes traveled across the countertop to a battery-operated hand mixer laid out beside a colorful set of red and white mixing bowls. Several store-bought floral dish towels were folded next to a large crystal pitcher filled with tea. Anna briefly wondered what happened to the old Tupperware one they'd always used.

A lovely calendar with landscape pictures and a scripture reading for each month decorated the wall at the end of the counter. Next to it hung a cuckoo clock with a small blue jay barely poking his nose from behind a box. Anna presumed he would come out and crow on the hour.

There was more. Lots more. Anna was still taking it in when her grandmother walked into the kitchen with a pink sweater draped over her shoulders and wearing a silver necklace. Anna just stared at her. She couldn't speak.

"Cat got your tongue, dear?" *Mammi* put her hands on her hips and scanned the room. "Speaking of cats, where is my little Patches? I haven't seen him all day." She blew out a breath of air, gave her head a quick shake, then walked to the oven and pulled it open. "New recipe tonight—pepperoni lasagna. A little Italian dish I've been wanting to try for a long time." She pulled out a pan, and Anna breathed in the aroma. It reminded her of the pizza place in town.

"*Mammi*? Are you feeling okay?" Anna couldn't stop looking around the kitchen. Each time she noticed something new. Daadi *is going to go crazy when he sees all this.*

"I've never felt better, dear—except it's really too warm in here for a wrap." She pulled the pink sweater from her shoulders and draped it over the back of her chair at the table. "*Ach*, and I went to see Dr. Noah this afternoon so I can get a refill on my prescription." Her smile faded. "I do feel just awful about putting poor little Benjamin in danger. I'm sure Lucy will never ask me to babysit again. The doctor said that usually low blood sugar makes you pass out. In my case, my blood sugar was so *high* that I was near a diabetic coma. He said I was very lucky." She shook her head. "Blessed. I'm very blessed."

"*Mammi*, is all this stuff from your basement collection? What do you think *Daadi* is going to say?"

Marianne lifted her head, seeming to snap out of her thoughts about Benjamin and her health. "*Ach*, I suspect he'll make me get rid of most of it." She chuckled. "But I'm going to enjoy it for now and try to sway him into letting me keep a few of these things out."

Anna eased out a chair and slid into it, fearful she might actually fall down. "Uh, okay," she mumbled as she watched her grandmother pull the oven door open, take a peek, and shut it again. Her grandfather had never cared for Italian food, not even pizza.

She squeezed her eyes closed when she heard her grandfather's heavy footsteps coming up the porch steps. The screen door opened and closed and the steps continued, then stopped suddenly. *Daadi* was surely taking inventory of the new decor. Anna wished she could sneak out of the house before he made his way to the kitchen. But her grandmother just scuttled around the room with a smile on her face, seemingly unworried.

"Marianne?"

Anna slowly opened one eye and barely turned to face her grandfather as her heart thumped in her chest. He walked closer until he was standing between Anna and her grandmother. He repeated himself. "Marianne?"

"Hello, Isaac. Sit down. Supper will be ready shortly." *Mammi* placed a tray of sliced garlic bread on the table. Anna wasn't sure, but it looked like maybe it was the frozen kind you buy in the grocery store.

Her grandfather didn't move. He looked like a statue, frozen in a state of shock with his jaw hanging low, his eyes bulging. But then, to Anna's surprise, he slowly pulled out his chair at the end of the table and sat down. He met Anna's stare, closed his mouth, and frowned.

Mammi put the lasagna on the table, then filled the fancy serving bowl with salad. "Now, Isaac, I know that you aren't fond of Italian food, but this is something special. You try it. If you really don't like it, I won't make it again."

Daadi's face turned red as his eyes scanned the kitchen, his gaze landing on the cuckoo clock before he focused on *Mammi*. "Woman, have you completely lost your mind? What is all this?" He recklessly waved a hand around the kitchen, then stared at the pink sweater draped over *Mammi's* chair. "And what is . . . that?"

Anna held her breath as her grandmother walked over to her chair, slowly picked up the sweater, and draped it over her shoulders again. She put her hands on her hips and gave him a thin-lipped smile before she spoke. "We are changing a few things around here, Isaac."

Daadi turned even redder, and Anna thought he might self-combust. "Are you trying to give me a heart attack? You have spent your entire life being a *gut* example of how a good Amish *fraa* should behave. Why would you disobey me after all these years and turn to the ways of the *Englisch?*"

Anna pushed back her chair. "I'll come back later."

"Sit." Her grandmother pointed a finger at her. "Everyone is going to eat this fine meal that I have prepared."

Anna did as she was told, but she'd lost her appetite. *Mammi* squinted her eyes as she peered at *Daadi.*

"You listen to me, Isaac. There is nothing wrong with anything in this kitchen. I might have gone a little overboard in the living room." She paused, tapping a finger to her chin. "We can discuss it later and hopefully come to a compromise."

"Where did all of this come from?" *Daadi* put a hand to his chest.

"I've been living with your intolerance for most of my life, Isaac. I've amused myself by purchasing a few extras over the years . . . with my own money that I've collected from the bakery deliveries."

Anna put a hand over her mouth, trying not to grin. "A few extras" was a huge understatement. Anna had never been more thankful that her grandfather couldn't make it down the basement steps to have a look at those few extras.

Daadi lowered his hand from his chest, placed both palms on either side of the china plate, and sat taller. "Is this all of it?"

Anna held her breath.

"*Nee.*" Her grandmother raised her chin. "I've got an entire room full of things I've bought. It used to be quite challenging—ordering things from catalogs, getting money orders to pay for them." She shook her head and smiled. "But now that I have a credit card and the Internet, it is so much easier. And my iPhone, of course."

Daadi pounded his fist on the table, rattling the china and the crystal glasses. "All of this will go, Marianne. When I come in from the fields tomorrow, I expect to see all of this gone and things back to normal."

Anna didn't know what to do. She looked back and forth between her grandparents, wishing she could disappear. But she didn't dare move.

"I don't think so, Isaac." *Mammi* leaned her face close to *Daadi's.* To Anna's surprise, he actually backed away, his lip turned under. "I have decided to share the wealth, as the *Englisch* would say. Much of this I bought just because—*ach,* I don't know, because it was forbidden, I guess. But much of it could be put to better use than being hidden in an old broom closet."

"What exactly do you have down there?" *Daadi* spoke cautiously, in a tone of voice Anna had never heard him use. *Oh,* Daadi, *if you only knew.*

Mammi tapped a finger to her chin. "Let's see. I have my radio, my comfy chair, lots of pretty jewelry and trinkets, and—"

"*Nee! Nee!*" *Daadi* laid his forehead in his hands before he looked back up. "Say this isn't true, Marianne."

Mammi stood straight up, walked to the crystal tea pitcher, and began filling all their glasses. "*Ya,* Isaac. I enjoy listening to country gospel music. I wanted a television, but without electricity, that was proving to be a challenge. When I was at the diner several years ago, the television was on, and I watched a game called

Jeopardy." She sighed before she placed the pitcher on the counter. "I think playing that game along with the television would have kept my mind sharp."

She pulled out her chair and sat down. "And another time, when I was at Barbie Beiler's *haus,* she was watching a program called *Dr. Oz.* How do you think I learned about taking cinnamon pills for my diabetes?" She put her napkin in her lap. "There is much to be learned from the television. It's not all bad, Isaac."

Anna felt like she were living on another planet, surrounded by people she didn't know. Yet here they were—her grandparents— facing off about a decades-old secret her grandmother had been keeping. She had to admit that *Daadi* was taking it better than she would have expected. Anna badly wanted to ask him about his conversation with Jacob, but this surely wasn't the time.

Following silent prayer, Anna and her grandfather began picking at their food. *Mammi* ate like she hadn't eaten in a month of Sundays, but Anna noticed that she didn't have any bread and she left most of the noodles. *Daadi* just kept staring back and forth between Anna and his wife. When they were done, *Mammi* started cleaning up, and Anna stood up to help her, but her grandfather nodded for her to follow him.

"I'll be back to help you clean up, *Mammi.*" Anna pushed her chair in, dreading a private chat with her grandfather, but also hoping he would shed some light on his conversation with Jacob.

"No worries, dear." *Mammi* smiled as she cleared the table. "I'm sure you and your grandfather have a lot to talk about."

Anna glanced at *Daadi.* He was shaking his head as he left the kitchen. She followed him to the front porch, closing both the screen door and wooden door behind her. *Daadi* fell into one of the rocking chairs, but not before tossing a new decorative red pillow onto the decking.

"Something must have happened to her in that *Englisch* hospital. They must have done something to alter her mind." *Daadi* put his elbows on his knees and held his head. "*Mei* poor Marianne."

Anna picked up the pillow and slowly took a seat in the other rocker. "*Daadi*, they didn't alter *Mammi's* mind at the hospital." She said the words, only half believing what she was saying. She could have never predicted this behavior from her grandmother. *Good for you*, Mammi.

Her grandfather looked up at Anna. "Then where is this behavior, this defiance, coming from?"

Anna fought the urge to ask him about Jacob. "*Daadi*, maybe it's because she has lived with your ways for so long. Maybe she started hiding things from you because she didn't dare tell you what she thought, and then just couldn't stop."

Her grandfather stood up and began pacing back and forth across the porch. "You will talk to her tomorrow, make her understand that this silliness will not be tolerated. All these fancy things must go." He stopped and glared at Anna. "You will do this, Anna."

"*Daadi*, I can't make *Mammi* get rid of all these things. Besides, I bet she has thousands of dollars of stuff down in—" *Daadi* whirled around, a scowl on his face, and Anna knew she'd messed up. He walked to where she was sitting.

"You knew about this disobedience, that she was hiding things from me?"

Anna took a deep breath. "Not until recently."

Daadi pointed a finger at her. "You make her fix this. I will not have *mei* own *fraa* flaunting such prideful things in our *haus*. You fix this, Anna."

Anna pushed her foot against the decking and nervously kicked the rocker into motion. "*Daadi*, it's not my place to fix this. And *Mammi* hasn't really done that much that goes against our ways."

Daadi gasped. "She has a pink sweater with little white balls for buttons."

"Pearls," Anna said softly.

"And who is this Dr. Oz?" He shook his head and started pacing again. "The devil has gotten inside her, I say."

Anna grinned, but quickly covered her mouth with her hand. "*Daadi, Mammi* is the most devout Christian woman I know. She just needed to be able to express herself."

Daadi grunted. "*Express* herself? See, even you are too influenced by the *Englisch* world. You will get her to get rid of all these things."

Anna opened her mouth to argue, but *Daadi* spoke up again. "Jacob Hostetler will be joining us for supper on Saturday. We have a wedding to plan. And I will tell you what I told him. No more sneaking around. And no more kissing until after you are married!"

He pointed a finger at Anna. "Help *Mammi* get our home back to normal before then."

Blackmail. That's what it sounded like. But Anna was glowing inside and out. *Jacob wants to marry me.* Everything else would fall into place one way or another.

20

CORA SPENT THE DAY THROWING UP. IT WAS A MIRACLE no one had suspected that she was pregnant. Not even her husband seemed to notice. But then, John barely noticed Cora was alive these days, so why should he take notice that she was ill? She thought about last night, when he'd almost acted like the old John, the wonderful man she'd fallen in love with. But that moment had been so short-lived that it was hardly worth storing in her memories.

She closed the lid on the toilet and ran a cold rag over her face, certain that she'd never been this sick during the first trimester of her other pregnancies. She heard the bedroom door close, so she knew John would be wanting to bathe. After she changed into her nightgown, she unpinned her hair and left the bathroom. Would he notice that she was pale again? Would he offer kind words to make her feel even a little loved?

He didn't say anything, but merely passed her on his way to the bathroom, closing the door behind him. She longed to talk to Marianne again, but tomorrow was Thursday, and Marianne would be entertaining Lucy and Benjamin. A wave of anger swept through Cora as strongly as the nausea. Anger that Lucy was who she was. Anger at losing their friendship as a result. And anger at herself for allowing herself to get close too soon—a mistake she wouldn't make again.

She took a deep breath and told herself to focus on the good news. There was going to be a wedding. Jacob had told the family about his conversation with Bishop Byler. The *kinner* were excited, and Cora thought a wedding would be *gut* for all of them. Such a blessing, and a nice distraction from the grief they'd all been drowning in. Cora looked forward to getting to know Anna better, though she couldn't help worrying that having the bishop as a father-in-law—especially someone like Isaac Byler—could cause problems for her son.

Cora was lost in thought about the pending nuptials when John came out of the bathroom. This time he'd already dressed in his night clothes.

"How was your day?" Her words were clipped, and she didn't much care how his day was. But she was aching for any kind of conversation, even if it turned into a fight.

"Fine." He walked around to his side of the bed, climbed in, but didn't cover up. As they both lay atop the white sheet, Cora closed her eyes and enjoyed the breeze streaming through the open window. It was miserable this time of year, but tolerable when the sun set on a breezy day. She'd be glad when fall arrived.

She opened her eyes and took a deep breath. "So what do you think about Jacob marrying the bishop's granddaughter, Anna Byler?"

"We don't even know the girl." John reached for his reading glasses, and Cora could feel him disengage from the conversation.

She gritted her teeth. "Jacob is very happy. And it will be fun to plan our first wedding." As soon as the words slipped out, she knew what her husband was thinking. *Leah was the oldest. She should have been the first one to get married.* Cora had already let that thought weave through her mind, then dismissed it. This was Jacob's time, and she refused to let any regrets get in the way of making this a special occasion for her son.

"Since Bishop Byler is now allowing Jacob and Anna to see each other, I'm sure we'll get to know our future daughter-in-law in coming weeks." Cora pulled the drawer of her nightstand open and reached for her hairbrush.

"Hope Jacob knows what he's doing, marrying the bishop's granddaughter. Especially a bishop like Byler. Jacob may never have any peace."

"He loves Anna, and that's what is important." Cora brushed her hair. "And Bishop Byler's wife, Marianne, is quite a dear person. I'm thrilled she will be Jacob's mother-in-law—though I suppose she's really a grandmother-in-law."

"Not much time to plan a wedding." John opened a book he was reading and pulled out a small piece of paper he used as a bookmark.

"I know." Weddings were always held in October or November, and September was almost here. "But the twins will help, and we'll be able to get it done. We have much work to do on this *haus* to get it ready, though. Even though the wedding will be at the Bylers' *haus*, we might have out-of-town guests."

"It's fine the way it is." John's attitude was grinding on her nerves more than normal. Maybe her hormones were out of whack. Or maybe she'd just had enough.

"*Nee*, it's not fine the way it is. We need to do a *gut* cleaning, and we need a fresh coat of paint on the far barn."

John grunted. "No one is going to notice if that barn on the north side of the *haus* needs fresh paint."

Cora took a deep breath. "We are going to paint it anyway because I will notice."

"Whatever."

"I dislike that word, John. It's something the *Englisch* say, and I don't want our *kinner* using it."

John closed the book, looked up at her, and repeated, very slowly and deliberately, "Whatever."

Cora kept her head down for a few moments, torn between crying or smacking him—an emotion that was rearing its ugly head more and more these days. Her bottom lip trembled, but she was not going to give him the satisfaction of crying. Besides, she had a trump card to play.

She turned to him and made herself smile. "Well, I have news. Maybe you would like to hear it?"

John shrugged. "I guess so."

"*Ach, gut.* Because I've been wanting to tell you." She kept her eyes on him, didn't even blink for fear of missing any part of his reaction. "I'm pregnant. What do you think about that?"

She waited, wanting him to suffer the way she was suffering, to feel anger and guilt that they were having a child to replace the one they'd lost, to share the little bit of hope she was beginning to feel about the new little one.

John slowly looked up and blinked several times. "Really?" he asked.

This was not what she was expecting. "*Ya.* I am with child." She paused, keeping her eyes on her husband. "At my age."

She studied him, this man she'd been married to for most of

her life, and she could not, for the life of her, tell how he felt about this news. She waited for him to say something else, but he opened the book again and started to read.

Cora felt her blood boil. She glared at him, then reached for her pillow and stood up.

"I'm going to go sleep in the sewing room."

John looked above the rim of his glasses and slowly said, "Whatever."

Marianne felt a little sorry for Anna. Her sweet granddaughter was trying so hard to get her to comply with Isaac's wishes, and Marianne had to admit she'd gone a bit overboard. But she wasn't ready to back down. Not yet.

"*Nee*, I'm leaving everything as it is for today," she said as Anna stood in the kitchen, arms folded across her chest. "You aren't the boss of me," she added, then chuckled, and was glad to see Anna smile.

"Well, I tried. *Daadi* can't say I didn't try." Anna walked to the counter where Marianne was sorting cookies for delivery.

"That's right, dear. You did what your grandfather asked." She handed the last bag to Anna. "Now go make your deliveries, and tell Jacob we will be having zucchini sausage lasagna for supper Saturday night." She ran her hands under the faucet. "I am going to get rid of some of these things. It's too hard on your grandfather's heart to have to see it all every day." She laughed. "But I have Lucy and little Benjamin coming for a visit later, so I'll take care of it after they leave."

"That will be *gut*. Thank you." Anna collected her baked goods, packed them up, and kissed her grandmother on the cheek. "Enjoy your visit."

"I will."

Anna looked up at the wall. "Are you going to keep the cuckoo clock?"

Marianne grinned. "I love that little fellow. He cheers me up when he pops his head out and crows on the hour. That might be one of the things your *daadi* and I will have to compromise about."

Anna smiled before she headed out the door.

Marianne set about making coffee for Lucy, and she'd baked a pineapple cheese torte. She was sure she could never make up for putting that little one in danger, but she was going to make sure they had a lovely visit. She wasn't planning to have any of the torte herself, though. *Gotta watch my blood sugar.*

Lucy had to reassure Marianne repeatedly that she didn't harbor any ill will about what had happened.

"Everything turned out fine, Marianne. And the doctor said you were very close to a diabetic coma, so you were lucky." Lucy took a sip of her coffee and watched Benjamin playing with his toys in the middle of the living room. "Are you taking your pills like you're supposed to now?"

"*Ya, ya.* The hospital sent me home with some samples, and I went to see Dr. Noah so I can get my prescription refilled. I'm watching my diet too."

"I'm glad." Lucy set her cup on the coffee table. "Everything looks really nice in here."

"*Danki.* Too bad my husband doesn't think so." Marianne's

infectious laugh warmed Lucy's heart the way it always did. *I wish I had a mother like you.*

"You know . . ." Lucy paused, hesitant to broach this new subject, but she needed another opinion. "Noah has asked me a couple of times to bring Benjamin and go to his home." She shook her head. "But I just don't think it's a good idea. Benjamin is Noah's nephew, so I can understand why he wants to see him. But I would just feel so uncomfortable." She hung her head. "About what happened and all. I know what they must all think of me."

"Lucy . . ." Marianne's voice was soft. "You must forgive yourself before you can expect others to do so."

"But I will never be part of that family, so it's hard for Benjamin to be a part of it."

"Family is a gathering of people who love and accept each other for who they are, whether related or placed together by God for His own good purposes."

Lucy hung on Marianne's optimism and wished that she could believe everything the older woman said. "They're never going to accept me, Marianne." She paused, chewing on her lip. "Why do you?"

Marianne reached over and took her hand. "You see, my dear, this is what you have to stop doing—doubting yourself. You are a lovely person, you're a *gut mudder* to Benjamin, and you're trying to take care of your own *mudder* under very trying circumstances. The Lord sees all of this, and so do others. Give yourself some credit."

"I always feel good when I'm around you." Lucy settled back in the couch and breathed in the aroma of Marianne's house—always the smell of something baked lingering in the air. "I like it here."

"I'm so glad." Marianne walked over to where Benjamin was

playing and squatted down beside him. "I don't know what I would have done if anything had happened to this little fellow. I'm so sorry."

Lucy shook her head. "Now, Marianne, I'm going to quote you. You must forgive yourself. It wasn't your fault."

Marianne ran her hand through Benny's hair, then stood and walked over to the window. "I thought I heard a buggy rolling up the driveway." She put a hand to her forehead. "It looks like Cora."

"Uh-oh." Lucy jumped up and joined Marianne at the window. "I don't think Cora wants to be around me these days."

Marianne didn't answer. She just walked to the door and waited for Cora to come up the steps. "Hello, dear." Lucy sat down on the floor beside Benjamin, wishing she could just scoop him up and go home.

Cora came storming into the living room looking like she'd just ridden on horseback to get there. Her prayer covering was on sideways, her brown dress was wrinkled, and Lucy wondered if she knew she had a smudge of dirt on her cheek.

"Hi, Lucy." Cora walked over and squatted down next to Benjamin. "Hello, little one." She ran a hand through Benny's hair, then flung herself into a rocker and pushed hard with her feet until Lucy feared the rocker might take flight.

"I have had it!" Cora's face was beet red. "I'm telling you both, I'm going to smack my husband. I really am. It's not our way, but I can feel it coming!"

Lucy glanced at Marianne, who was standing nearby with her hands folded in front of her, eyebrows raised. "Now, now, dear. Maybe tell us what the problem is."

Cora shook her head so hard that her loosened prayer covering almost fell off. She haphazardly reached up and attempted to move it into place. "John is . . . he's . . ." She grunted loudly. "He is a . . ."

"Easy now, Cora." Marianne edged closer and put a hand on her shoulder. "The Lord is listening."

Lucy didn't move. She pretended to help Benjamin build something with his blocks, but she was completely tuned in to what Cora was saying.

"He is a mean man. A cruel man. I finally told him last night that I am pregnant." Cora's face twisted into an expression that was both frightening and almost comical. "Do you know what he said?"

Marianne remained quiet. Lucy did too, though her mind was racing. *Pregnant?*

"He said, 'Whatever.' I am carrying his child, and that's all he has to say: 'Whatever.'" Cora abruptly stopped rocking and sat up straight. "I wish he would just leave. Go somewhere. Like to another country."

Lucy bit her lip. She'd never heard an Amish person talk like this. She didn't even think it was allowed. Before she could process that thought any further, Cora jumped from the chair and started to pace. Lucy stayed close to Benjamin. She jumped a little when Cora stopped abruptly and gasped.

"Marianne, what have you done in here?" Cora walked to the mantel and ran her hand over the new figurines above the fireplace. She turned to Marianne. "And what in the world did Isaac say?"

"Well, he wasn't thrilled." She gave a little laugh. "And I'm going to work out a compromise with him. It won't all stay." She shrugged. "I was just tired of keeping the secret."

Cora adjusted her prayer covering again, which didn't help. Several hunks of brownish gray hair were hanging loosely. Lucy wondered if she should tell her about the smudge on her cheek. She decided not to.

"Maybe that's what I need to do—overhaul my household." Cora walked to the couch and plopped down. "Either that, or buy John a one-way ticket to *wherever*."

Lucy handed Benjamin another block, unsure what to say, if anything. She knew she wasn't on Cora's list of favorite people. In fact, she was surprised that Cora had spoken to her and Benny at all.

"Maybe you should give him a *gut* talking to." Marianne sat down on the couch beside Cora.

Then Cora shook her head and buried her face in her hands. "I feel so awful."

Lucy slowly got up off the floor, wound around the coffee table, and sat down on the other side of Cora. She still didn't say anything. But Cora was so upset and not acting herself, Lucy couldn't help wanting to offer her some sort of comfort.

"This is embarrassing." Cora was weeping now. "But I didn't know where else to come. I was up all night, thinking about what we've become. But I can't have my *kinner* seeing me like this."

Lucy glanced at Marianne, who looked back at her and shrugged. For once, Marianne seemed at a loss for words.

"Maybe, uh . . . maybe your husband just needs some time to get used to the idea of another child." Lucy shifted her weight on the couch, not sure if she should have added her two cents.

"Well, he better get used to it. This *boppli* will be here in seven and a half months!" Cora lifted her head from her hands and leaned back against the couch cushions, sniffling.

Marianne patted Cora on the leg. "Honey, are you sure you're pregnant?"

Cora actually rolled her eyes. "Uh, *ya*. I missed my period. I never miss my period unless I'm pregnant."

"Did you do a pregnancy test?" Lucy asked.

"A what?" Cora frowned as she turned to face her.

"You know, a pregnancy test." Lucy got up off the couch, picked up several blocks Benjamin had thrown across the room, returned them to him, then sat back down.

Cora turned to Marianne. "Do you know what she's talking about?"

Marianne shook her head. "*Nee*, I don't."

"It's a little kit you buy in the store. Walmart has them," Lucy said. "You urinate on the little stick, and if it shows a plus sign, you're pregnant. Or if a minus sign shows up, you're not pregnant. They're pretty accurate."

"That's disgusting," Cora shivered. "I'm not going to . . . you know . . . on a stick."

"Well, if you did, you'd know for sure if you are. Sometimes people miss their period for other reasons."

Marianne took in a deep, loud breath. "Cora, how old did you tell me you are?"

"Too old to be having another *boppli*." Cora sighed. "I'm forty-three."

Marianne chuckled. "I was that age when I started going through the change. Honey, you might not be pregnant at all." She grinned. "Your hormones certainly seem out of whack, but that could be because you are entering menopause."

Cora's face brightened. "Do you think that's it?"

Lucy stared at Cora, confused. Cora seemed so *happy* about the possibility of a false alarm. But that didn't make sense. Many

Amish families were quite large, and Cora obviously loved children. Surely a new baby would be a gift in the troubled household.

"I think it's wonderful that you might be pregnant," Lucy said softly.

Cora turned to her and frowned. "That's easy for you to say. You don't already have six—I mean, five—children. And I'm a *few* years older than you." She pointed a finger at Lucy. "And I have a husband who has checked out, flown the coop!"

"At least you *have* a husband," Lucy said under her breath, not looking up at Cora.

Cora let out a heavy sigh. "Yes, Lucy. I have a husband. And right now, I wish I didn't!"

"*Ach*, now. You don't mean that," Marianne said.

"What I mean is I want the old John back. The John I married. The man he was before Leah died. I need him right now, and he's nowhere to be found." The tears were starting again.

"I can go get you a pregnancy test," Lucy blurted out. "You'll know within a few minutes if you're pregnant." She glanced over at Benjamin, who had curled up on the floor and looked like he was almost sleeping.

"So . . ." Cora tilted her head. "All I have to do is, um, *go* on a stick, and this stick will let me know if I am with child?"

Lucy nodded. "I'll go right now if you want me to."

Cora stared at Lucy long and hard. "You would do that for me? I mean, after the way I treated—"

"It's no problem at all." Lucy stood up, not wanting to hear what else Cora had to say. "Can you watch Benjamin?"

"Of course," Cora said.

"We both will," Marianne added.

Lucy picked up her purse, still talking directly to Cora. "If he wakes up, he will probably be hungry. There are some snacks and juice in the diaper bag."

"Lucy, we'll all be fine." Marianne stood up. "I promise you I won't faint. I'm in *gut* shape. And even if I do, Cora will be here."

"I'm not worried." Lucy headed for the door, happy for the chance to help—to do something to work her way back into the friendship circle. Despite Marianne's earlier words, Lucy still felt that she needed to prove herself worthy of Cora's friendship.

"I'll be back."

"I was awful to her," Cora mused as they heard Lucy pull away in her car.

"*Ya*, dear. You were." Marianne never minced words.

"It's just that I know her type."

"And what type is that?"

Cora looked over at Benjamin to make sure he was sleeping before she spoke. "The type who steals another woman's husband."

Marianne sighed. "*Ach, ya*. I'm sure it was all Lucy's fault and Ivan Stoltzfus had nothing to do with it. I'm sure Lucy seduced him with her wiles and robbed him of his innocence."

"Don't mock me, Marianne. That's probably exactly what happened."

"Oh pooh!" Marianne chuckled. "You don't know that."

Cora shrugged. "Either way, adultery is a sin."

"And you are free of sin?" Marianne's smile had a sly edge. "You, who was ready to smack her husband or send him to another country?"

Cora couldn't fight the smile on her own face. "I never said I was perfect. But I really do know the type. John . . ." She paused, embarrassed again. "John had an, uh . . ." She shook her head. "I know the type. Trust me."

"So John had an affair. He cheated on you. And you don't like Lucy because of this?"

Cora stomped her foot from her place on the couch. "Don't make me out to be the bad person here. I never cheated on anyone."

"Well, you shouldn't take out your frustrations with your own past on Lucy. She's trying very hard to walk God's path, and no one has beat themselves up more about what happened with Ivan than Lucy herself. She doesn't need you to beat her up too."

"I never said I wanted to beat her up. I just know her kind, and I don't trust her."

They were both quiet for a while before Marianne spoke up again.

"Well, she did offer to get you this urination test." Marianne shrugged. "Sounds to me like she is trying very hard to be your friend. And before you knew about Lucy's past, you were very fond of her."

"I know." Cora rolled her eyes.

"Then let it go. Live in the here and now. Only God can judge, and if He has forgiven Lucy, then I would think you could too."

Cora didn't answer, just sat quietly for a while, her hands across her belly. When she spoke again, she changed the subject. "So do you think I'm really pregnant?"

"I don't know, dear. But I suppose we will know soon enough."

Cora followed the instructions on the pregnancy test, wishing she'd had one of these when she was pregnant with Abe. She'd spotted throughout her first trimester and hadn't been completely sure she was pregnant until her belly started to get round. The waiting had driven her crazy. This waiting wouldn't take nearly so long—if it worked.

She could hear faint voices in the living room while she sat there on the edge of Marianne's bathtub and watched for the plus sign or the minus sign. In the quiet of that bathroom, those minutes of waiting, she felt something shift in her spirit. It was like a tight place inside her had loosened, freeing her to turn toward God.

She closed her eyes.

God, forgive me for all of my bitter thoughts about another child. I just miss Leah so much, and bringing a boppli *into the family seems almost like leaving her behind. I know it wouldn't really be like that. But it just feels wrong to be happy when we don't have my precious girl in our lives anymore. I've prayed to You continuously to heal my family, and as angry as I am at John, I ask You to please help us find a way back to each other. Whatever the results of this test, I promise to accept it as Your will.*

She paused.

And, God, please forgive me for the way I treated Lucy. Help me love her instead of judging her.

Even as she prayed it, she realized how much she wanted it. She'd missed being around Lucy and Benjamin, and she did want to put judgment behind her. It was time to look forward instead of back.

No matter what the little stick tells me.

Is it time? Slowly, she opened her eyes and looked at the results. She took a deep, cleansing breath and walked back into the living room. Lucy and Marianne stood up when she walked in, neither saying a word.

Cora smiled. "I'm pregnant."

Nobody moved. Both women just looked at her.

"And it's okay." Cora touched her stomach. There was a new sense of peace, and Cora knew that peace was always the work of the Holy Spirit.

Marianne walked up and slowly wrapped her arms around Cora. "God has a way of working things out, and maybe this child is the blessing you and John need."

Cora thought about John's reaction to her pregnancy and her stomach tightened, but then she tried to focus on that freedom she had felt while waiting for the stick to give its message. She chose to walk in God's light, not her husband's darkness. She would continue to pray for John, but she couldn't be responsible for every feeling he had. She had enough to work through on her own.

Lucy came over with a shy smile and placed her hand on Cora's stomach. Cora stiffened a little. Amish people just didn't do such things. But Lucy clearly meant well, so Cora tried not to flinch. And when Lucy smiled, Cora couldn't help but smile along with her.

"I hope I'm able to have more children someday." Lucy pulled her hand back, then glanced at Benjamin. "I didn't use to want children, but kids change you. For the better."

Cora reached for Lucy's hand and squeezed. "You're a *gut* mother, Lucy. And a *gut* person. I'm sorry."

Cora was surprised when Lucy burst into tears and threw her arms around her. "I've missed you," she said. Cora froze, shocked yet flattered at how deeply their estrangement had affected the younger woman. She pulled her friend into a hug. "I've missed you too."

21

SATURDAY NIGHT ANNA WAS AS NERVOUS AS SHE WAS excited for Jacob to be joining her family for supper, especially now that she knew a proposal was in order.

She hoped *Daadi* would behave. He was still unhappy over *Mammi's* new decor, even though they'd talked and made some compromises. The cuckoo clock had gotten to stay, but most of the knickknacks had been boxed up and carted back to the basement.

Jacob arrived right on time.

"Wow. This room doesn't look at all like it did before," he whispered as he walked into the living room. "It's really pretty."

Anna shivered happily at the sound of his voice, and butterflies danced in her stomach as she thought about being Jacob's wife. "You should have seen it a couple of days ago," she whispered back.

Jacob's chuckle stopped abruptly, and he stiffened when Anna's grandfather walked into the room. "Did you remember our conversation?" *Daadi* asked.

"Yes, sir."

Anna felt her face turning red.

"*Gut.* Now come into the kitchen. For some reason, we are being forced to try another new recipe. Probably something Italian, French, Chinese, or from some other foreign place." *Daadi* shook his head. "If you came for a *gut* meat and potatoes supper, you might be out of luck."

He shuffled toward the kitchen, motioning for Anna and Jacob to follow. "Marianne has taken leave of her senses." He looked over his shoulder, pointing back toward the living room. "As you can see."

"Now, *Daadi*," Anna said. "*Mammi* did take down most of her decorations and trinkets. I think it's a nice compromise."

Her grandfather pointed to the cuckoo clock on the kitchen wall as he took his place at the head of the table. "That bird makes me jump every time it bursts out of that—"

"Hello, Jacob." *Mammi* turned from the stove to give him a welcoming smile. "You just ignore my husband and sit yourself down."

Anna nodded toward the chair across from the one where she normally sat. She glanced nervously at her grandfather, wondering if he would snap at her grandmother for putting him in his place in front of company. But ever since *Mammi's* awakening—as Anna liked to call it—*Daadi* had changed too. He still grumbled, complained, and gawked. But he also deferred to his wife far more than Anna would have ever thought possible. *Mammi* had managed to keep the items that were most important to her—her lace curtains, kitchen gadgets, and all of her china dishes and crystal glasses—and with surprisingly little effort. Maybe it was as exhausting for *Daadi* to enforce the rules as it was for them to follow them.

The meal was pleasant and uneventful. *Thank you, Daadi.* Afterward, Jacob led Anna out onto the front porch. She knew what was coming, at least she thought she did. But that didn't make it any less special when it happened.

"I love you, Anna. I want to marry you, to love you, and raise a family with you." Sweat dripped from Jacob's brow even though a cool front had left the evening mild and breezy. He took one of her hands in both of his. "Will you marry me?"

"I don't know. You look awfully nervous." Anna burst out laughing when his expression fell. "*Ya*, Jacob. Of course I will marry you. I love you very much."

He put his hands on either side of Anna's face and then leaned closer. Her lips parted and she closed her eyes. But then . . . nothing. Jacob eased away without following through.

"I promised your grandfather I wouldn't kiss you again until we were married."

"You what? But, Jacob, I—"

"Shh." He glanced around nervously. "I feel like he is lurking around somewhere, hoping I'll break my promise. I got permission to marry you, and I don't want to blow it now, even though there is nothing I want more than to kiss you right now."

He breathed out a huge sigh, then grinned. "So how fast do you think we can get married?"

She giggled. "Jacob Hostetler, you know I need time to plan." She cupped his cheek with her palm. "But we'll have the rest of our lives soon."

"I'm ready to start my life with you."

Anna smiled. "Me too. Let's go inside and tell *Mammi* and *Daadi*."

Holding hands, Jacob and Anna turned back toward the front door. And sure enough, as they walked past the big front window, they spotted Anna's grandfather poking his head around the white lace curtains.

It took everything Lucy had the following week to walk into Noah's clinic, but jobs in Paradise—and even neighboring Lancaster—were hard to find. The receptionist job at Noah's office paid four dollars more per hour than her shifts at the diner—plus it was a consistent schedule with no weekends. If she was careful with her money, she might be able to start saving some of her salary. She tucked the newspaper with the classified ad in her purse as she walked in the door.

The same woman was sitting in the receptionist area as the last time Lucy visited the clinic. Lucy explained why she was there, and a few minutes later Noah walked into the empty waiting area.

"Come on back, Lucy." Noah motioned for Lucy to walk with him down the hallway. "Where's Benjamin?"

"He's with my friend Cora." It felt good to be able to say that. She was striving to stay on the path God was laying out for her. And having good friends for the journey seemed an important part of His plan.

Noah pointed to the tan chair in front of his desk, and Lucy sat down. She waited until he was seated behind his desk before she said anything. "I totally understand if you're not interested in me working here, but my day care is right down the street, and this pays more than I'm making now. I also found out that my mother will be moving into a new facility soon, and it's near here as well. So . . ." She paused, bit her lip. "That's why I'm here."

"Do you have any experience in a medical environment?" Noah scanned the application she'd dropped off the day before.

"No." She resisted the urge to just get up and run out of there. She should have known this would never fly.

"That's okay." Noah looked up and smiled. "Francine didn't either, and she would be able to show you how to do the insurance coding." He sighed. "I wasn't even going to replace Francine. I thought my wife, Carley, could fill in or my nurse and I could run the clinic by ourselves. But Carley has been wanting to try some freelance writing assignments, and Gloria often needs to be in the exam room with me. So I still need someone to take calls and manage appointments, even if business isn't exactly booming."

Lucy thought about Marianne's transformed house. "Maybe that will change soon."

"I don't know why it would," Noah said sadly. "Anyway, you know what the pay is, and I can provide you with insurance. We typically don't pay for dependents' insurance, but in this case—"

"No. I'll pay for Benjamin. And you can take what Mother and I owe you out of my first checks." She looked down. "I mean, if you decide to hire me."

"When could you start?"

"I've been at the diner for a while, so I wouldn't feel right not giving them at least a week's notice."

"Then let's plan on you starting a week from today. How's that?"

"Really?" Lucy twisted the strap on the purse in her lap.

"Yes, really. Francine won't be leaving until after Labor Day, so that would give her a few days to train you."

Lucy was quiet for a few moments. "I'm sorry I didn't return your last phone call. It's just that I . . ."

"No worries. There will be other family events, and I'll know where to find you." Noah stood up and extended his hand. "Welcome to Stoltzfus Clinic. See you soon."

Lucy felt the smile stretch across her face. "Thank you, Dr. Stoltzfus."

"Just Noah." He smiled. "We're family, after all."

Lucy could barely hold back the tears as she left the building. God was blessing her over and over. She was abundantly thankful for this new job and the way that Noah wanted to include her and Benjamin in his family.

But she wondered about Noah's sisters and his other relatives. Would they be as accepting? Or was she just setting herself and Benjamin up for more rejection?

Cora watched John shuffle from the bathroom to his side of the bed as he did every night. She thought about the way Marianne had stood up to her husband and the compromises they'd reached. Cora wondered if there was anything she could do to shock John back into being himself. If not, maybe it would be better for him to just leave. Divorce wasn't an option, of course, but maybe they could live apart for a while.

The truth was, John was making everyone in the family miserable. Mostly Cora. The *kinner* didn't say much, but Cora could tell they missed their father—the young boys especially.

She'd already bathed, so she slipped into her nightgown, sat down on the edge of the bed, and brushed her hair. Their routine was as predictable as the sun rising and setting each day. If there was any conversation forthcoming, Cora knew it would be stilted, if not just plain mean.

She still couldn't believe John's reaction to her pregnancy. *Whatever.* The more she thought about it, the more his attitude crawled beneath her skin and festered. By the time she finished brushing her hair, her heart was racing, her face flushed, and her hands were trembling. As her emotions spiked, she felt her senses take leave, and this new Cora was pulsing with enough adrenaline to squash John Hostetler into a million pieces if he wasn't careful.

She walked around to his side of the bed and stared down at him until he took off his reading glasses and closed the book in his lap.

"What?" His expressionless face seemed like a slap to hers. "Why are you just standing there staring at me?" He opened the book again and slipped his glasses back on.

At first Cora stood there frozen, her teeth gritted, her hands knotted into fists. Then something finally snapped. She felt like a dog gone rabid as she jerked the book from her husband's lap and heaved it across the room. It slammed into the wall and fell to the floor, spine up. Cora noticed for the first time what John was reading. *Entanglement* by Louise Parsons. An *Englisch* murder mystery. She had told herself that maybe the book he kept in his nightstand was a Bible study of some sort. Why hadn't she ever opened the drawer and looked?

"What are you doing?" John jumped out of the bed, threw his hands up in the air, and glared at Cora.

"*Nee*, John. What are *you* doing? I'm sick and tired of this! Everyone in this family misses Leah, but we don't have the luxury of just checking out of life like you have! You're not doing your job, John. You're not taking care of me or your family."

"How dare you." John's face reddened, and his lip trembled. "I provide a *gut* living for this family. I work long hours and—"

"Stop it! Just stop it!" Cora screamed and stomped her foot. "You know exactly what I'm talking about."

Panic crossed John's face. "Keep your voice down."

"I will not!" she screamed back at him. "Something has to change, John. We can't keep living like this." She realized she had her hands on her stomach. She hadn't even been aware of doing that. "We're having a *boppli*. He or she will not replace Leah, but there is a life growing inside of me, John."

He didn't answer. He turned away from her and stared out the window.

"We have to talk about this, John. About this child that is coming. And about Leah. We never talk about her anymore. Don't you think the rest of us are hurting too? We all miss her."

"But it's my fault she's gone." John spoke barely above a whisper, his face still turned away.

"That's not true." But that's what she'd told herself, wasn't it— that it was his fault? She'd needed to put the blame on someone. And that was wrong. She knew she needed to let go of the blame and trust in God's will. But knowing and doing weren't necessarily the same thing.

Could she let go now?

Could her husband?

"John, you can't keep blaming yourself like this. It was God's will that our beautiful *maedel* was taken. And you have other *kinner* who need you." She took a few steps toward him, wanting to wrap her arms around his waist. But she didn't.

She waited for him to say something. To turn around. Anything. But he didn't move, and neither did she.

"This is my punishment," he finally said, his head hung low.

Cora eased her way closer but still didn't touch him. "Punishment for what?"

John turned around, and Cora brought a hand to her chest when she saw the tears streaming down his face. "God took Leah because I cheated on you all those years ago. And I turned the plow too sharp. That's why she's gone. It's my fault on all accounts." He covered his face with his hands and wept.

Cora swallowed hard and moved closer. Part of her longed to reach out and embrace him, but she didn't dare. She was so used to him pulling away from her that she wasn't ready to set herself up for that, even though she wanted nothing more than to comfort him.

"It was an accident, John. It's not your fault. And God doesn't work like that. He doesn't punish an affair by killing a child. I Ie forgave you a long time ago, just like I did."

Even as she said the words, she found herself wondering if they were really true. Had she really forgiven John? She honestly didn't know. But she knew she had to forgive now.

"You have to come back to the world of the living, John. You're hurting yourself." She hesitated, then added in a whisper, "You're hurting all of us."

He pulled his hands from his face, his cheeks moist, his eyes puffy. "I feel so awful, Cora. Some days I don't want to get out of bed or to even live. I can't . . ." He clenched his fists at his sides. "I can't stand the pain. And it takes everything I have to keep going."

John began to sob so hard that Cora starting crying too. "We need each other, John. I know how you feel. I lost her too. I feel the pain you feel." Cora spoke the words, but she could see now that John's pain had taken him to a bad place, a place so dark that he couldn't seem to find the light anymore. And she didn't know how to bring the light to him.

She finally wrapped her arms around his waist, and her husband latched onto her in a way he hadn't done in months, burying his head on her shoulder. Cora stroked his hair as she'd done so often for the *kinner* when they were upset. John continued to sob as if Leah's death had just happened minutes ago. And for the first time, she realized that John was suffering in a different way than she was. He didn't just miss their daughter. He was blaming himself twofold. He was drowning in blame.

Cora finally got him tucked back in bed. He was still crying. Cora got into bed with him, cradling him in her arms until he finally fell asleep.

All this time she'd been wanting John to take care of her and the children. But her husband couldn't even take care of himself. And she didn't know if she had it in her to care for him the way he needed.

Once John was asleep, Cora sat up in bed. For a long time.

And as soon as it was daylight, she called the only person she could think of who might be able to help them.

22

ANNA RODE WITH HER GRANDFATHER TO JACOB'S house. They were quiet most of the trip, but then her grandfather spoke up.

"I don't think anyone ever gets over the loss of a child." Then he turned to Anna and smiled—something Anna hadn't seen him do since *Mammi's* overhaul of the house.

"You are a lot like both of your parents. Your mother was kind and loving, a gentle soul. And your father was a strong man with a willful spirit, but he always had *gut* intentions." He paused, a faraway expression on his face. "The Lord giveth, and the Lord taketh away. It is how we deal with the latter that defines our destiny. We can choose to survive. Or we can just die inside."

Anna knew that her grandfather wasn't just talking about John Hostetler. He rarely talked about Anna's parents, but he was obviously thinking of them now. From what she'd heard, he'd been in a bad way for a long time after her parents' death. If anyone could help Jacob's father, it was *Daadi*.

When they arrived at Jacob's, she helped her grandfather get the horse and buggy settled, then followed him up the walkway to the Hostetlers'. She wasn't sure why *Daadi* had asked her to come along. He'd even asked her *mammi* to make the bakery deliveries today so that Anna could join him on this trip. Jacob was at work, so it wasn't that *Daadi* thought she'd want to see him.

Jacob's mother was waiting for them at the door. "*Danki* for coming, Bishop Byler." She opened the screen and ushered them inside. "All of the *kinner* are busying themselves, so it's just John and me at home." She smiled at Anna. "And I'm so glad you came with your *daadi*. We're very excited about your upcoming marriage to Jacob, and we are looking forward to getting to know you better."

"*Danki.*" Anna smiled as she continued on into the living room. Cora's eyes were swollen, but her welcome was genuine, and Anna said a quick prayer that her grandfather would be able to help Jacob's father.

"He doesn't know you're coming, Bishop. I told him to take a break from work today, and surprisingly he agreed. He's in our bedroom." Cora nodded toward a closed door. "Should I go tell him you're here?"

Anna's grandfather shook his head. "He won't be happy to see me. And that's all right. I'll just go on in, if that's all right with you?"

Cora nodded. "*Ya.*"

Anna now knew that it was her role to keep Cora occupied, to distract her from what was going on in the other room. Cora's eyes were fixated on the door, so Anna spoke up.

"Did Jacob tell you that we are thinking about having the wedding the last weekend of October?"

Cora turned to face her, joy beaming through her worry. "*Ya*, he did. That's not much time to plan a wedding, but what fun we'll have doing it. I know your *mammi* will be doing most of the work, but I hope you'll let me help. We . . . we've never had a wedding in our family."

Anna and Cora spent the next hour talking about the wedding and glancing from time to time at the bedroom door. Every once in a while, Anna heard faint voices, but she couldn't hear anything that was said. Finally, the door opened.

Cora stood up from where she and Anna were seated on the couch, and Anna did too. *Daadi* and Jacob's father walked into the living room together. "*Danki* for coming, Bishop." John Hostetler reached out and shook her grandfather's hand.

Daadi simply nodded, then told Anna it was time for them to go.

"Is he going to be okay?" Anna asked as they headed home.

Her grandfather flicked the reins and picked up speed. "It will take some time. These things are not easy."

"But he'll get better?"

"*Ya, mei maedel.* I believe he will."

They were quiet the rest of the way.

Lucy unpacked her mother's things at the care facility. Her mother hadn't spoken one word to her in three days, ever since Lucy told her she would be moving here. Cora had offered to watch Benjamin while Lucy got her mother settled.

"So, are you ever going to speak to me again?" In some ways, Lucy wished she wouldn't.

Mom didn't move from her spot on the twin bed. Lucy felt sorry for the person in the other bed, who seemed to be sleeping. That poor soul would awaken to find Alice Turner as her roommate, a fate Lucy wouldn't wish on anyone.

She recalled the way her mother used to be, and guilt nipped at her. She reminded herself that Mom wasn't mean by nature.

It was the stroke—or maybe Alzheimer's. Noah had said there were some new treatments they could try. But even then, Mom would probably never be her old self. Something had changed in her brain. She couldn't help being the way she was.

"I have all your toiletries in the bathroom, and all your clothes are unpacked in the dresser. Can you think of anything you need?"

"A daughter who loves me. That would be nice." Mom frowned as she glared at Lucy.

"You have a daughter who loves you." Lucy stowed her mother's red suitcase in the small closet on her side of the room.

"Really?" Lucy's mother looked all around the room. "Because I don't see a daughter who loves me. The only daughter I see is one who is locking me up in an old folks' home."

That stung, but Lucy couldn't think of an alternative arrangement. Just last week her mother had caught a kitchen towel on fire. It was bad enough living with mean, but Lucy couldn't have her mother being a danger to Benjamin.

"Mom, you know why you got kicked out of the last place, right?" She wasn't sure if her mother would remember or not.

"Yes. I smacked a woman who deserved it."

"Can you at least try to get along with everyone here? This is a very nice place, and you're only in here because I'm not able to take good care of you like they can."

"You don't *want* to take care of me." Her mother waved an arm toward the door. "Just get out of here. And don't ever come back. You're a worthless daughter."

Lucy bit her tongue the way she'd been doing several times a day. Her tongue was practically growing scar tissue from being bitten so often. But she was getting better at holding her temper. Maybe a little more patient. *Maybe I really am a daughter of the promise.*

She kept her voice gentle. "Don't you want to see Benjamin?"

Mom glared at Lucy through squinted eyes. "Are you stupid? Of course I want to see my little Benny."

"Well, he can't drive here himself. I'll have to bring him."

Silence, and her mother stared at the floor.

"I'm going now."

Mom kept her head down. Lucy said a quick prayer that her mother would be kind to the staff—and her roommate. She turned to leave. But before she made it to the door, she turned around again.

"I love you, Mom."

Her mother didn't look up. And Lucy left.

That Saturday Marianne had invited Cora and Lucy over, so Lucy picked up Cora around mid-morning. Mary Jane had insisted that she and Anna Mae would keep Benjamin, and Cora could tell that Lucy was glad to have some time to herself, especially since she had started her new job on Wednesday.

"Marianne has something on her mind," Cora said as they stood on the front porch waiting for the door to open.

"Why do you say that?"

"I can just tell. It might be that she's just lonely because we haven't been around as much. I know you've been busy learning your new job. And I see her at church service, but other than that—well, I've been enjoying being with *mei* husband lately."

Cora smiled, forever grateful to Bishop Byler for whatever he'd said to John. Things were far from perfect—John wasn't going to be healed of his depression overnight. But the bishop's visit had helped, and surprisingly, the bishop had suggested that John go to Lancaster and talk to a professional counselor. Even more surprising was that John had agreed to do so. He'd had his first session last week.

"Come in, come in." Marianne ushered them into the living room with an urgency that Cora hadn't seen before.

"Is everything okay?" Lucy pulled the filmy scarf from around her neck and laid it on the couch.

Cora untied her black bonnet and hung it on the rack by Marianne's door.

"*Ya, ya.* Everything is fine. But I need you two to help me with some things."

Cora glanced around the living room, surprised that the bishop hadn't made his wife get rid of all her new things. The lace curtains were still hanging, and a few other decorative pieces graced the mantel.

Marianne motioned with her arm for Cora and Lucy to follow her.

"Does this door go to the basement?" Lucy asked as Marianne pulled open a door beneath the stairs.

"*Ya.*"

Cora and Lucy stepped carefully down the narrow steps until they reached the concrete floor. There were some boxes, pipes, and a row of columns that apparently ran the length of the house— nothing unusual for a basement that hadn't been finished out. To their left, tucked behind the staircase, was a door with a shiny knob. Cora knew that Marianne was about to share her secret room with Lucy, even though she wasn't sure why.

"This way." Marianne walked to a door, stood on tiptoe to reach above its frame, and pulled down a key. She turned it in the lock, pushed the door open, then picked up a flashlight right inside. She shone it inside until she found her battery-operated lantern.

Cora looked at Lucy, who'd brought a hand to her chest. "Where in the world did you get all this . . . stuff?"

"Oh, here, there, and yonder," Marianne said as she picked up a radio. It looked like it must be thirty years old. "This is one of the first things I purchased. I had to go to the Sears and Roebuck and pay them cash to order it from their catalog. Then they mailed it to me."

Lucy was wide-eyed as she scanned Marianne's inventory. Cora recalled her own reaction the first time she saw this room. She'd probably looked just like that.

Lucy picked up a box filled with jewelry. "Is all this stuff allowed?"

Cora grunted. "Of course not! Why do you think she has it hidden down here in the basement? Only reason her husband didn't know is because he has bad knees and can't make it down here." Cora thought about the ballerina jewelry box she'd bought with Marianne awhile back. It had given her great pleasure, and she'd come to believe there was nothing wrong with a little pleasure. Perhaps Marianne had gone a bit overboard. Cora suspected Marianne had invested quite a bit of money in this, um, hobby of hers.

There was one chair in the room, a cushy upholstered one. Marianne sat down in it and gestured around her. "I've decided to get rid of these things." She frowned. "Not all of it. But most of it. I've put the things out around the *haus* that I believe to be acceptable, and Isaac and I have compromised on some things—like *mei* little cuckoo clock." She flashed a grin, then gave a businesslike nod. "But the rest of this stuff I really shouldn't have, and maybe it can benefit someone else." She pointed to Lucy. "So you first, *mei* dear. I want you to take anything you'd like."

"What are you saying?" Lucy's eyes grew even rounder. "No, Marianne. I can't do that."

"Sure you can." Marianne stood up and reached for the box of jewelry. "Start with this. I bet most of these things would look very pretty on you."

Lucy shook her head. "No, I'm not taking these things. But I bet you can sell a lot of it."

"You mean like have a garage sale?" Marianne scowled. "That's an awful lot of work, and Isaac would see everything I've bought over the years. I don't think his heart could take that. He's still adjusting to the new things in the house."

"Not necessarily a garage sale," Lucy said. "You can sell things on eBay or something."

Cora looked at Marianne, and they both shrugged. "What's this eBay?" Cora asked.

"It's an Internet site where you can put things up for sale, and the highest bidder wins. You send the item to the buyer, and they send you the money." Lucy smiled. "Usually, they send you the money first, and—"

"Good grief, Marianne. How long have you been collecting these things?" Cora had been sorting through some of the items on the shelves. She picked up a beautiful sculpted lighthouse. It was about twelve or fourteen inches high, varnished in maroon and white, with a glossy finish. "This is lovely." She twisted her mouth from side to side. "But why?"

Marianne took the lighthouse from her. "Because I've always wanted to go to the beach." She put it back on the shelf. "I think I'll keep that one."

"What about this?" Lucy lifted a colorful silk flower arrangement. "It's really pretty."

"You take that, dear." Marianne held her palms up. "I insist."

Lucy held on to it. "Why don't I sell it for you on eBay and see how much I can get. Then you can decide if you want to sell some of these other things."

"Is it easy to do, the eBay?" Marianne's eyes kept scanning the shelves full of her treasures. Cora knew this had to be difficult for her. She'd been finding refuge here for such a long time. But now that her secrets were out of the closet—so to speak—perhaps Marianne wouldn't feel the same need to indulge herself behind her husband's back. An honest relationship was so much better than one full of hidden things.

That was true in Cora's life too. Cora thought about the way John had held her close last night. They still hadn't talked much about the *boppli* on the way, but they were making some progress. There was still much pain, but at least they weren't hiding from each other anymore

Lucy nodded. "It's very easy to sell things on eBay. I've done that and bought some stuff too. I'll put this flower arrangement online, and anything else you'd be comfortable selling." She looked around, shaking her head. "I'll bet this stuff is worth a lot."

Marianne tapped a finger to her chin. "I want any money I make to go to something important. I don't need it." She chuckled. "Isaac hasn't missed it, and neither have I. We already have a nice nest egg put away for Anna."

"What about putting the money in the community health fund? Several of our members back in Ohio had cancer, and their chemotherapy really depleted our fund." Cora picked up a box of Christmas ornaments. Why in the world had Marianne bought these? Their people didn't even put up Christmas trees! She shook her head and put the box back on the shelf.

Marianne nodded. "That's a *gut* idea. We've also had quite a few folks with serious medical issues." She looked over at Lucy. "How much money do you think I could get for all *mei* things?"

"I have no idea. Really. There are so many boxes in here, and I don't even know what's in them all. You probably have an idea about how much money you've spent over the years. But things depreciate, and the marketplace changes." Lucy shrugged. "I really don't know."

"Would this help?" Marianne squatted down, reached her arm to the back of the bottom shelf, and pulled out a brown ledger book. She opened it up, flipped through a lot of pages, then pointed to the last one. "Seventeen thousand, six hundred twenty-two dollars, and forty-eight cents. That's how much I've spent. Including shipping."

Cora's jaw dropped. She glanced over at Lucy, whose mouth also hung open.

"Seventeen *thousand* dollars?" Cora had seen the room before, so she knew about the radio and what was visible on the shelves, but Marianne apparently had a fortune tucked away in some of the boxes.

Marianne ignored Lucy's and Cora's shocked responses. "Let's sell a big item," she said, "enough for Jacob to get a buggy of his own. He and Anna are getting married soon, and they'll need a buggy." She glanced around the room, her voice rising. "And when the Lapp farm burned a few months ago, we rebuilt it, but they lost a lot of equipment, and to *mei* knowledge, they haven't replaced it. I'd like to help them do that."

Cora was only half listening. All she could think of was the sheer amount of money Marianne had spent over the years. And just about everything she'd bought was right here in this little basement room.

"Let's start moving all of this upstairs." Marianne's face was bright with excitement. "We'll send as much home as we can with Lucy so she can sell it at eBay. I'll store the rest in *mei* sewing room. Or whatever will fit. I'm sure we'll have to leave some of this down here for now." She tapped Lucy on the shoulder. "Now, the only way I'll agree to do this is if you take you a commission. You know, like those realty people do when they sell a house."

"Absolutely not." Lucy shook her head emphatically. "I want to do this for you."

Marianne frowned. "We'll talk about it later."

For the rest of the afternoon, the women hauled up boxes and bags from the basement. Cora was careful not to carry anything heavy, at Lucy's and Marianne's insistence. she was happy to oblige. With each passing day, she was growing more excited about the child she was carrying.

They put all the items in the middle of the living room floor so they could sort them into categories and decide what to sell. They broke for a chicken-salad sandwich during the lunch hour, then got back to work.

When it was all sorted, they sat down on the floor, eyed their efforts, and started making lists. First, they wrote down how much they thought they could collect, then they began debating where the proceeds should go. This led to a conversation about Anna and Jacob's wedding and the plans that still needed to be finalized in the coming weeks. By this point they'd all lost track of time, so they were all surprised when Bishop Byler walked in the door. The poor man grabbed his chest, put a hand to his forehead, and eyed the piles of inventory spread throughout his living room.

"*Nee*, Marianne. *Nee!* You can't possibly expect to put all of this in the *haus!*"

Cora and Lucy both jumped up from where they sat on the floor, and Lucy extended her hand to Marianne to help her up. Once on her feet, Marianne answered her husband.

"Of course not, Isaac. These things are going to eBay." Marianne stretched, stiff from sitting on the floor.

Isaac slowly pulled his hand from his chest, but his expression was no less anxious. "Where is this eBay? On the coast? And where did all of this . . . this—where did it all come from?"

"Let me say good-bye to *mei* friends, and I'll explain everything." Marianne turned to Cora and Lucy. "I'm too tired today to load any of this in Lucy's car. Can we do it sometime next week?"

"I can help on Monday," Lucy offered. "That's Labor Day, which means I'll be off work."

Cora nodded, then Marianne walked Cora and Lucy to the door, and once they were at Lucy's car, they both waved at Marianne, who closed the door.

"I'd love to be a fly on the wall in that house right now." Cora laughed as she got into the car.

"Me too," Lucy said, then giggled.

23

MARIANNE LOOKED UP AT HER HUSBAND, HANDS ON her hips. "I will not change one thing in this *haus*, Isaac. You and I agreed that much of what I had collected was unnecessary, and that's what Lucy has been selling on the eBay. What's left here are things we compromised on." She waved her arm around the living room.

"Marianne, we have a wedding here today. What kind of example are we setting for the district?" Isaac drew himself up to full height and put on his sternest, most forbidding demeanor. "I am the man of the household, and you must do what I say."

"Oh pooh! Don't play that card with me, Isaac. Let our home be the new standard for the district. There isn't anything in this *haus* that takes away from our faith, and there is nothing wrong with having a few nice things that lift the spirit or make life a little easier." She backed away and waved her hand at him. "Now, shoo! There is much to be done, and all of our help should be arriving soon."

Isaac hung his head like a little puppy as he walked out the door, but Marianne wasn't overly concerned. She had managed to hold her ground for nearly two months, and she wasn't backing down now. The congregation would no doubt be surprised when they saw the house, but that was okay. How Isaac handled their surprise would be up to him.

"How do I look?"

Marianne turned when she heard Anna's voice. She eyed her beautiful granddaughter dressed in a perfectly pressed new blue dress that Marianne had made for her. "You look beautiful. Jacob is a lucky man."

"I'm the lucky one." Anna walked to Marianne and gave her a hug. "I'm so proud of you for showing *Daadi* everything in your broom closet. And it's wonderful the way you are using the money from selling things to help the community." She looked around the room. "And all of this looks very nice. It's not too fancy, and it makes our home a little brighter."

"It won't be your home for long." As Marianne said the words, she felt a lump in her throat.

"It will be for a little while, though—until we have enough money for our own place."

Marianne allowed herself a small smile, enjoying her secret. Her granddaughter and new grandson would be getting their own place sooner than they knew. An antique German jewelry box Marianne had purchased thirty years ago—at an *Englisch* garage sale, of all places—had turned out to be worth a lot of money, enough for a down payment on a house. And Marianne had already purchased Jacob a new buggy. All he had to do was pick it up in town.

Her secret hobby had ended up being a savings account of sorts, and being able to do for others gave Marianne much more pleasure than all her years of collecting had. She'd finally convinced Lucy to take a percentage of their eBay sales, and the extra income was helping Lucy purchase some things she hadn't been able to afford before, like a swing set for young Benjamin.

"*Mammi*," Anna called from the porch, "the wedding wagon is here." Marianne looked out to see a wagon loaded with all the tables, chairs, dishes, and utensils they would need for today's wedding. The kitchen table and counters were already piled high with food brought in by members of the community.

There was plenty of everything, especially joy.

It was going to be a grand day.

Lucy carried Benjamin out to her front porch to wait for Noah's car. Amish weddings started early, so Noah, Carley, and Jenna were supposed to pick her up at eight that morning. Lucy had argued and said she could take her own car, but ultimately Carley had convinced her to ride with them. "I have a huge surprise for Noah—and for you."

Getting to know Noah's wife had turned out to be an unexpected benefit of Lucy's new job. She and Carley had gone to lunch together several times, and they'd had long talks about all kinds of things. Carley had told Lucy about her own spiritual journey and about what it meant to be a daughter of the promise. Her words had echoed what Marianne had said, and they resonated deep within Lucy.

Apparently it didn't matter if you were Amish or not. Anyone could find plain peace. Lucy had found it through both her Amish and her non-Amish friends. She was on a new path, and God was lighting the way. She knew He had forgiven her for her past sins, and she was slowly forgiving herself.

If she had any regrets at all, they concerned her mother. It would have meant the world to see Mom back to normal, the way she'd been before the stroke, but the doctors said that was unlikely. Chances are she would be angry and spiteful the rest of her life. But Lucy did her best to visit her daily, even though most days she had to push herself to go. She brought Benjamin to visit at least once a week. Her mother was happiest on those days.

At the end of every visit, no matter how nasty Mom had been that day, Lucy made a point to say, "I love you, Mom." Her mother never said it back to her. And that hurt, even though Lucy knew her mother couldn't help it.

Noah parked his car at the Bylers', and they all got out. Carley ran into the house while the rest of them picked up boxes of food and slowly made their way inside. Benjamin quickly found a dozen or so children in the living room, and Lucy knew there were plenty of eyes watching him, so she headed for the kitchen, where Carley was talking to Marianne.

"Oh no! Really?" Marianne didn't sound happy.

"What's wrong?"

The two women jumped at the sound of her voice. "Nothing," Marianne said quickly, exchanging a glance with Carley.

"Everything's fine," Carley told Lucy. "You'll just have to wait a bit longer for the surprise, that's all."

The two women were clearly in on a secret they didn't want to share. And that was okay. A few months ago Lucy would never have been invited to an Amish wedding, much less been welcome at the home of a bishop. She felt honored just to be here. But she didn't know what to think about this surprise. What kind of surprise could Carley have planned for both Lucy and Noah?

Whatever it was, Carley and Marianne sure were excited about it.

Anna waited at the bottom of the stairs while everyone assembled in the living room and beyond. Some Amish houses had panels that could be opened up to create one large room, but her grandparents' house wasn't like that, so they'd set up benches in the downstairs bedroom and even on the porch. Later those same benches would transform into tables for the wedding meal.

She didn't notice her future in-laws walk up until they were right beside her. Cora looked beautiful, practically shining with happiness. *Mammi* had said that pregnancy does that to a woman— it makes her radiant. Anna loved that idea, and she couldn't wait to have a child of her own.

John Hostetler was actually smiling, and as he leaned over and kissed Anna on the cheek, she silently thanked God for the healing powers that were surely working in that home. "We are so happy to have you joining our family," he said. "May today be a blessed day. Today and always."

Anna thanked him, then watched them walk away together. Her people weren't big on public affection, especially the older ones, so she found it particularly touching to see John latch onto Cora's hand.

Anna watched them walk up to Jacob in the crowd. He looked up, they locked eyes, and he broke out that smile that always made her stomach swirl. She couldn't believe that this kind, responsible, *gorgeous* man would be her husband soon.

And as she looked around the room, she thought about all

the changes they'd all gone through the past few months. *Mammi* had finally stood up to her grandfather after years of hiding things from him. They'd almost lost *Mammi* when her diabetes got so bad. Her grandmother had become friends with an unlikely *Englisch* woman they'd all grown to care about. Jacob's family was on the mend. And two weeks earlier Anna and Jacob had both been baptized, confirming their choice to live by the *Ordnung* in this peaceful community.

Even *Daadi* was making some changes. Though still strict, he was listening more and even softening his rules—a little. In return, people in the community were beginning to recognize what a loving and faithful leader he could be. And Sarah Jane Miller had made a recent visit to their house, saying she'd heard a nasty rumor that *Daadi* had practically killed her stepmother, Lizzie. "All rubbish," she'd said, adding that she would set those in the community straight.

"It's time." Emma had come up behind her. She locked her arm in Anna's. "Come on. Let's go."

Anna forced herself to peel her eyes away from her future husband. She walked with Emma to the front row of benches.

"I'm so happy for you," Emma whispered as they took their seats.

Anna took a deep breath. "I can't believe this day is finally here." She reached into the pocket of her white apron and rubbed the flattened dime between her fingers. It didn't have any magical powers, but it would always be a treasured keepsake.

The wish she'd made before leaving it on the railroad track that day had been fulfilled so beautifully.

But what about Jacob? Had his wish come true as well?

After the ceremony and the meal, Noah walked toward the barn, where he knew the men had gathered to tell jokes and sometimes smoke cigars. He missed those times. He'd felt uncomfortable about attending this wedding, since Bishop Byler had been the one to enforce his shunning and had almost caused his practice to go belly-up.

Noah was actually surprised that the bishop had allowed him in his home. But Lucy had told Carley that the bishop was going to be making some changes, and that one of them involved Noah.

He'd no sooner had the thought when he heard the bishop's deep voice behind him. "I was hoping I would find time to talk to you."

Noah turned to the tall, stooped man. "What about?"

"I want you to know that I will be making announcements to our congregation at the next worship service. Some of our people are letting their health go because they don't want to go to any other doctor besides you." He paused, stroking his gray beard. "Including *mei fraa*. So I will be allowing our community to seek your services." He looked toward his house and rolled his eyes. "And it looks like other changes will be in order as well. My wife has seen to that." One side of his mouth crooked up a bit before he walked away.

Carley came running up to him, her beautiful face glowing with excitement.

"The bishop just talked to me, so I know the surprise." Noah kissed her on the cheek. "He's going to let the people in his district come back to the clinic."

"Oh, we suspected that." She grinned. "But that's not the surprise." Noah recalled that the surprise was for Lucy too. He couldn't imagine what his wife had up her sleeve.

"There's your surprise." Carley pointed to her left, and Noah grabbed his chest. "I can't believe this." He started walking toward the figure crossing the yard, speeding up as he got closer.

"Samuel!" He threw his arms around his brother and held on. Finally, he eased away and turned to his sister-in-law. "Lillian, it's so good to see you. What a wonderful surprise this is." Noah turned to Carley and pointed a finger at her. "Sneaky, sneaky. When did you all plan this?" Without waiting for an answer, he turned back to Samuel. "And where are Anna and Elizabeth?"

Lillian spoke up. "We left them with our dear friends, Martha and Arnold. The girls love staying there and, well, Samuel and I are thinking of this as a vacation." Lillian giggled, and Noah couldn't help but think of the day she arrived in Paradise so many years ago, a young girl without a clue about the Amish—or herself. She'd made a remarkable transformation and was a wonderful wife to Samuel, stepmother to David, and mother to Elizabeth and Anna, and even grandmother to David and Emily's twins.

"We made plans last month when we heard about the wedding," Samuel added. "Since we've known the Bylers all our lives, this was also a *gut* excuse to come see all of you too. We were supposed to be here for the wedding, of course, but our flight was delayed."

"I'm just glad you're here. It's a wonderful surprise." Noah hugged Samuel again, but as he looked over his brother's shoulder, tears filled his eyes. He edged slowly toward his nephew as memories of the time they'd both spent in the hospital filled his mind.

"How's that kidney of mine working?" He grabbed David and pulled him into his arms.

"Great, *Onkel* Noah. Just great." Samuel's son stepped back, and Noah looked him up and down, remembering the boy he'd watched grow up, the fifteen-year-old who had received Noah's kidney. Then Noah spotted Emily. It had to be her. She was pushing a stroller with twins. How had so much time had gone by?

His two sisters walked up, and Mary Ellen and Rebecca were both grinning from ear to ear. Noah could barely see someone behind them, and when his sisters separated, he saw Katie Ann. Her face shone as she walked up to him and gave him a hug.

"We're all together. This is just *wunderbaar!*"

The word from Noah's childhood came to him naturally, and he smiled at the comfort of it. But then he spotted Lucy standing off to the side, her eyes wide, staring at Katie Ann.

And he couldn't help but wonder how *wunderbaar* she felt at that moment.

This is the big surprise?

Lucy stared at the Stoltzfus clan, thinking about Ivan. She didn't dare approach them. Noah and Carley might have accepted her, but she felt sure the others didn't, and she surely couldn't face Katie Ann.

Lucy had felt so good about herself lately. But seeing Katie Ann reminded her of who she was, who she'd always be. A woman who'd had an affair with a married man. Who'd borne a child out of wedlock. The woman her mother told her daily that she was.

Glancing around, she scanned the area looking for Benjamin,

whom she'd last seen with Cora and Marianne. She wanted more than anything just to find him and go home. But she had come with Noah, Carley, and Jenna, so she was stuck here until they were ready to leave.

She was looking all around when she noticed Katie Ann walking toward her. Lucy automatically changed course to avoid her. But then Katie Ann called her name.

Lucy sighed. She owed it to the woman to stop and listen, though talking could never change what had happened. Lucy had already apologized several times, but apologies could only go so far. And neither of them would ever completely know why Ivan had done what he did. Or who he truly loved.

Lucy had always wondered if the house she lived in had really been meant for Katie Ann and Ivan, if they'd planned to reconcile. The house was completely different from what Lucy and Ivan had discussed, almost as if he had built it for someone else.

Katie Ann had told Lucy she'd never had any intention of reconciling with Ivan. But Lucy would always wonder if that had been on Ivan's mind when he died. *Part of my penance, to have to always wonder.*

"Hello, Lucy."

Katie Ann was as beautiful as ever, even with her plain clothes and no makeup. "Hi, Katie Ann." Lucy could hardly look her in the eye.

"How have you been?"

Lucy swallowed hard as she wondered what the point of this was. Did Katie Ann want her to apologize again? Did she want to tell her what a horrible person she was? Lucy could handle that. She'd had lots of practice. "I'm fine. How have you been?"

"*Gut, gut*. Eli and I stay very busy with Jonas, Eli's children, and all our grandchildren. We really love living in Colorado."

"That's good." Lucy felt that scarlet *A* burning on her chest. She wished Katie Ann would just walk away. But no, things were about to get worse. Ivan's two sisters, Mary Ellen and Rebecca, were walking toward them, and so was Lillian, Samuel's wife. She recalled the way those women used to look at her when they'd run into her somewhere with Ivan. Or even without Ivan.

For a brief moment, she had to remind herself that the Amish were pacifists. This was not going to be like a playground fight, and there would be no pulling of hair or anything like that. Still, it was their job as Katie Ann's relatives to put Lucy in her place. Again. She waited.

But they all greeted her with a smile. So did another woman who walked up to join them. "Lucy, do you know our friend, Sadie?"

Lucy shook her head. "Nice to meet you."

Then another woman walked up. Lucy felt like she was standing in quicksand. And they were all going to watch her sink.

"This is my mother, Sarah Jane," Lillian said. "Since you are part of the family, I thought it would be *gut* for you to meet everyone."

"So nice to see you again, Lucy," Lillian's mother said. Lucy didn't remember ever meeting her.

Lucy couldn't speak. *Part of the family?* Her nerves settled a bit when Carley walked up. "Wow. Look at all of us. Daughters of the promise."

Lucy bit her bottom lip. Was she being forgiven? Included? Was she really going to have a family that accepted her? How could that be after what she'd done to Katie Ann? Maybe they just wanted to see Benjamin. They would have to tolerate Lucy to have that.

But this didn't look or feel like grudging tolerance. It felt like . . . friendship, smiling at her from amidst a group of women who'd always disliked her. It was all very confusing, and as they talked among themselves, Lucy barely heard anything. But she did hear Katie Ann ask her if they could take a walk.

"Oh, I don't know. Benjamin is here somewhere, and I'd hate to leave him, and—"

"There he is." Lillian pointed toward the house. "The bride is holding him."

Lucy nodded. There was no getting out of it, so she got in step with Katie Ann.

Katie Ann stopped when they got far enough away from the crowd not to be heard. "You look nice. I like your hair that color." Katie Ann was obviously trying to make her feel comfortable, although she had no idea why. She touched her brown hair, knowing she'd looked very different last time Katie Ann saw her.

"Thank you. It's easier to take care of shorter. And I don't color it anymore. I stay busy with Benjamin and work." She shrugged, knowing Katie Ann would get to the point, but dreading it just the same.

"Lucy, I've talked to Noah, Mary Ellen, Rebecca, and Samuel— all of Ivan's siblings. They all want very much to have little Benjamin in their lives. And you." She paused and took a deep breath. "I have told them all that I hope you can be a part of the family. And that I hold no ill will against you."

"How can you say that?" The words slipped from Lucy's mouth before she had a chance to think.

"I'm no saint, Lucy. I carried around a lot of bad feelings about you for a long time." Katie Ann's voice was stern but not harsh. "And if I lived here, I think it would be hard for us to be friends. But I understand from Carley that you're a daughter of the promise, and this means a great deal to us. It's a journey that all of us have traveled at some point in our lives. It's sacred and dear to us." She smiled. "And not always easy. I know that sometimes on our journey, forgiveness is a large part of the process." She paused. "It took me a long time to forgive you."

Lucy hung her head. "I'm so sorry. I'm so very sorry." She looked up, tears filling her eyes. "But I love Benjamin so much. And I did love Ivan, despite what we did."

Katie Ann pressed her lips together, and Lucy wished she hadn't said that last part. But then Katie Ann nodded. "Of course you love Benjamin. And Ivan would want his family involved in Benjamin's life. So I'm hoping that you'll let them be a family to you."

A family? Lucy had never had anyone but her mother. She had always dreamed of having a big, loving family, but this was an unlikely source. She hung her head again, and this time she started to cry.

Katie Ann put a hand on her arm. "Forgive yourself, Lucy."

Lucy sniffled, unsure what to say.

"Because I forgave you a long time ago."

Lucy didn't move as she watched the other woman walk away. She was thinking that Katie Ann might be the best person she'd ever met. How could Ivan have loved them both? She slowly made her way back to the house. Children seemed to be playing everywhere around her. Adults gathered in groups of three or four, laughing and talking.

Lucy looked up at the bright blue October sky. *Am I really a daughter of the promise?*

She spotted Marianne and Cora near the porch, chatting with a group of women. Marianne was holding Benjamin. As Lucy grew closer, she recognized Katie Ann, Lillian, Mary Ellen, Rebecca, Carley, and Sarah Jane. She walked up just as Marianne set Benjamin down on the ground in front of another little boy.

"This is your *bruder*, Benjamin." Katie Ann squatted down and pointed at Jonas. He was older now than when Lucy saw him last. "His name is Jonas."

Lillian walked to Lucy, put her arm through hers, and pulled her to the group. "Look at these two," she said in a bubbly voice. "They really like each other."

They all laughed as Benjamin tugged at the jacket Jonas was wearing. It was impossible not to see the resemblance.

Katie Ann looked up at Lucy and winked. "Welcome to the family."

Lucy bit her lip, and it took everything she had not to cry. Then everyone *awwed* when Benjamin hugged Jonas. Lucy closed her eyes for a few moments, thankful for this new circle of people in her life, for the changes she'd made within herself, and for all that God had blessed her with. She closed her eyes and silently spoke to God, knowing that He had been hearing her all along.

Anna and Emma were chatting with Cora and her daughters when Jacob walked up.

"I'm stealing my bride." He grabbed Anna's hand and eased her away from the group.

Emma grinned, her hands on her hips. "And where are you two off to?"

Jacob just smiled and pulled Anna along with him. They rounded the corner of the house, and the instant they were out of sight, Jacob pulled her close and kissed her the way a husband kisses his wife.

"I kept my promise to your grandfather, but I couldn't wait one more minute." He pulled her close and kissed her again. "Can you believe we have our own buggy and the down payment for a *haus?*"

"I know!" Anna bounced up on her toes. "*Mammi* has been doing so much for everyone, and she seems so happy doing it."

"I love you, Anna Hostetler."

"I love you too, Jacob Hostetler." She was sure the smile on her face was going to be there forever.

He kissed her again, but Anna eased him away. "I have a question for you." She reached into her apron pocket, pulled out her dime, and held it up between two fingers. "What did you wish for the day we put the dimes on the train track?"

Jacob reached into the pocket of his black pants. "This dime?" He smiled.

"You have yours today too," Anna said softly.

"Of course." He kissed her tenderly on the mouth, his hand cupping her jaw. Then he nodded. "Come on. I'll show you."

He pulled her around the corner to the yard where most of their guests were in view. "Look." He pointed to his parents. Both of them were laughing and chatting within a circle of about ten people, including his sisters. Then he nodded to his left, where Abe and Eli were also enjoying themselves with a group of kids.

"I wished that we'd all heal somehow. That's what I wished for. For peace. Leah would have wanted that."

Anna wrapped her arm around his waist, wondering if he was going to ask her what she'd wished for that day at the tracks.

"But a dime on a train track didn't make all this happen." He draped an arm around her shoulder and pulled her close. "I prayed for it every day." He turned to her and kissed her on the cheek. "I prayed for healing. And I prayed for you. For you to love me."

Anna had to blink the happy tears away as gratitude washed over her.

"And I do." She glanced toward heaven as she said it.

Thank You.

Reading Group Guide

1. Early in the story, Anna overhears Ben and Rubin talking badly about her grandfather. How do you think things would have played out if Anna had not heard this conversation and decided to ask Jacob out?

2. Bishop Byler is a stern man who is imposing rules that are already in place. What are some of the forces driving his actions?

3. Marianne believes her husband's strict ways have driven her to keep secrets. Do you agree with this or does Marianne need to accept some of the responsibility for her actions? Are you keeping secrets from a spouse or loved one, and if so . . . is it a burden or a necessity? And is there ever really a *good* reason to keep secrets?

4. Were you ever concerned about Glenda, the receptionist at the lumberyard? Did you see her as a threat to the relationship that was developing between Anna and Jacob? And what about the jealousy that Anna was feeling? Was it justified? Is jealousy ever justified, no matter the situation?

5. John can't cope with Leah's death, largely in part because he blames himself. Were you angry at John throughout the story?

Did you feel sympathy for him? Were you rooting for him to come around or wishing he would just leave the family?

6. Jacob is taking up the slack and trying to be the head of his grieving household when his father checks out emotionally. What are some of the ways that Jacob does this?

7. Lucy is clearly the Daughter of the Promise in this story. What are some examples of the ways Lucy is bettering herself in the eyes of the community and in the eyes of the Lord?

8. Cora is a woman with the best of intentions, but her bitterness often shows through, and she is guilty of judging others. Besides Lucy, who does Cora judge?

9. Forgiveness is a major theme throughout the book. What are some examples of this? And how does forgiveness of one's self affect several of the characters?

10. Why do you think that Cora and Marianne hit it off so well and became friends quickly? Was it their situations with their husbands? Or was there more to it?

11. Can you name all the Daughters of the Promise?

Plain Perfect _____

Plain Pursuit _____

Plain Promise _____

Plain Paradise _____

Plain Proposal _____

Plain Peace _____

Amish Recipes

Cora's Chicken Bundles

1	pkg. cream cheese, softened
1/4	cup sour cream
1	teaspoon dill weed
1/2	teaspoon salt
1/2	teaspoon pepper
1/2	cup celery, chopped
1/4	cup onion finely chopped
1/4	cup butter, melted
1/4	cup seasoned bread crumbs
3	tubes crescent rolls
4	cups chicken (cooked and cubed)

Beat cream cheese, sour cream, dill, salt, and pepper. Stir in chicken, onion, and celery. Unroll each tube of crescent rolls and roll out like stromboli, rectangular shape. Fill with chicken mixture. Fold sides up over chicken and pinch to seal. Brush with butter and sprinkle with bread crumbs. Bake at 350 for 15-20 minutes.

Marianne's Cherry Crumb Cake

1/2   cup butter, softened

3/4   cup sugar

2   eggs

1/3   cup milk

2   cup flour

2   teaspoon baking powder

1/2   teaspoon salt

2   cans cherry pie filling

I   teaspoon vanilla

Cream butter, sugar, and eggs. Add dry ingredients and milk with vanilla. Spread half of the batter on bottom of 13 x 9 baking pan. Pour pie filling on top of batter then pour remaining batter on top of pie filling. Mix the following until crumbly:

2   tablespoon butter, softened

1/2   cup brown sugar

1/2   cup flour

Spread on cake. Bake at 350 for 45-60 minutes.

Marianne's Pepperoni Lasagna

1 1/2   lb. ground beef
1   small onion, chopped
2   1/2 cup water
1   (8-ounce) can tomato sauce
1   (6-ounce) can tomato paste
1   teaspoon beef bouillon granules
1   tablespoon dried parsley flakes
2   teaspoon Italian seasoning
1   teaspoon salt
1/4   teaspoon garlic salt
2   eggs
1   (12-ounce) pkg. small curd cottage cheese
1/2   cup sour cream
8   lasagna noodles, cooked and drained
1   (3 1/2-ounce) pkg. sliced pepperoni
2   cup shredded mozzarella cheese
1/2   cup grated parmesan cheese

In a skillet, cook beef and onion until done, drain grease. Add water, tomato sauce, tomato paste, bouillon, and seasoningss. Bring to a boil, then reduce heat and simmer uncovered for 30 minutes. In a bowl, combine eggs, cottage cheese and sour cream. Spread 1/2 cup meat sauce into a greased 13 x 9 x 2 baking dish. Layer with four noodles, the cottage cheese mixture, and pepperoni. Top with remaining noodles and meat sauce. Sprinkle with mozzarella and parmesan cheeses. Cover with foil and bake at 350 for 35 minutes. Uncover and bake 10 minutes longer. Let stand 10 minutes before cutting. Yield: 12 servings.

Cora's Raspberry Swirl Cheesecake

1   (8-ounce) pkg. cream cheese, softened
1   (14-ounce) can sweetened condensed milk
1   egg
3   tablespoon plus 1 teaspoon lemon juice, divided
1   (6-ounce) chocolate pie crust
1/2 cup raspberry preserves

Beat cream cheese until fluffy. Gradually beat in sweetened condensed milk until smooth. Add egg and 3 tablespoons of lemon juice. Mix well. Pour half the batter into the crust. In a small bowl, combine 1 teaspoon lemon juice and preserves. Spoon half the preserves over batter. Pour remaining batter on top. Using a knife, swirl remaining preserves in a decorative pattern of your choosing. Bake at 300 for 55 minutes. Cool before serving and refrigerate leftovers.

Acknowledgments

I HAVE A YOUNG FRIEND WHO SIGNS HER EMAILS—*I AM a Daughter of the Promise.* I just love that. I hope that my books have helped at least a few people travel the path that God set them on in an effort to become a Daughter of the Promise. I know that each book I write ministers to my own soul in that regard. Writing this series has been a blessing and a dream come true for me. These characters are family, and God laid them on my heart to tell stories that glorify Him.

It is an honor to dedicate this book to my dear friend Richard Gabler. Mr. Gabler, you are truly one of God's special people, my angel on earth. I love you dearly.

There are always lots of people to thank, and I hope I don't miss anyone. It takes a team to get the books on the shelves!

Thanks always to my fabulous publishing team at HarperCollins Christian Fiction, to my wonderful agent, Natasha Kern, my irreplaceable assistant Janet Murphy . . . and to my family and friends for their continued support. Special thanks to Barbie Beiler for always answering my questions and for the friendship that we share.

I'm blessed to have great editors helping me with this project.

Sue Brower, Natalie Hanemann, and Anne Buchanan—you're the best!

And to my fabulous hubby, Patrick . . . love you forever and ever. ☺

To my wonderful Lord and Savior—thank You for all that You are in my life and for Your many blessings!

The Daughters
of the Promise Series

What would cause
the Amish to
move to Colorado,
leaving family and
friends behind?

The Land of Canaan Series

Also available in e-book formats

"You may think you are familiar with Beth's wonderful storytelling gift but this is something new! It's a story of how God can redeem the seemingly unredeemable. It's a message the world needs to hear."

—*Sheila Walsh, author of* God Loves Broken People

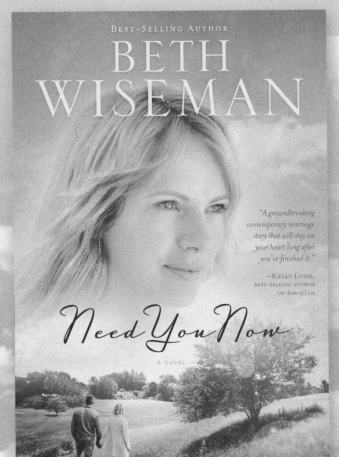

Brooke has only loved one man,
her late husband.
Owen's rebuilding after a painful divorce.
Can a mysterious house bring them
together for a second chance at love?

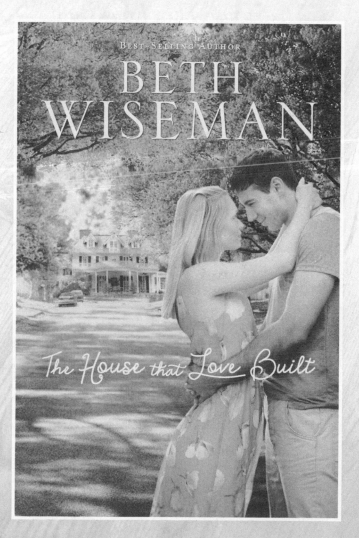

BEST-SELLING AUTHOR

BETH
WISEMAN

The House that Love Built

AVAILABLE AS PRINT AND E-BOOK

An Excerpt from
The House That Love Built

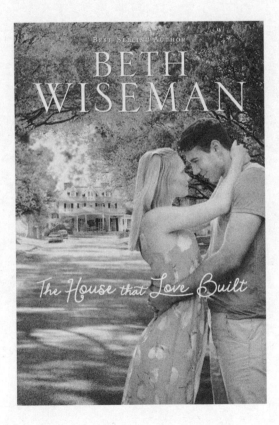

Excerpt from
The House That Love Built

BROOKE HOLLOWAY WOKE WITH A START, THEN FELT her stomach lurch when she recalled her dream. She rolled over and threw her arm across Travis's side of the bed, wishing she could will him to be there. She lay there a few more minutes before forcing herself to get up and dressed before she went downstairs.

She pressed the button on the coffeemaker before facing off with the calendar that hung on the wall to the left of the refrigerator. She reached for the black marker dangling on a string nearby and drew a big X across today's date, as she did every morning, then scribbled "45" in the upper-right-hand corner of the square. The kids liked to keep up with the countdown to July 10.

Two cups of coffee later she still yawned as she headed back upstairs and down the hall to Meghan's room.

"Up, sleepyhead." Brooke flipped on the light and walked toward her precious six-year-old, whose blond hair crumpled in a mass on the pillow. "Time to get up." Brooke sat on the bed and kissed Meghan on the forehead, Travis still fresh on her mind. He used to wake up the kids each morning, said that seeing their faces first thing always made for a better day.

"Two more days of school after today." Meghan sat up and pulled down the pajama pants that had inched up her calves during the night.

"I know." Brooke stood and clapped her hands together. "So let's don't be late."

She headed down the hall to Spencer's room. Brooke had learned, after being reprimanded more than once, to always knock first.

"Come in."

Spencer was already sitting on the side of the bed when Brooke took two steps into his room. He no longer wanted her hugging and kissing him in the morning. Or any other time, for that matter. He'd grown up too much these past couple of years. Brooke wondered how much of that was her fault, if she'd handled Travis's death correctly with the kids, particularly Spencer. Either way, her ten-year-old son had made it clear she couldn't be "huggy and kissy" with him anymore.

"Glad to see you're up. I'm going to make some eggs and bacon, so I'll see you downstairs. Okay?"

Spencer nodded as he rubbed his eyes and yawned.

Thirty minutes later they were eating, and running late as usual. Brooke glanced at her watch, hoping the kids wouldn't miss the bus. Again.

"I miss Grandma," Meghan said through a mouthful.

"I know. Me too." Brooke stuffed the last bite of bacon in her mouth, chewing as she got up and tossed her paper plate in the trash can. "We'll go see her tomorrow after school. She's playing bingo this afternoon."

"She'd rather play bingo than see her grandkids?" Spencer stood up and also tossed his plate in the garbage.

Brooke looked at her watch again and grinned. "Yes. I believe she would." She snapped her fingers. "Now, chop-chop. We need to go."

Brooke had tried repeatedly to talk her mother out of moving to the assisted living complex here in Smithville, but once Patsy Miller had a notion in her head, there was no changing her mind. "They have bingo, card games, pottery, and painting classes," Mom had told her. "And Gladys told me they have dances too. You never have to cook, they give you rides to the doctor, and they have a maid service. Sounds like heaven to me, and I'm going to live there!" she'd said. That had been two months ago.

"We're going to miss the bus again." Meghan grabbed her backpack by the front door and slipped it over her shoulders.

"Not if you hurry!" Brooke kissed her on the cheek. "Love you."

Then she grabbed Spencer and planted a kiss on his forehead. "I know, I know," she said when he squirmed away. "But humor me every once in a while."

Brooke watched from the porch until the kids were safely on the bus, then started her ten-minute walk to Miller's Hardware Store.

Francis Tippens, affectionately called Big Daddy, was unlocking the door when Brooke walked up. At almost seven feet tall, the man commanded respect, and no one dared to call him by his given name. Even though he had a permanent scowl on his face, Brooke was pretty sure he would go to his grave to protect her and her children.

"Mornin', Ms. Brooke." Big Daddy held the door open for her. As she reached for the light switch, she tripped over the entryway rug. *Gonna get rid of that thing one day.*

Brooke stopped at the counter while Big Daddy walked toward

the back of the store to begin unloading a recent order. "Have a good day, Big Daddy."

He didn't turn around, just waved. Brooke walked behind the front counter, sat on the wooden stool, and unlocked the register. She pulled yesterday's cash from her purse and was loading it in the machine when the door flew open again.

"Good morning, sunshine." Brooke put her hands on her hips when Juliet came scurrying in, shaking her head. Brooke braced herself for whatever excuse Juliet might have for being late.

"I am so sorry." Juliet brushed a strand of long blond hair away from her face, hair that didn't look like it had seen a comb this morning. She readjusted her silver purse on her shoulder and tucked her pink blouse into the short blue-jean skirt. "I couldn't find my keys this morning." She let out an exaggerated sigh. "Then I remembered it was Wednesday and I had to put the trash out."

"It's okay."

Juliet had grown up in Smithville and had worked part-time at the store during her high school years. Now she attended Texas State in San Marcos, but Brooke hired her to help do inventory and catch up the filing in the summers.

"I'll go start the coffee." Juliet headed toward the back office. "Want some?"

Brooke nodded. "Yes, please. Thanks."

She closed the cash register and stared out the plate-glass windows that ran the length of the store. Across Main Street she could see Travis's old business, the windows boarded up. Right out of high school, he'd used inheritance money from his grandparents to open the Treasure Chest, a store he'd filled with old books, photographs, antique toys, and other vintage items. Brooke would joke that most of the inventory consisted of stuff Travis had collected since he was a kid. She was pretty sure he'd overpriced everything in the store because he really didn't want to sell any of it. Luckily, they hadn't depended solely on Travis's income.

Brooke wished someone would lease the space and open something new. Maybe a candy store. Then she'd just eat herself happy.

The story continues in The House that Love Built, *by Beth Wiseman*

About the Author

Photo by Saxton Creations

BETH WISEMAN IS HAILED AS A TOP VOICE IN AMISH fiction. She is a Carol Award winner and author of numerous best-sellers, including the Daughters of the Promise and the Land of Canaan series. She and her family live in Texas.